LAST FLIGHT OF THE PIGEON

A JOURNEY ACROSS CHINA BY BICYCLE

SIMON CLODE

ISBN: 978-0-9954615-0-5

Published by Simon Clode

To my Nans and Adam Cogan, the 17th best centre-back I've played football with.

1. There is No Pigeon Flying

It should not be difficult to buy popular things. The annual hysteria over a particular year's most wanted Christmas present is a good example of such perplexities. For people of my age, the pinnacle of Christmas hysteria was caused by Tracey Island. That situation, which drove parents to brawl in toy shops and, worse still, actually make Christmas presents by hand, should not be a feature of any festive period.

This was orchestrated by intellectually superior, yet morally inferior, marketing puppeteers. They pulled at heart strings to loosen the purse strings. Surely, though, the margins on plastic pieces of crap are so great that it would have been better to manufacture too many. Brains would have received a bigger bonus and parents wouldn't have gone on wild goose chases to mythical toy shops in faraway, hostile, places like Stoke. Fundamentally, no child would have been presented with a gift that looked as if it had been sponsored by a vast array of cleaning products.

Yet somehow this situation persists. My predicament with popularity involved a bicycle. The most popular bicycle in history. It should not be a difficult task to buy the most popular bicycle of all time. It especially shouldn't be such an imposition in China, where the bicycle in question is made. At no point on this particular customer journey should I have been required to speak with a man in Barcelona.

The object of my desire was a Flying Pigeon PA-02, the best-selling bicycle of all time[1]. An icon, the PA-02 is the bicycle

---

[1] (Koeppel, 2007, p. 66)

responsible for the stereotypes, myths, and that awful song about transportation habits in Beijing. Weighing slightly less than a tug boat, this single-geared embodiment of simplicity looks as though it was created using instructions no more technical than the road markings for cycle lanes. This isn't *a* bicycle, it's *the* bicycle.

The saga began in the autumn of 2014, six months after I had moved to Beijing. A love of bicycles had led me on a search for a classic Chinese bike. It did not take long to decide that the PA-02 was the bicycle for me. It is not only the most popular bicycle in history but arguably the most important too. The fact the Flying Pigeon nest was only down the road in Tianjin sealed the deal.

The plan was straightforward. I would travel from my new home to Tianjin and buy a PA-02. Then, at first light on the following morning, I would begin my triumphant return to Beijing by cycling through the beautiful shades of red and gold of northern China's ephemeral autumn. It was to be a romantic endeavour somewhere between carrying a new wife across the threshold and dragging a fridge into place.

At its most impressive, China's high-speed rail network can take you a distance equivalent to that of Edinburgh to Tangiers in just eight hours. On a less grand, yet equally astonishing level, my journey from Beijing to Tianjin took as long as the ten-stop metro journey that had preceded it; just thirty minutes.

Despite being home to the Flying Pigeon factory, I failed to see a single PA-02 for sale in Tianjin city centre. Here, as with elsewhere in China, Giants now rule. A Taiwanese brand with an apt name, Giant is the biggest bicycle manufacturer in the world. Giant's domination on the mainland is only tempered by Merida, another manufacturer from Taiwan.

In the Darwinian world of the modern day Chinese bicycle market, a 21kg, single gear, sit up and heave bike like the PA-02, cannot compete with Giant's multi-coloured, multi-geared, mountain bikes and their grasp of basic ergonomics. I had hoped that here, though, in the city where they are made, Flying Pigeons would still be available. However, even here in their hometown, Flying Pigeon have been crushed by Giant.

Giant's conquering of Flying Pigeon meant my first quest was as effective as a super injunction. Four hours of aimless wandering around Tianjin had left me disappointed and chronically bored. Having reached the very limit of a man's ability to shop for anything, I returned to my hotel. Once I was safely ensconced in my assemble-by-numbers room, I did as much research into the bicycle outlets of the city as my limited Mandarin could manage. Eventually, I located a bicycle market, which was far enough away to delay my visit until the following morning.

Determined not to waste the evening, I used room service to carb-load ahead of my return. In the Great British tradition, I paired pizza with a side of chips, as if that's an acceptable thing to do.

With no need for breakfast, I checked out early on Sunday morning and headed out to the bicycle market. Upon arrival it was clear that the grubby market was decidedly lacking in bikes, particularly PA-02s, of which there were none.

Dejected, and now short of the time to cycle home even if I chanced upon a Pigeon elsewhere, I skulked off back to Beijing. On the train, I sent a text to a friend whose girlfriend owned a relatively new PA-02. With the romance of cycling home from Tianjin slipping away, the option of just buying one in Beijing seemed an acceptable cop out. Perhaps I could even take it on a pilgrimage to Tianjin for a weekend.

The PA-02 in question had been purchased from the inventively named Bicycle Shop, which was close to my flat. In addition, the bike had been purchased only a year previously, so I was hopeful of my chances. After stopping off at home to lavish Holly, my girlfriend who had been at a hen party the night before, with bottled water and faux self-righteousness, I cut across Workers' Stadium to visit the Bicycle Shop.

After the pre-requisite deep breath that precedes speaking someone else's language very badly, I entered the shop and openly directed my questions to all three of the salesmen inside. After glancing around one another, the shop assistant who was silently elected spokesperson was absolute in his assurances that they didn't have a PA-02, nor would they ever get another in. Furthermore, he had no idea where I might find one.

After a lot of nodding to pretend I had understood everything I had been told, I took a quick look around the shop. It was full of modern city bikes and even a few luminous coloured fixies. Even here in its natural habitat of the state-owned Bicycle Shop, the PA-02 was conspicuous by its absence.

Outside the shop, another reason for the reduction in demand for Flying Pigeons was only a matter of metres away in the shape of Beijing's city bike scheme. As lighter, more maneuverable bikes, with none of the burdens of ownership, they've stolen one of the PA-02s remaining roles in life – popping. Whether the destination is the shops, work or school the city bike scheme allows you to pop there with great convenience. The bright red bicycles of this scheme cost only 10p an hour, which has proved cheap enough to contribute significantly to the drop in demand for their ancestors. Something illustrated by the increasing number of locked, rusting, PA-02s around the city, whose baskets have unintentionally become quasi-artistic, make-shift bins.

The next day I visited a dozen bike shops in Beijing. In six hours of searching, I had seen more £10,000 triathlon bikes than PA-02s. My pursuit of a Flying Pigeon was descending into a farce. Disheartened, I resorted to Taobao, a monolithic internet marketplace. The romance of my quest was dying, but this was

2014, surely I could satisfy my lust on the internet. The first object of my desire was a man from Tianjin, which felt right. We chatted very briefly before he revealed that he too didn't have any PA-02s in stock. The tease. This pattern was followed with three other sellers; optimism preceded short-lived hope and eventual disappointment.

Determined not to become the kind of person who couldn't find the needle in the medical waste, I decided to refocus my search. I targeted the group of people with a propensity to dwell on the recent past for reasons of identity and a misunderstanding of irony; students. So I headed to Wudaokou, a kind of University Disneyland, which combines the campuses of many universities in the northwest corner of Beijing.

My suspicions were well founded; there were more aging models in Wudaokou than a Marks and Spencer's advert. The first signs weren't promising, though, these were mostly rusty mountain bikes, but gradually the odd Flying Pigeon landed alongside them.

Inside the bike shops of Wudaokou however, it was a different story to the bike racks outside. It is not just Giants and city bike schemes killing off the PA-02, it is also the omnipotent electric scooters, which represent the next rung on the vehicle social mobility ladder in China. If anything they were more prevalent than pushbikes in the retailers of Wudaokou.

As I wandered amongst the shiny Giants and partially bubble-wrapped scooters, my task became the laughable equivalent of a Chinese man wandering around an Audi forecourt on the outskirts of London; if he was asking the youthful sales assistants for a Morris Minor and the Morris Minor was only £100 cheaper than the cheapest Audi. My hunt for the past was making me look like a clown in the present.

***

In many walks of life, China is developing faster than it takes the seeds of nostalgia to yield affection. Somewhere between China's relationship with its own history and the rapid economic growth, a gap is being left into which even icons can fall.

Nowhere is this more evident than in private transport. In Beijing, each and every road is a cross-section of society. China's social mobility ladder is illustrated by any of the roads in the capital's centre. In the side lane the PA-02s are being overtaken by Giants, who in turn are being surpassed by electric scooters, who themselves are being left behind by petrol scooters; all of whom are warily looking out for taxis. On the other side of the tree-lined partition, on the road proper, more taxis weave amongst the minivans, who are being overtaken by 4x4s and family estate cars. If you wait a few minutes someone in a £100,000 sports car will come along to complete the spectrum and allow you to jealously tick off Ferrari in your *Eye Spy a Prick* book. If you've got an hour to kill, I guarantee you will see both a Ferrari and a Rolls Royce. You shouldn't really spend an hour watching traffic, though, that would be ridiculous.

China doesn't just do everything bigger than the rest of the world, it does it faster. In 1998, 60% of Beijing's commuters cycled to work. Four years later that figure was 20%[2]. Rapid just doesn't do China justice.

It was becoming clear that to find a new PA-02, I'd have to try a little harder than merely go shopping. So I sent a message to my friend Mr Zhang. Now in his late 50s, Mr Zhang is a man who I first met after Holly hired him to drive us to Ikea and with whom I now share a relationship that is close enough for us to go for beers and for him to send me pictures of himself in speedos. It's not like

---

[2] http://www.worldometers.info/bicycles/

they're photos of him lying on a tiger skin rug with a curled finger beckoning me over or anything, he just loves to go wild swimming in the boiling hot summer months.

Mr Zhang has an incredible zest for life. The first time I met him, he ducked under my waving arm and hugged me, which is not the norm for a first meeting with a 50-something man in Beijing. But Mr Zhang is not the norm, he's hyper-charged.

A natural extrovert in all senses, he improves the sourest of moods. Even if you're feeling a little slow or grumpy - you could, for example, be going to Ikea at 9am on a Sunday morning - his relentless zest for life will cause you to smile. Eventually everyone in his presence becomes as happy as Mr Zhang. If anyone could find a new Flying Pigeon in Beijing, Mr Zhang could.

In the early days, before I could speak any Mandarin, Mr Zhang and I would mime at one another and occasionally he would shout at me in Mandarin. Incredibly he would always manage to smile whilst yelling, something that defies all of the sciences. Gradually we began to talk in basic Mandarin and use the messaging app WeChat. WeChat is the sound of China today; the *bingdingbong* of a new message may as well be the national anthem. Rather than decipher my childish Mandarin, Mr Zhang preferred to rely on WeChat's translation system. This must work better going from English to Mandarin than vice versa because I once stepped off a plane and received a message from him that read "I look forward to receiving you in my mouth", instead of what it actually said, which was "meet you at the gate".

I sent Mr Zhang a message to see if he knew where I could get a new PA-02. This time the imperfections of the translation function produced a rather more prophetic response, which read "there is no pigeon flying".

Regardless of his own doubts, Mr Zhang set about hunting one down and located second hand bikes from two of the other big four bike brands in China, Yongjiu (Forever) and Fenghuang (Phoenix). I went to look at the Phoenix as it was in the same second hand shop where another friend had suggested I may find a second-hand PA-02.

Outside the shop, there was a number of bikes for sale in something resembling the sales of stolen bikes that police hold in Britain. Only in this instance the police hadn't been involved at any stage. Inside there was a few second hand Flying Pigeons, though these were exclusively the Light Roadster model – weighing in at a feathery 18kg - and not the unforgiving behemoth that is the PA-02.

Just as I was about to give up, a week later I had an unexpected breakthrough. As part of the online endeavours that had led to my failed Taobao romances, I had found the last remaining corners of Flying Pigeon admiration. Perhaps unsurprisingly they were based in Los Angeles, London, Tallinn, Toronto and Barcelona; the kind of cities where the true fuel of nostalgia - disposable income - exists in enough pockets to warrant a supply of iconic, but fundamentally useless, bicycles. Without too much hope, I had sent out speculative e-mails to ask the foreign importers about their suppliers.

I received a reply from a man called Antonio, who lived in Barcelona. He imported classic Flying Pigeons to sell throughout Europe and was fantastically helpful and supportive. He kindly put me in touch with the recently retired export manager of Flying Pigeon, Mr Wang.

After a couple of phone calls and e-mails, Mr Wang explained that unless they were specifically ordered in a flock of 200 or more, Flying Pigeon no longer made classic models like the PA-02. This was a quantity that no domestic agents were interested in purchasing. He did, though, go on to provide the exciting offer of being able to get one from the factory, or if this wasn't possible, he could "present one from his collection". Finally, I had caught a pigeon.

Mr Wang was, however, far less convinced of my plan to cycle the bike home to Beijing. "This bike is no good for a long journey" he said convincingly, whilst unconvinced. Undeterred, whilst being deterred, I was going back to Tianjin.

1.1 My Cycling History

I do not possess an impressive Palmarès. If I was to commit the highlights of my cycling career to paper, the proudest entry would be 34th place in the youth category at round six of the Midlands Electricity Super Series downhill mountain bike race in 1999. This is sadly a claim that can still be corroborated by the internet[3]. I did once come far higher up the rankings, making it to the heady heights of 13th place. Yet this was out of 14 starters, one of whom retired injured. In short, I am rubbish at cycling.

Despite my ineptitude, I have always loved bicycles. Like the rest of Britain, my formative cycling years were dominated by Raleigh. Britain's most famous bicycle producer provided my first three bikes; from a tiny yellow BMX, through a blue mid-sized monstrosity that claimed to be a mountain bike, and finishing with the even more horrendous Activator II; a bike so bad that even the heaviest of teenage customisations couldn't rectify any of its many faults.

Next came a Kona Lava Dome, a bright green mountain bike, which I still remember fondly. This affection is most likely due to the Kona arriving at an age when life is almost exclusively about a narrow band of obsessions. Sadly for the Lava Dome, I split my obsessions between my first true love, football, and riding bikes. However, it still got enough attention for me to snap its frame at my local jumps[4]. Its replacement was the outlandish Spooky Bandwagon, which arrived just in time for sixth form, part-time jobs, the discovery of booze, the ability to fall in love on a daily basis, and not very much cycling.

---

[3] http://www.mikrotime.com/mtb/bcf/meb9906.html

[4] Taken from the Saxon word meaning 'teenage boys hanging around mounds of mud'.

University may not have revived my cycling career, but it did bring the Tour de France back into my life. As the Spooky sat dormant in the utility room or hallway, annoying housemates with its presence, I would take advantage of the minuscule amount of time a law degree calls upon students to be present and a job where all of my shifts began at 6pm, to watch drug-fuelled monsters storm up a mountain without the slightest hint of physical pain. Many happy afternoons were spent sitting through hours of swooping helicopter views of valleys and pixelated shots of mountain ascents that troubled the technology of the time. Though these were the Tour's years of shame, it was still exciting. It was certainly better than studying law.

Despite Lance and co I still love cycling. I am just old enough to remember the Tour de France in a nostalgic, if naïvely fond, way. The highlights show on Channel 4 in the late eighties and early nineties was a key part of my attempt to exclusively watch or play sports for the first 16 years of my life. I am equally fortunate to be young enough to go and watch the post-shame tours in person, without the guilt of handcuffing any children to radiators to facilitate such a trip. Nowadays, the grand tours are in my life full-time thanks to a rare sports-related time zone dividend. The last four hours of most stages take place between 8pm and midnight Beijing time, which is the perfect way to alienate a loved one in the summer months.

With the financial security of getting myself onto a graduate scheme, only a matter of months before Northern Rock went under and the concept of financial security didn't seem quite so laughable, I bought an expensive mountain bike. At a time where others may have been saving for a house deposit, or buying engagement rings, I was advancing my salary to buy a bicycle. A bicycle designed for mountains no less. Two months before I was due to move to London. It was the cycling equivalent of a Chelsea tractor. I deserved to have it stolen.

At least it was insured, because of this, I could afford to admire the lengths the criminals went to in removing it from the concrete bike storage facility outside my flat. They cut through steel bars, slipped themselves and the bikes through a narrow gap that was at least four feet off the ground. All on top of cutting off the locks. The police knew the thieves but had no hope, or at least no intention, of getting the bike back.

At this point, most people give up on owning a real bike in London, but I decided to buy one that was more attractive and easier to steal. At least it was suited to the purpose of commuting this time. My Bianchi was the first road bike I'd ever ridden. It is also the best bike I have ever owned. It just felt so much faster – because it was – than anything else I'd experienced before. When it was stolen, I was not so admiring of the thieves.

Though I should have been. This time they had to get through two separate doors requiring a separate key card and manual key. Once through there, they had to get into a metal cage with a number code and then cut off the motorbike lock I used to secure it.

This time the police were more optimistic. After reporting the crime, the police officer asked if there was anything else he could do for me. I shocked him by responding that they could, if it wasn't too much trouble, help find my bike.

"Oh, is it a real bike then, not just an insurance thing?" The policeman responded.

"Yeah, it's a Bianchi. I'm very fond of it." Said the emotionally stunted 26-year-old.

"A Bianchi, oh right. OK, well go to Redacted Market on Saturday. If it's going to show up anywhere, it will be there. Call us if you see it, don't try and steal it back."

"I wouldn't be stealing it, it's mine."

"OK, well don't try to get it back or buy it back or anything, without us present."

"I'm definitely not going to buy it back."

Sadly, my beloved Bianchi wasn't at the market. Every so often I would see the same model, in about the same size and would stare intently for the large blood stain on the right-hand grip, which would have all but identified it as mine. This unique record of ownership was the result of an incident involving whiskey, the hour of the morning known as 4am and MI6. Though the latter was only really involved because a pothole catapulted me over the bars in Vauxhall and my friend Ali and I ended up fixing the bike under the entrance to Vauxhall Cross' helpfully bright lights.

Its replacement – and again I wasn't for quitting on owning an expensive bike in the bike stealing capital of Europe - was the new model of the same bike. Inexplicably, it was appalling. If I was as narrow-minded as someone reviewing cars on the television with xenophobic panache, it would be tempting to attribute this inconsistency to its Italian origins, but it was made in Taiwan. Slyly, Bianchi hides the genuine place of birth by placing the *Made in Taiwan* sticker under the bottom bracket, whilst the red white and green "Italian Designed" label fools nobody on the seat tube.

I hated that bike, and worst of all, so did everybody else. Even the bike thieves wouldn't steal it. They took the £200 BMX, which I had bought because I couldn't face riding the Bianchi, but wouldn't take the cursed bike from the very same cage.

So it came to be that the worst bike I've had in nearly twenty years came with me to Beijing. It's no wonder I wanted a different bike. The only question was what bike to get.

Confession time. The Pigeon was not the first classic Chinese bike over which I had lusted. When I worked in Shanghai four years earlier, a company started renovating the old Yongjiu China

Post bikes. These, as all of the classic Chinese bikes did, bore an extremely close resemblance to a PA-02. There is, however, one crucial difference with the China Post bicycles, they are a rich, deep green with gold trim. A classic colour combination, which made them more than stand out in the sea of black.

Eventually, I was dissuaded from buying one by the cost of shipping it back to Britain at the end of my time in Shanghai. They looked magnificent though, and the idea of buying one stuck with me. In truth, the original search for a classic bike to bumble around Beijing on had started by rekindling my quest for a China Post bike. However, once I became caught up in the history of it all, it wasn't long before my attentions moved on to Flying Pigeon and specifically the PA-02.

2. PIGEON FANCIER

In the broadest of broad brush strokes, Flying Pigeon's history is a microcosm of China's recent past. Beginning life as a foreign company in the 1930s, it was nationalised in the 40s, revolutionised in the 50s, survived the 60s and 70s, grew in the 80s and 90s, before diversifying in the noughties.

In 1936 an individual, whom the official history of Flying Pigeon records simply as 'a Japanese businessman', started a factory known as Changho Works that began producing bicycles under the brand name 'Anchor'.

In one of history's more linguistically satisfying moves. the triumphant Nationalists nationalised the factory after World War 2. Doubtless aware of the historic parallels between winning a war and taking over a bicycle factory, the Nationalists renamed the company 'Victory'. This would be the one time that the company would have anything like an aspirational moniker.

After the civil war, the victorious Communist Party (CCP) took over the factory and Liu Shaoqi[5], Vice Chairman of the Government, declared that it would be the first bicycle manufacturer in post-Civil War China.

Presumably stumped for ideas following their own triumph over the Nationalists, the Communists initially struggled for a name.

"But we beat them Captain Man Er Ling".

"I know that Corporal Zhong, but we can't call it Victory can we? Victory is their name."

The new company opted to rebrand as Zhongzi[6], though this did

---

[5] Mao's heir apparent and President of China until he was purged in the late 1960s. Liu Shaoqi's reputation was posthumously rehabilitated in 1980. Door, horse, bolted etc.

[6] To be clear it was not named after a fictitious Corporal in a Chinese version of Dad's Army.

not last long. Very shortly afterwards, they once more took inspiration from the battlefield to rebrand. In reference to the Korean War on their border, the brand logo became a white dove of peace in flight. So in 1950 the Flying Dove was born. At least it would have been if there were separate words for dove and pigeon in Mandarin, or if the person responsible for the translation had seen a logo. As it was, an oversight left the English-speaking world with the most underwhelming of brand names; Flying Pigeon.

Is it a plane? Is it Superman? Is it a...nah, it's just a pigeon.

Underwhelming a name though it was, at least it was accurate. Bulky, ubiquitous and often covered in the dirt of urban or rural environs, the first of the brood to arrive - the PA-02, was always going to be a pigeon and not a dove. This was not a bike made for exporting, this was a bike to carry the revolution forwards. Born in the days before intellectual property litigation bored the life out of everybody, the PA-02 was *closely modelled* on the 1932 Raleigh Roadster. The PA-02's design is credited to an employee called Huo Baoji, of whom the rather concise history of Flying Pigeon tells us no further information. Though it seems safe to assume he was a dab hand with tracing paper[7].

The PA-02 officially hatched on July 5 1950, the same day that the United States engaged in the Korean War. Which came first, the pigeon or the war, isn't clear. Though there's more than a hint of a political advisor rushing the press releases out after hearing that the Battle of Osan had kicked off.

The PA-02 is not an only child, the PA-06 and PA-13 (in China

---

[7] http://www.flying-pigeon.cn/EN/about.aspx?pcateid=164&cateid=165 – though the English translation has been edited since the version I used. Frustratingly it now includes the juicy titbit that Pigeons are used as a dowry for brides, which could have given the book a whole new narrative.

surnames come first) completed the traditional family photograph. The younger sister, PA-13, is a poetry reading, flowing-dress wearing girl, who dreams of leaving her miserable industrial town for a better life in Europe and has the Dutch-style, curved, step-through frame to prove it. PA-06, the little brother, is the over-fed sibling who's staying behind to run the farm and has an additional top bar designed to withstand the weight of carrying a pig straddled across the bicycle's frame. This widespread story about the double top bar's primary purpose being to accommodate swine is probably an urban rural myth, but it's a fantastic one so I'm all for perpetuating it.

However, it was the first born who would grow up to be the icon. Mao's successor, and exonerator of Liu Shaoqi, Deng Xiaoping used it as the key performance indicator of prosperity, where China's economic development would amount to a "Pigeon in every household". In fairness to Deng, in Mandarin he could have been saying dove, thus it would have sounded slightly less like having an avian pest problem was an indicator of economic progress.

In the 1980s, having survived China's hardest times in living memory, the PA-02 and the generation born with it, propelled China along the first creaky pedal strokes towards being the world's biggest economy again.

In 1994 Flying Pigeon was designated the honour of being a 'national key trademark brand under protection'. Intentionally, or not, this coincided with the beginning of the PA-02's end, where China's economic reforms and great opening up would start to build the environment that delivered the diverse makeup of China's transportation today and eventually lead to the present situation where it was nearly impossible to buy a new PA-02 in its homeland.

***

By the time I returned to Tianjin to meet Mr Wang, the beautiful colours of autumn had given way to the naked branches and freezing temperatures of early December. The city was under endless blue skies, which were complemented by the kind of wind chill that caused me to dedicate an unusually large amount of time to wondering where my testicles might be hiding.

With almost 15 million inhabitants in the municipality, Tianjin is probably the biggest city you know about, which some smug cretin living in China thinks you've never heard of. I had arranged to meet Mr Wang at Yang Wu Zhuang metro station, which was on the very southern outskirts of the city. He was already in the car park when I arrived. He trotted over to me at speed and after a warm handshake we jumped into his little white minivan and headed further south to the Flying Pigeon factory.

Mr Wang worked for Flying Pigeon from 1969 until his recent retirement. We joked about our differing career patterns. He had spent 45 years with one company, whereas I, at the age of 30, was about to start working for my 10th different employer. Nowadays, Mr Wang did some part-time consultancy work for Flying Pigeon, presumably handling the requests from London, Los Angeles, Tallinn, Toronto, and Tono in Barcelona, as well as dealing with the odd clown like me.

We spoke about Flying Pigeon's export markets in 2014. For the company as a whole, Asia was the largest market, followed by Africa, where most of the classic style bikes like the PA-02s were sold. Anti-dumping measures meant they exported relatively few bicycles to the EU. Mr Wang was warm and engaging, he was interested in my family and why I was in China. He was also making a huge effort to help me out. Not only was he driving me to the factory but he had also bought two new tyres and inner tubes with him from a "special shop" because he knew those on the model I was picking up were not good enough.

All of which made me feel like a complete bastard for spending the afternoon carefully avoiding the truth about my real intentions for the bike. When Mr Wang asked if I would return by train that evening, aware of his previous doubts, I answered honestly that I would be staying in a hotel. After he told me the 30km from the factory to the hotel would be too far to cycle, I hastily fibbed that a friend would pick me up the following day in a mini-van similar to his. My lie was met with further, undeserved kindness. Mr Wang said he would drive me and the bike to my hotel that afternoon.

From mere embarrassment, my feelings were upgraded to outright shame as it became abundantly clear that Mr Wang was the kind of decent human being everybody adored. As we entered the building, a woman in her early twenties, with eyes full of affection, ran up to him to say "hello boss". Then, when the young guard responsible for the factory showroom was a fastidious bore, Mr Wang just coolly phoned the manager, handed over the phone and headed in. He didn't even beat the youngster around the face with his own hat, which was the very least he deserved.

In the showroom, Flying Pigeon's current flock of bicycles were all on display. Children's bicycles, fixies, mountain bikes, fat-tyred cruisers, and time-trial bikes were all on show. There was every type of bicycle but for a BMX or penny farthing. At the very top end of the long, thin room it was heartening to see that pride of place on the tallest plinth was a PA-02.

There were four PA-02's left, all of which had originally been made for a Ugandan auto-parts company, with the magnificently misleading name of Nile Fishing Company. Like its 20th century history, Flying Pigeon continues to tell part of China's economic story in the new millennium, where China is now the supplier to Africa's own development.

Mr Wang and I set about squeezing tyres and brake levers, rotating the pedals by hand, and generally fiddling with bits of metal in a way that unites people the world over. If he was ever in the position to go on a house viewing in Britain, Mr Wang would definitely be checking the anti-slam action on all the kitchen draws in an outwardly nonchalant, yet secretly attentive, manner.

After a few minutes, I decided upon a particular PA-02, which prompted Mr Wang to ask if I wanted to keep the saver forks. The saver forks are the chrome, spring-topped, stanchions, which sit in front of the main forks. They look exceptionally cool. I definitely wanted them for aesthetic reasons, but wanting to show some deference to Mr Wang's expertise I asked what he thought. "Well, they were made for a time when the roads were much worse. But they are very useful when the forks snap." I looked at the sharp angle near the bottom of the actual forks, imagined them snapping mid-way between Tianjin and Beijing the next day, noted my testicles had only just re-descended in the warmth of the showroom, then opted strongly in favour of keeping the saver forks.

With the decision made it was time to pay. On Mr Wang's insistence, we would fit the superior tyres in the factory. I say we, but at this point, a man in his twenties called Zhang appeared and set about tuning the chosen one.

As we started trying to pay, there was initially some problems with the model not being made to domestic market regulations, as it was originally intended for export to Africa. Eventually, these issues were resolved. However, I can't tell you what the solution was, as the Vice General Manager had insisted I sit in an office next door to have a rest. I'd like to think the solution was a pragmatic, yet creative, one. Perhaps it was decided that since I was a foreigner, the bike was, for all intents and purposes, still being exported after all. I fear, though, they just had to put reflectors on the pedals.

When I popped to the toilet I noticed that the red bicycles of Beijing's bike scheme were also assembled here! Like one of the great stories from Chinese history, much of the cause of PA-02's downfall was coming from within its own family. Which is my shameless excuse to shoehorn in some historical smut.

At times, Chinese history is up there with some of Caligula's very best efforts. It's filled to the brim with treachery, filth, and debauchery. My favourite debauched tale is centred around a Chancellor named Lu Buwei.

Around the time Rome and Carthage were having fisticuffs over who could have all the olives and wine, Lu was playing pull the noodle with a particularly appealing concubine.

Unfortunately for Lu, the Crown Prince also had eyes for the same woman, eventually making her his bride. Prior to this marriage, one of the two men fathered a child with the concubine-who-would-be-queen. Lu outlived his royal rival but for one reason or another – perhaps many years being the court archery board had taken the shine off her allure – Lu decided he had no interest in the now dowager queen. Wanting to be rid of her, Lu orchestrated a scandal to sully her name beyond repair by tempting her into the bed of another man.

All those years studying the Queen's likes and dislikes came in useful to Lu. Following a search, of which the details are sadly lacking, Lu found a man with an unusually large penis. To draw his former lover's attention to the man with the Great Wallop of China in his pants, Lu had him walk around with a wooden wheel on his giant, presumably erect, phallus.

Sure enough, hearing about a man who could impersonate an axle peaked the Queen's interest. This interest ultimately led to the Queen having two more sons, which caused her first son (now King and possibly Lu's son) to view his new half-brothers as a threat to his rule. The new King decided to clean things up in the way powerful families have done for eternity, through brutal, fraternal violence and cruelty.

The sordid tale ends with death for the King's half-brothers, exile for his mother and suicide for Lu. Though Lu's fate sounds quite favourable compared to our friend in possession of the equineesque endowment, who was pulled apart by two chariots. No mention is made as to whether one of the wheels on the chariot was the same one that got him into this trouble in the first place. His rivals, whether genuine or imagined, now dead. The all-powerful King goes on to become the First Emperor; you know, the unifier of China, terracotta warriors and all that[8].

Anyway, I deliberately digress. It eventually transpired that Mr Zhang and a colleague were tuning the whole bicycle, which was good for my chances of making it back to Beijing alive, but much worse for my increasing levels of deceit-filled shame. Eventually Mr Wang returned with receipts for the bicycle and tyres. The bicycle cost about £31, the tyres around £7. I had change from £40, after buying a new bicycle and extra tyres, in 2014.

£31 is roughly the double the price it cost to buy one at the peak of its desirability in the 1980s. At this time getting a Pigeon was even more of a struggle than even my own present-day travails, which had lasted only a couple of months. At times there could be a waiting list of two years, in spite of Flying Pigeons costing the equivalent of many weeks' salary for the majority of Chinese workers at this time.

I went to inspect the bicycle with Mr Wang, who immediately started to dismantle the front end so it would fit in his minivan and my imaginary friend's equally fictional vehicle the following

---

[8] *Fact warning!* – Like lots of great history this story is almost certainly a total fabrication. For a sober account read (Keay, 2009).

day. Though I was keen to get to the hotel and get to sleep, this presented a major problem. I would have to reassemble the bike myself at a time when I didn't have a spanner, which is the key tool when you're essentially dealing with the world's largest set of Meccano.

I took out my phone and hastily searched for bike shops near my hotel and saw that there was a Giant shop within a mile. Mr Wang explained he had to meet someone for dinner, so he would drop me off at the metro station and then deliver the bike to my hotel before 9pm. This was good as it gave me a little time to get to the Giant shop and buy Mr Wang a gift, which was as representative of my guilt as it was my thanks.

It was gone 7.30pm by the time I reached the shuttered windows of the closed Giant shop. I resolved the best thing to do was get Mr Wang a gift, check-in, stay an extra night, set the bike up the following day and then return to Beijing the day after that. I sighed and set out back towards my hotel through the dark, cold and hectic streets of Tianjin.

Walmart was not my first choice of establishment in which to buy Mr Wang a gift. Initially, I was going to give him my Team Sky Racing Jersey, but given he is in his sixties I had decided that the newest Zhang in my life would be better suited to it and so went elsewhere to find Mr Wang a gift. Walmart exceeded expectations in some fashion. I managed to find a presentation box of two bottles of French wine. Better still, on my way in I had noticed an advertisement for bicycles. I headed up to the second floor and from the edge of the escalator could make out a group of children's bikes. Behind those however, was a puncture repair kit that contained a multi-sized spanner. The dream was alive again! It also meant I had a puncture repair kit, which was also previously on my longer than helpful list of idiotic oversights. Though seen as this list still had 'pump' on it, the puncture repair kit may as well have remained on that list.

As I picked up the puncture repair kit, Jingle Bell Rock began to play on the tinny shop speakers, causing me to trot to the tills beaming with festive, spanner related, joy.

With Mr Wang not due for an hour or so, I put October's dress rehearsal into practice. In preparation for the following day's exertions, I set about eating pizza, chips, and a big bowl of garlic flavoured broccoli. As promised, Mr Wang arrived just before 9pm, and I went downstairs to meet him. We carried the different bits of bicycle across the foyer, passing the many and varied mouths-wide-open expressions of the hotel's reception staff.

After negotiating the tight turn through the hotel room door, Mr Wang shook my hand and offered any help he could give me whilst I was in China, which was very kind of him. Then again, he didn't really know what I was up to. I imagine me calling him at 3am requesting an air ambulance at a location I couldn't describe, wasn't quite what he had in mind.

As soon as the door was locked, I set upon the bits of bicycle like a child on Christmas day. The spanner was of the cheap and nasty kind that would cause sleepless nights if you had used it to assemble your bed, but it was just about good enough to get the bike together. Though the seat collar really required a second spanner to get the job done properly, everything was attached in the location it should have been.

I stood back and admired all £38 of bicycle in front of me, and Holy Mao! It is one big bird. At over six feet long and with 28-inch wheels, it was taller than any bicycle I'd seen before. That considered, box fresh, with its brown saddle and shining chrome rims, pedals, cranks, bell, bar, and brakes, it is an incredibly stylish bicycle[9]. One thing I hadn't expected was that the stanchions holding up the rear luggage rack would be twisted like a Victorian churchyard gate; a brief moment of flair amongst the otherwise unrelenting brutalism.

With the bicycle assembled and my belly full, I got into bed to maximise the amount of sleep I would get before my intended 5am departure. However, my sleep was delayed by the phenomena of the region that is static electricity. In winter, North East China becomes a great big game of Buzz Wire, where something climatic that I don't understand means you get two or three static shocks a day. Having slipped into bed wearing a fluffy bathrobe I had a potential power output similar to Sizewell B. As I leant over to turn the bedside light off I caught the metal edge of the bedside table first, causing my hand to recoil so quickly I slapped myself on the nose.

This incident delayed my sleep by a good 45 minutes. The morning encore, however, meant that I would be leaving Tianjin wide awake.

After terrifying the dozing receptionist by clattering 21kg of steel out of the lift, I pushed the Pigeon out into the freezing fresh air of the empty city just after 5am. I awkwardly rolled down the wheelchair access ramp, seated higher than ever before on a bicycle. A feeling that lasted approximately 15 seconds longer, before the loose seat post collar gave in and my lardy mass pushed the seat right down into the frame. As I crossed the road in order to head north, I weaved and wiggled around with all the self-confidence of a man washing a large courgette by hand.

---

[9] On my first outing with the Pigeon in Beijing, whilst locked to a tree outside a coffee shop, it drew the attention of a very attractive lady. The lady spent the majority of her phone call caressing the saddle and squeezing the Pigeon's brakes like something out of an innuendo laden advert for chocolates.

Almost immediately I passed under my favourite Chinese road safety sign, which instructs motorists not to tell jokes and drive. I could not be certain that a passing motorist commenting on my present situation would be in contravention of this rule. It might sound like a strange traffic regulation to have, and I don't know the exact numbers, but the thing about being such a populous country is that a number of drivers and passengers will actually die laughing. In 2010, over 275,000[10] people died in road traffic accidents in China. The equivalent of wiping out the entire population of Derby in one year. This was something I tried not to think too much about as I swayed across the icy road.

I wobbled a little further along but quickly got into a rhythm that saw me leaving the Tianjin city area by sunrise. On the very edge of the city limits, I stopped on a bridge to take a photo and had a chat with two pensioners on their early morning walk. They loved the bike and gave nods of approval when I explained my aim was to cycle 140km to Beijing.

By my breakfast stop in Wuqing district, I had covered 35km in two hours, at this rate I'd be home in just six more hours. Already, though, the single gear and enforced low seat position were asking challenging questions of my knees. Questions that caused them to glance at one another, shrug, and then stare blankly ahead in complete befuddlement as to what was going on.

A further two hours later, 50km into the ride, I had my first genuine difficulties. With my knees starting to ache, I stopped at a petrol station in what has to count as the middle of nowhere on China's densely populated eastern seaboard. Using skills learnt during my time as an amateur nutritionist, I purchased a can of cattle branded energy drink famous for misleading customers

---

[10] (WHO, 2013, p. 244)

about its ability to facilitate flight and two bars of chocolate famous for being called Snickers, for a grand sum of 65p. I stood in the warmth of the shop to consume them as the bemused cashier stared at my bobble hat.

The next nine hours were not the most fun I've had in my life. Getting to half way was not the fillip you may think it would be. Yes, my glass was half full, but it was half full of gone off milk, which someone else had already spat back into the glass and I was now gleefully glugging the lukewarm contents, inclusive of chunks.

I became more and more fearful that if I stopped my knees would seize up and I'd be stranded embarrassingly close to home. The lowest of low points came between 80km and 90km, where an ugly headwind slowed my progress to 5kph for two hours. This unfortunately happened on a long straight, which made the experience all the more crushing. It felt like the empty high-rise flats of the impending ghost suburb, awaiting a million or so inhabitants from Beijing's overspill, would never be reached.

I unleashed Led Zeppelin on my ears and battled through. By now it was as much a mental task as a physical one. Fortunately, my first paid job that didn't involve delivering newspapers was working for a large American giraffe who sold toys. My role there was, essentially, to do nothing for nine hours a day. It was in this nurturing environment I learnt the art of turning my brain off for long periods of time. Though useful for long haul flights, conferences, and clothes shopping, it was on this first flight of the Pigeon that this experience really paid off.

Although my mind was resiliently numb, my knees were the very opposite. 30km from home on the edge of Beijing near the area of Tongzhou, they gave up in protest. The angle at which they were squeezing out the power to move me was causing them to burn with pain. I slowed down very gradually, before stumbling off the bike and sitting on the curb for 20 minutes. I was only 4km from the start of the Beijing metro. The safe zone. No matter what, if I made it to Tongzhou, I had technically made it to Beijing. If it came to it, in Tongzhou I could lock the bike up, get the metro and then return the next day to collect the Pigeon[11].

Sometimes in China, just when you need a bit of inspiration, something monumentally large will turn up. Tongzhou had one such perspective provider in the Grand Canal. Impossible to confuse with its Venetian namesake, the Grand Canal is almost as unfathomably bonkers as the Great Wall in its scale. It was almost certainly more useful.

Tongzhou is the northern end of the 1776km waterway. It is the start of the most northerly section that links the capital with Tianjin. The canal then goes on to link the Yellow and Yangtze rivers and runs all the way south to Hangzhou. Like the Wall though, this monumental endeavour wasn't created in the industrial age. It was linked together at some point around the same time that the Roman Empire ceased to be a living memory in Europe.

Admittedly, the route passed through existing bodies of water, but still, imagine joining the famous canals of Venice and their yet-to-be infamous cousins in Birmingham by the year 600. You can have the English Channel, the Thames, the Rhine, the Swiss lakes and the rest as a starter. It is still an incredible amount of digging.

Full of faux perspective for the sake of narrative, I raised myself from the kerb as if I'd been thinking about the Grand Canal and not pizza for inspiration. As it turned out, my knees hadn't seized up, and if anything, by continuing without breaks it appeared I'd

---

[11] Honesty footnote - this would not have happened.

made the situation worse. What they needed was a rest. Hardly rejuvenated, but less annoyed with me, they resumed bending. After a little more progress, I passed through Tongzhou and followed the Batong metro line into the centre of Beijing. The final 20km took over two hours and involved the ignominy of having a crowd of thirty or so people watch me empty two sugar sachets from the hotel tea and coffee making facilities into my bright red face at a set of traffic lights as I tried to persuade my legs to stop wobbling.

By sunset, I could see the hazy silhouette of the CCTV building[12] in central Beijing and with great relief knew I was definitely going to make it back. For the final thirty minutes, I crawled along the roads I used daily, desperately trying to maintain the level of vigilance a Beijing bicycle lane requires. Bicycle lane is a misnomer, given that scooters, taxis, motorbikes, the Death Star, pedestrians, mobile food stalls, rickshaws, cars, and everyone else utilise them. Direction of travel is also a matter of personal choice. Eventually, I arrived home unscathed, some 13 and a half hours after leaving Tianjin.

Exhausted, I began running a bath before examining the wear and tear inflicted upon the bike and my body. The bike, besides one or two loose bolts, was in pristine condition. From the front, I looked dishevelled, but acceptably so. The view of my rear was far less conventional. As I craned over my own shoulder to look towards the mirror I could see that my backside was emblazoned with a crescent of six, equidistant red dots from the saddle's studs. I may have bought the Pigeon, but the Pigeon clearly owned me and it had branded my arse as a reminder.

---

[12] CCTV; China's satirically named state broadcaster. Locally known as the big underpants, the CCTV building is an iconic piece of architecture. From some angles it does look like a huge pair of metallic shorts.

When I first came to China in 2011, I could not believe just how much everybody seemed to be moving. It is relentless; I can't think of a moment where I've been outdoors in China and I couldn't see someone else moving. From the 80-somethings trotting down the street for their morning exercise to the man carrying a fridge-freezer on an electric scooter; China is a country that feels like the population is physically moving it forward themselves. It is true that if everybody in China jumped at the same time the world would shake, but only because everybody had stopped moving.

Like the generation who spent years propelling them, the PA-02 has reached retirement age. That same generation still makeup the vast majority of the model's owners. The PA-02 is having a dignified time of it in 2015, often being pedalled at such a gentle speed around the cities, towns, and villages, that it seems implausible they can be upright. They're still moving, though, always moving.

Agony or not, completely the wrong tool for the job or not, branded backside or not, the Pigeon had triumphed by making it back from Tianjin. Perhaps because it played so hard to get, I had become smitten with the Pigeon and this burgeoning romance had allowed my imagination to fly away with itself. As I soaked my aching knees and stinging backside in the bath I decided to take the Pigeon on a much, much, much bigger journey across its homeland in the months leading up to its 65th birthday.

2.1 MAPS

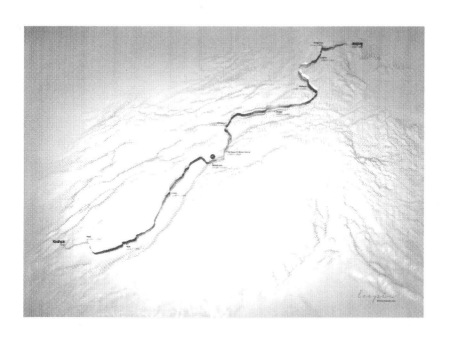

3. HIBERNATION AND PREPARATION

For a country that still contains a number of mysteries for the foreign visitor, there is one definitive absolute about China. It is massive. I could concoct a fictional discussion with myself over which path I decided to take, but from Beijing, there is one very obvious route to take for a ride across the country. You make like a Pet Shop Boy and go west.

To go south would mean endless days of heavy pollution along the industrialised eastern seaboard. To go southwest would have meant mountains too high for the Pigeon to fly over. To go north or northeast, looked too short. To go east looked far too much like the ocean.

Going west offered cleaner air and quieter roads. Most of all, going west meant an incomparable mix of cultures, geography, and history.

I plotted a route out of Beijing, through Hebei, into the grasslands and desert of Inner Mongolia, down into tiny Ningxia, before joining the Silk Road in Gansu, then finally travelling through colossal Xinjiang to finish in Kashgar on China's western border. It was a route that tested the full-colour scheme of geographical maps, from the everyday greens and yellows to exotic purples. There were mountains, deserts, a plateau, there was even a depression.

For the ultimate romantic ending, I would have arrived in Kashgar on July 5, for the Pigeon's birthday. However, I had a narrative unfriendly deadline of a wedding on June 27, on the opposite side of the world in New York. Following some rough calculations and an algorithm involving the date of Holly's birthday and how long it would take to get a suit made for the wedding, my planned start date revealed itself to be April 7.

Though my knees weren't quite ready to hear it, 60 days seemed to be a reasonable estimate to cover the distance. At approximately 4500km as the pigeon flies, this made for a very manageable looking 75km a day. Though as soon as ten rest days were subtracted, that total crept up to 90km a day; precisely 10km short of the distance my unprepared body fell apart at on the ride from Tianjin.

Allowing for an average additional 10km a day for getting in and out of cities, snack-chasing, and getting lost, I was left with a palatable average of 100km for 50 days cycling and ten rest days. 40km less than the journey I had undertaken in December.

This all sounded manageable but the ride from Tianjin had taught me a number of lessons about both the PA-02 and myself, which would make 100km a day far more challenging than it looked on the glow of a laptop screen.

After the ride from Tianjin, it had taken a full 48 hours before I could contemplate a gentle 2km ride to a café. It was not only the Pigeon who was not designed for long journeys. In my current state, I would require 100 rest days, not ten.

I also had relatively kind conditions for the ride from Tianjin. It was flat, the wind was low and the pollution was only classified as dangerously unhealthy. In addition, I was only carrying a light rucksack, and though it was freezing cold, this was a blessing in disguise for my levels of hydration and comfort.

Not being the Communist Party or an even a lesser being, such as God, I wouldn't be able to affect the gradient, climate, distance or pollution. I could, however, limit the load and get myself fit enough to survive.

Though limiting the Pigeon's additional load appears to be the equivalent of drinking a mineral water with a second helping of burger and chips; every kilogram would matter, no matter how ironic they seemed.

Limiting the load that I would carry on the Pigeon's back was relatively easy. A giddy fifteen minutes in the business model conundrum that is Sports Direct provided all of my camping gear with the exception of a tent. I also picked up two cycling shirts that were the same colour as the consequence of mistaking a glow stick for a novelty cocktail.

I turned to one of the internet's bike shop leviathans for the bits that really mattered — in other words, the items that would protect and maintain either the Pigeon or my genitals. You can't mess around when it comes to your own kids after all. Especially if they've not yet been conceived. I also purchased some bits and pieces I'd never used before like rehydration tablets and muscle recovery powder, to see if they really do help; and chamois cream, which I really needed to help.

A tent, changes of clothing, a wash bag, sun cream and luxury items like a camera and laptop would finish the additional load, which all weighed in at an indulgent 20kg. I was, after all, going for enjoyment and interest. I would not be going for any records with one gear. Another thing that was a product of indulgence was my own weight, but there was at least something I could do about that.

Someone once told me that the pollution shrouding Beijing was a filter to keep boring people out. This is certainly true for the foreigners living there, but I'm pretty sure the relaxing of residency rules for Chinese people plays a much bigger role. Whatever the combination of causes, Beijing, pollution aside, is a phenomenal city.

It is one of three existing capital cities to possess a wonder of the world. Of the others, Rome feels like a city resigned to history, even if its resignation is beautiful and full of great food and wine. The other, Istanbul, puts up more of a fight in the categories of vibrancy and modern relevance, but I missed being blown up by only two hours on my last visit to Turkey, so I'm a little down on it for the time being. Also, Efes, yuck.

In the near future, Beijing is not going to feature alongside Vancouver, Melbourne or any of the beguiling entries given to Swiss cities on lists of the best places to live. But do you really want to live in the far flung extremities of Western civilisation, or worse, Switzerland? Or do you want to live in the most important city of the 21st century?

I'd choose Vancouver too.

That, though, is not the point. Beijing is booming in the way cities in Britain have never done in my lifetime. It's impossible not to get caught up in it. As a physical entity, it is completely imitable; the city's grid form and concrete horrors could be erected anywhere. The colour of Beijing is grey. Yet as a living, breathing, city it is inimitable. That same grey monotony hides a very real city and provides the perfect background to allow its colours to stand out.

Beyond the great history, the availability of the many and varied - but all excellent - cuisines of China, and the near total absence of violent crime, Beijing is also becoming a global city. It's sourcing the best bits of other global cities, tweaking them and leaving the worst bits out.

As Jonathon, a friend who later joined me for a week of the journey said of Beijing "It was like Shoreditch. Just without any twats. Well, except you." Imagine that, a world where progress has got as far as fairly priced craft beer and Korean-Mexican fusion food, but stopped itself well short of cereal cafes and beard glitter. Come to Beijing it's a polluted utopia[13].

Just don't come between November and February. In deep

---

[13] One caveat: you can't get a good Indian/Bangladeshi/Pakistani curry anywhere. Complete nightmare.

winter Beijing goes into hibernation. Thick, draft-excluding curtains cover doorways, rickshaws transform from open-top carriages to tin-can coffins in waiting and even the trees are dressed in thick coats.

In many ways this Beijing's winter is the ideal situation to lose weight and train for a marathon bike ride, as the body is forced to work harder to keep itself alive. On the other hand, it's really cold. Crawling along at 10kph for hours on end in temperatures of -10 or colder does not make for a life filled with smiles. Beijing winters also come with a Catch-22 weather situation. To clear the pollution and have air clean enough to exercise in, Beijing needs a northerly wind. Sadly, north of Beijing is Siberia, meaning the cleanest air is also the coldest. The cleanest days often come with a wind-chill factor in the minus-twenties or minus-thirties.

Not wanting to lose my nose to frostbite or have my lungs go the way of a pit canary, I decided to let the Pigeon hibernate through winter. A cowardly move but one that would also reduce wear on a bicycle that would be getting more than enough abuse in spring.

So my preparation started indoors. I had a head start in terms of building the right muscle groups for endurance cycling thanks to a purchase I made two years earlier; a turbo trainer. This was the kind of purchase that should make a man in his late twenties wonder if marriage and fatherhood are necessary steps to put a stop to such frivolity. Instead, throughout the 2013 Tour de France I spent many happy hour-long stints, wine in hand, cycling along to the stage highlights after work. Though a silly indulgence at the time, it would now be used for the purpose that it was always intended. Suffering.

These early training sessions allowed me to test out some chamois cream, an anti-bacterial substance, designed to keep the region you don't want covered in bacteria, clear of such trouble. It had become known as "gooch cream" the first time it was discussed with a critical mass of male friends, thanks to *Jackass* popularising gooch as a not exactly pleasant term for the perineum. The same conversation was so linear that it was only seconds before my own perineum had been rechristened as Graham.

Despite Graham's gooch cream keeping him and his close associates happy throughout training, it couldn't stop one terrifying phenomenon of the turbo trainer. Regardless of my position on the bike, the gear I used, or the resistance I set it at, without fail the tiny vibrations I was producing would eventually leave me numb where I least wanted to experience no sensation. The first time this happened I genuinely thought I'd lost my own balls; a sensation that caused such panic that I failed to unclip from the pedals as I rushed to dismount and rummage around my shorts. The bike and I crashed to the floor. A frantic catastrophe that left me with no answer to the pressing question about the location of my nads. Instead, I was left lying underneath the bicycle like a tortured upturned tortoise; a sight you occasionally still see on the streets of China's capital.

Despite the occasional moments of fear that I'd become a eunuch, I pressed on. After all, my literature review had made it abundantly clear I needed to lose a lot of weight. Tyler Hamilton and Daniel Coyle's excellent throwing-shit-and-watching-it-stick book *The Secret Race*, a tell-all about professional cycling in the late nineties and early very naughties, highlights just how important minimising weight is in cycling. There is no greater proof of this than how much more time Michele Ferrari, the godfather of EPO in cycling, focused on a rider's weight than he did on the contents of Lance Armstrong's other fridge.

Hamilton agreed with Ferrari too *"My body, which was being pushed like never before, didn't understand— it needed food, now! But here, as in so many things, Ferrari was right: as my weight dropped my performance improved. And kept improving."*[14]

Bradley Wiggins, looking a bit sneezy and red-eyed, in off-white Fred Perry garb, precariously perched on cycling's other shoulder agreed *"my weight loss means I'm carrying the equivalent of six bags of sugar less up a mountain. Shedding that weight is all that I can do to give myself the best chance on the climbs other than taking drugs, and I'm not going to do that."*

I am not quite a man who would name the scotch egg as his favourite variety of apple, but after Christmas I returned to Beijing a festively-fat, scale-testing, 85kg of cheese and stout. I had at least 10, if not 15kg to spare. I was carrying at least another half a Pigeon, or 10 bags of sugar in the Wiggins approved analogy for needless weight, for no reason whatsoever.

Weight loss is not a mystery. You just have to burn more calories than you consume, consistently, day after day. For me, it meant three very simple rules: less beer; almost no cheese; and a dramatic increase in the amount of exercise I did. I also began to take my vegetables in liquid form and try to forget just how much I love pizza and pasta.

In January I focused purely on weight loss. I consumed no cheese and reduced my alcohol intake to the amount I formally declare to doctors and employers. If I didn't have the chance to exercise, I skipped a meal. It was a basic system but by the end of January, I had dropped to 80kg. *Just* 2kg more than Bradley Wiggins weighed before he started his own weight loss regime, whilst standing a whole 15cm taller than me.

In February, I began to train for the ride itself whilst continuing the weight loss efforts. I started with hour long stints on the turbo

---

[14] (Coyle, 2013, p. 137)

trainer, grinding out a big gear with high resistance to replicate the Pigeon's unique punishment for legs.

Once deepest, darkest winter was over I also embarked on weekend training rides to the many and varied sights on the outskirts of Beijing. One of which took me to Marco Polo Bridge, a crossing over the almost barren Yongding River by the fifth ring road, so named because the wandering European was apparently an admirer of its 12th-century predecessor.

In anticipation of traversing much of his own route across China I had purchased a copy of Mr Polo's occasionally interesting but mostly mundane travel memoirs. His views on the bridge are indicative of his ability to build up excitement then disappoint. Marco thought that in its day there were "few bridges in the world that compare to it or match it in beauty". How does Marco, a man who had grown up amongst the canals and bridges of Venice, justify his gushing review? By confusing medieval military intelligence with aesthetics and pointing out "ten horsemen can easily ride across it a breast"[15].

The modern replica was also made of stone and wide enough for many a horse. However, as the stagnant water below gave the air its unique fragrance that afternoon, the decidedly less romantic Chinese name for it, Lu Ditch Bridge, seemed more appropriate.

The bridge occupies a more significant position in history than merely being spotted by a passing Venetian who was oddly prone to hyperbole and understatement all at once. As part of the agreements that followed the Boxer Rebellion, Japan was entitled to station troops in Beijing to secure the railway line to Tianjin; presumably helping factories like the recently established Changho Works to operate. One of the places that the Japanese

---

[15] (Cliff, 2015, p. 141)

troops were garrisoned was very close to Marco Polo Bridge. Following a textbook military history incident whereby some misunderstanding, escalation, brinkmanship, duplicity and stubbornness won out, the second full-scale Sino-Japanese war kicked off at this very place. The scars of the first shots can still be seen on the walls of the fortress sitting on the east bank of the bridge.

Other than an incident where I accidentally sent £20 worth of sushi to Holly's work address, rather than our flat, my diet continued pain-free. I persevered with the funny coloured vegetable drinks, as well as the relationship testing expenditure on protein from raw fish. After the festivities around Chinese New Year at the end of the month, I had only dropped a further 2kg to 78kg, but things were still going in the right direction.

Though in my defence, February also saw the closure of my gym. In traditional Chinese fashion, the gym and pool where I had a membership closed indefinitely after the owners simply didn't return after Chinese New Year. Not wanting to join and pay for another gym, this meant a total lack of variation in my exercise.

The gym was a brilliantly ramshackle establishment, where the chaos within was exaggerated by neighbouring a kickboxing gym full of muscular twenty-somethings working out in perfect synchronisation. The gym had many problems; from technical issues like some treadmills operating in miles per hour and others in kilometres per hour, but never declaring which; to fellow users who were so unprepared for exercise that I saw people running in flip-flops more than once. The tone was set by the management team of the gym. I once arrived to find a member of the team, still wearing his shirt and tie, sat on an exercise bike, eating a bucket of KFC.

So I was left with just cycling. In March I cycled for as many hours as I could. Whilst sat on the turbo trainer, I watched enough crime dramas to add 'Swedish - Business Proficient' and 'Danish – Native Speaker' to my LinkedIn profile.

The most efficient employee in China is the person who presses the button to change Beijing's season from winter to spring in the middle of March. By the time the button has recoiled to the position it maintains for the next 364 days, 23 hours, 59 minutes and 55 seconds, all the trees have had their coats taken off, the blossom has bloomed, and every pet dog has had their booties removed.

To celebrate the change of season; one weekend I headed northwest to Beijing's botanical gardens for another training ride. During this ride, a fierce wind whipped up the barren winter's entire deposit of pollution. This kind of pollution is not the persistent heavy metal stench that embraces Beijing on a nearly daily basis but a larger, dustier compatriot. Without the metallic stench, I was lured into a false sense of security.

Forgoing the mask that I usually would have worn if the smell had been more pungent, I headed into the wind for 90 minutes. It was only after arriving at the gardens when Julian – a friend who had joined me for the ride – looked at his phone and announced the pollution reading was 895 (eight hundred and ninety-five) particles of filth per whatever.

On a day to day basis, you can normally guess how polluted Beijing is by how far into the distance you can see. In general, it hovers around 150-200, which is broadly just very unhealthy for everyone. To give a sense of scale; big, dirty London rarely breaches 100. Above 300, where the health guidance runs out and the alarming adjectives finish, is considered hazardous; over 500 and the schools are closed. So 895 is an apocalyptic number. I desperately hope the majority of it was sand rather than metallic debris.

In my final week of preparation, I increased the number of

Chinese lessons I attended and focused on learning the more important phrases I would need: "no officer, I am not a spy"; "where is the hospital?"; and "you'll have to phone my mother using this number, when the screaming has stopped, ask her again what blood type I am."

By April 7, amongst the purple, white and yellows of Beijing's spring, after three months of consuming many green things, weighing in at 75kg and able to say "Just don't tell her how much blood I've lost", I was ready.

3.1 Diet of Champions

When I wasn't sending £20 of sushi to my girlfriend's work address by accident, or being berated for spending £20 on sushi, I would source protein in more economical and relationship friendly ways. Here are some of my favourites dishes to help you become a champion cyclist too.

3x3 Chicken Wings

Before Jamie Oliver MBE invented lemon, garlic and chilli, food in Britain was awful. This is my poultry-themed homage to him.

Ingredients

- 3 lemons
- 3 chillies
- 3 gloves of garlic
- 9 chicken wings

Method

Ideally, your chicken will be in an indeterminate state of refrigeration somewhere between frozen solid and dangerously half-cooked. I find over-priced Western supermarkets in China provide this as part of the service, but you may wish to freeze four or five wings and leave the remainder out near to a window facing the sun for maximum effect. Place the chicken into a Tupperware container, which can barely contain them; please note that you should use new Tupperware, which you yourself have purchased. You should not use the Tupperware your mother bought in the eighties, which has been masquerading her attendance at an Ann Summers party ever since.

Next, squeeze the three lemons over the chicken without taking care to avoid any pips entering the container. Nonchalantly chop the chillies and add to the mix. Do not scratch your genitals or engage in an intimate act with someone. Use the brilliant trundle wheel garlic chopper you received for Christmas. You may wish to imagine your kitchen side is a school field, which you've been asked to measure by a teacher incapable of dealing with your natural energy and desire for attention, whilst rolling this device. Shake the garlic into the container, then spend ages picking the remaining 80% of garlic out of the no longer brilliant chopper.

Place the lid on the Tupperware, enjoying the four satisfying clicks as you seal it. If making this dish more than once, on occasion you may wish to close two sides in tandem in order to revel in the stereo click. Shake the Tupperware vigorously, but not so hard you tear the skin off.

Cycle for four hours.

Pre-heat the oven to 180. Place the contents of the Tupperware on a baking tray. Turn the chicken wings skin side down and place in the oven for three minutes.

After three minutes remove the tray. If you are around 173cm tall, male, and naked after four hours of cycling you will want to take care of steam emitting from the top of the oven. Nobody's penis needs to be exfoliated with that intensity of heat. Turn the chicken wings skin side up and top with pepper, which of course is black, because nobody should be caught dead using white pepper. Return the wings to the oven.

After another three minutes, in which time you should have put on some boxer shorts and/or pyjama bottoms, remove the wings and drizzle with the leftover chilli and garlic infused olive oil that you used to dress last night's salad with. Return the tray to the oven.

Every three minutes, raise the oven temperature by three degrees, remove the wings and baste with the juice which is now cremating the edge of the tray in a manner so severe that you are glad you gave into your girlfriend's demands to get a cleaner because your own efforts were "frankly, appalling". Repeat this three times.

Following three further minutes of what footballers do in hotel rooms, remove the chicken for the penultimate time. I shouldn't need to say this, but by now your oven should be at 192. After one final basting, grind some sea salt over the wings. You may also take this opportunity to place a perfectly formed salt crystal on your tongue and enjoy the sensation of it dissolving. You should now turn the oven up to its full power. It really doesn't matter what temperature this is, what's important is that you've used something to its unnecessarily high, full potential.

Wait a further three minutes before removing the wings for the final time. Place the wings on a plate. Devour.

Scrambled eggs

Ingredients

- Eggs

Method
Make scrambled eggs.

Dirty Salmon

Cynics may suggest that due to its high alcohol content that this isn't a meal for an athlete, but they'd be wrong. An alcohol based meal can be the fuel of champions if prepared correctly. Jockeys - and despite my own reservations, horse racing is a sport because it was on Grandstand - frequently live like alcoholics to keep their weight down and presumably also to blank out the boredom of being involved with horse racing. Cyclists recognise that if you're sleeping, you're not eating and if you're not eating, then you're losing weight. The aforementioned Tyler Hamilton also recounts the days where cyclists would take drugs (obviously) to sleep through the hours they weren't cycling in order to keep their weight down. I have no interest in sleeping pills but I do love a Martini, which in the right quantity has the same effect.

Ingredients

- 100g of smoked salmon
- 1 lemon
- Olive brine
- 1 thimble of Martini
- Twice your daily allowance of alcohol units in vodka form.

Method

Fill whatever vessel you desire to drink from with ice and top up with mineral water. If you live in the first world tap water is also fine to use. Put to one side. What vessel should you use? A mug would be bolshie, yes, but you need a glass. And you should use a glass, this isn't the war you know. If this drink uses the last of the brine it is acceptable to drink your Martini from the olive jar like a hipster toe rag.

Remove the salmon from its packaging, place on a small plate and dress with the juice of one lemon and a bit of pepper. Note: it is of great importance that you dispose of the evidence, particularly the sticker denoting the price of this delicious fish that has travelled some 10000km to be with you tonight. You do not want another conversation like that which followed the £20 sushi order after all.

Decant the olive brine into a plastic cup that was left unused after a house party. At this stage be indecisive about what to do with the olives. Eat an olive, then another and another. Stop eating the olives.

Remove the lid from the cocktail shaker and add two large ice cubes. Add a thimble sized amount of Martini. Two significant points here. So significant I'm going to have to use bullet points.

• You will notice I am using Martini and not an unspecified dry vermouth. This is because I am in the market for sponsorship by that particular brand.

• You may think using the lid of the Martini bottle is an acceptable way of judging a thimble sized amount of liquid. Do not do this! Seeing the liquid in the lid will spark one of two muscle memory reflexes from your teens; you will either A) vomit, or B) neck the Martini. Neither of which is helpful.

I have decided not to tell you which vodka to drink, though I have told you to drink vodka. Traditionalists harp on about gin being the true base of a Martini cocktail. This is nonsense, gin is a flavoursome delight to be reserved for gin and tonic. It is acceptable to have a vodka/gin mix in a Martini, such as the Vesper Martini, but if you know about Vesper Martinis I don't need to tell you anything because you've been to the place a Vesper Martini takes you, which is the floor, and survived to forget everything.

The reason I haven't told you what vodka to use is because I'm ashamed. In my formative Martini nights, I unwittingly got hooked on a cheap French vodka called Eristoff. Do as you want because I have no authoritative platform from which to speak, but my advice is to find a vodka with as little flavour as possible. The brine and Martini will deal with flavour, the vodka's there to send you to sleep.

Eat a few more olives.

Remove the vodka from the freezer. If your vodka isn't in the freezer stop reading this, go to the highest point in the building that your empty soul is poisoning and throw yourself off it.

Guestimate how much vodka you could drink neat and add to the cocktail shaker. Twice.

Add three thimbles of brine to the mix.

Now, this really is important. Though I have had some wonderful shaken Martinis, the pinnacle being a cocktail so well made by one Hong Kong mixologist that the Martini had a millimetre thin ice crust, which you had to crack to enjoy the drink, you are not going to be able to make a good shaken Martini at home.

What you can do however is shirl™ the contents. Shirl the contents in a clockwise (or anti-clockwise - there's no voodoo shit going on here) motion, being careful not to breach the structural integrity of the ice, but give the liquid contents more contact time with the cubes than they would have if you were merely stirring your drink. You are looking to produce an acceptable temperature whilst not watering down the flavour or strength. Smugly pop an olive into your mouth, chew, and swallow.

Your next decision is about the olives. Are you bothered? Should they continue to linger like a red herring in a Scandinavian crime drama? No, no they should not. Which means they're either in the glass, on the stick, or in your mouth. Put them in your mouth, chew, swallow, etc.

Empty your drinking vessel of ice and water.

Pour the contents of the shaker into the vessel.

Add additional brine to taste.

Consume quickly before someone discovers what you've been up to. If having this dish for breakfast, be sure to imbibe the right side of cleaning your teeth.

Anyway, enough of this bollocks, let's go on a bike ride across China.

4. WHEEZING DRAGON, DYING PIGEON

Loaded up with the necessary bits to keep me alive and the Pigeon moving, our combined mass was a very uncool 115kg. The kind of weight that normally causes a cyclist more concerns about the ups than the downs, but in the case of the Pigeon it is the downs that strike fear from your fingertips through to your ashen face.

The Pigeon is about as rudimentary as a bicycle can be. With a single gear, consisting of a 46 tooth chain ring and 20 tooth pinion, it was never going to trouble a speed camera but the braking system was certain to trouble every traffic light from Beijing to Kashgar. More presciently it was sure to make every descent filled with fear.

The only thing remotely funny about the PA-02's stopping system is its proximity in name to an emu-toting comedian; rod pull brakes had vanished from Britain's roads by the time I started cycling in the late 1980s and with good reason. They are operated by a series of linked metal rods. At the bottom of the rods sits a rigid arch, which pulls the rock-solid brake pads up into the gigantic rim simultaneously.

At least that's what happens when you squeeze them gently in a spare bedroom. Out on the road, all of the above happens briefly, before one pad stops making contact because the malleable steel rims are not straight and the pad making contact gets pulled out of shape. It almost always doesn't end with the bicycle stopping.

Riding back from Tianjin this had not been a problem. The journey was free of descents and I only applied the brakes at a handful of junctions before my speed dropped to such an extent I could halt the Pigeon by putting my feet on the ground, or simply let the gentle breeze bring me to a halt. The brakes would be tested early on my next journey, though, as the first day would involve mountains, which by their very nature call for functioning brakes.

I left Beijing at 6.30am dreading the second half of the first day's ride, which would involve getting the Pigeon over the mountains to Yanqing, some 90km away. With this in mind I left the story improving route out of Beijing, which would have taken me past Tiananmen Square and the Forbidden City to your imagination, and instead headed due north.

Beijing was having one of its rare pollution-free days. As I wobbled along at optimum speed all was well with the world. Until it wasn't. A puncture within 5km, in the shadow of the Bird's Nest Olympic stadium was not a great start. I fixed it, only for it to blow again after a further 2km. An elderly man cycled alongside me and advised me to turn left at the next corner where I'd find a bike mechanic. As I approached the corner another lady insisted on walking me there in person; the contrast between the £38 bicycle and the purposeful clothing, equipment and panniers clearly served only to highlight my hopelessness to helpful Beijingers.

Though it is an industry in evolution if not quite decline, Beijing still has a surprising number of road-side bike mechanics. Operating out of metallic cupboards stocked so heavily as to rival any garden shed, these mechanics are as much a part of the last two and a bit decades of economic boom, as the bicycles and electric scooters they fix for loose change.

The mechanic set about fixing the puncture as his token bloke on the street, which each of these mechanics come with as standard, lectured me on the various benefits of China's classic bike brands. Despite their tremendously *similar* appearance, the various brands each have wildly different reputations. The Pigeon, he said cheerily, was slow and unreliable.

Fixed up, I was on my slow and unreliable way. Almost immediately the second of these characteristics proved itself to be true, as the troublesome inner tube bulged out of a gap between the rim and tyre like a PE teacher's bollock from some obscenely small shorts. It was evident that the wheel couldn't take the direct weight of the panniers and me. The excess weight was causing the malleable steel rim to bend, which allowed the tyre to slip, leaving an escape route for the inner tube, which was inevitably leading to punctures.

Two hours into the trip I was faced with a dilemma that had arrived far sooner than I had anticipated. I was expecting to answer this question in Yinchuan or on the border of Xinjiang and I was expecting to answer it from a self-preservation point of view. I would give the Pigeon a fitting send-off by riding it into the ground. It wasn't a question I had expected to consider before lunch on the first day.

I called Holly, gave her some instructions that would ruin her day and that of our visiting friend Matt, before literally pushing on. After briefly exciting a public toilet attendant on the outskirts of Beijing by being the first foreigner to use her urinals, I spotted another mechanic.

Mechanic number two fettled with the whole bike. After fixing the puncture and hammering the rim back into shape he began to give the brakes a service and smear grease over the few moving parts with the affection a farmer reserves for his favourite lambing ewe. Perhaps, with this level of care, the Pigeon could be saved after all. This time I received a lecture from his hanger-on about how optimistic my goals were. I protested that I was enough of an idiot to try. Something that he and the mechanic agreed with as they laughed at how I'd put the saver forks on backwards. I thanked them for their help and wobbled off to the noise of the two of them laughing even harder.

Luckily, I was just out of sight by the time the teacher's testicle returned. I slowed to a stop, with the bulbous inner tube performing this task twice as well as the brakes. I heaved the Pigeon up off the road and inspected the wheel. It was already bent out of shape so as to not be round. I mulled over my predicament, whilst tucking in to my still warm pasta lunch. I was still just inside Beijing but my alien attire and choice of cutlery and transport was attracting stares from many in the bus queue opposite. Shortly afterwards I had everyone's attention as the Pigeon's inner tube exploded, producing a noise not unlike a bomb. As a nation of firework lovers, the Chinese rarely flinch at unanticipated loud noises, but the Pigeon's final squawk of disapproval terrified most within ear shot. The bang nearly caused me to drop more than my lunch.

Holly and Matt turned up to find me sat on the pavement amongst the remnants of the inner tube and my dropped pasta. Fortunately, they had arrived armed with morale boosting cheese sandwiches and the Pigeon's hastily arranged replacement. Even before the explosion, it had become clear that the Pigeon was not going to survive long enough to make it worth persevering with, I simply didn't have time; Mr. Wang had always been right, this bike really was no good for a long journey. Well, a time-limited long journey at least.

Unburdened by luggage I had made it back from Tianjin in one piece. This now seemed like a minor miracle, but there was no way that the rear wheel would survive the upcoming ordeal I had planned for it. I was trying to make a pensioner run a marathon, but unlike Britain's most infamous marathon bothering pensioner, the Pigeon had the decency to drop dead at the first attempt. I was just trying to make it do too much. Fail early, fail often, then start again.

I spent many hours over the following two months considering how far the Pigeon would have got and at what speed. I do think it can be done on a Pigeon but it would take at least three, not two, months and require an original 1980's wheel that's been rusted into some form of permanence. At least it went out with a bang.

Faced with the reality of Ollie and Jill's matrimonial deadline, the improbability of sourcing a new wheel once I'd exited the densely populated first week of my route, and the likelihood that this was my last chance to do something as silly ever again, I'd asked Holly to bring a replacement so I could complete the trip with only the minor disappointment of not having any reason to do so. *There was no reason. But who needs a reason when you've got a mountain bike?*[16]

Holly, Matt and I swapped the Pigeon for the bike I had been using whilst (pointlessly, it turns out) resting the Pigeon. A £180 Pigeon of its day; the Giant ATX860 even goes as far as to have meaningless numbers in its name to pay homage to its predecessor. It too is a do everything, no complaints, man on the Clapham omnibus of a bike.

If you were going to design a bike with the aim of people not bothering to look twice at it, the ATX680 is what you'd draw. It is not the bestselling bicycle of all time, it isn't even the bestselling bicycle of last year. Rather than being the iconic design in a world of no choice – famously the Pigeon was available in any colour you like, as long as that colour was black – it is lost in a sea of consumer choice where colour and tiny variations in componentry

---

[16] You may think I'm bastardising Irvine Welsh here, whereas actually I'm plagiarising seminal 90s mountain bike video Chainspotting, which admittedly had already bastardised Irvine Welsh.

create a situation where no single bicycle dominates the market.

Giant too, like all hugely successful companies, creates both the defining products of its time and defines what being that product means. At the ATX680's end of the market, there are no icons only icon-killers. It's a bicycle of this Uniqlo jeans, H&M t-shirt, Ikea dining table, big brands without any branding age. It even comes in sizes XS, S, M, L, XL, nothing so bespoke as your inches or centimetres here. You choose it in seconds, buy it in less, you don't even try it out because you just get the same size as last time, you sometimes forget what colour it is, you don't mourn if it's stolen, it's just a bike.

Though it lacked romance, it did at least work. Having spent seven hours reaching 40km, it was a relief to see the next 20km achieved in under an hour and without incident. Just north of the city I flew passed the many magnificent Ming Tombs, where the Emperors of that particular dynasty decided to park up for a final time. Perhaps I should have buried the Pigeon there too.

I also began to enjoy myself. Amongst the bright yellows, pinks and purples of spring I climbed through the mountains between Beijing and Yanqing. Now armed with disk brakes, the descents I'd been fearing earlier, became kilometre eating minutes of fun. The only break in my delight came in the shape of two tunnels.

The tunnels were not lit and following the brightness of the spring sun, I was totally blind for the first twenty or thirty metres until my eyes adjusted to the dark. Imagine the sensation when the lights go out before bed and it takes time for your eyes to adapt. Only you're not in bed, you're cycling on a slippery surface at the edge of a road, blindfolded, whilst lorries roar alongside. Isn't being in bed much nicer than that?

I arrived in Yanqing at dusk for what would become a familiar tradition of proudly exclaiming I had a reservation, only to be told that I didn't. Not that it ever mattered, there was always a room available. It transpired that by making my reservations in the Latin alphabet, somewhere in the system between the app on my phone and the paper forms in the hotel I would be disenfranchised on a near daily basis. This would have been fine, had it not then involved a daily tedious phone call with the travel agents responsible for the app calling me to ask why I hadn't checked-in and whether I aware that such actions would result in them taking customer loyalty points away.

Once inside the room, I admired the cigarette burn marks on the wall, showered, and waited for Holly and Matt, who had been to visit a nearby section of the Great Wall after rescuing me. By the time they arrived it was dark and we headed out onto the streets of Yanqing, which are yet to be illuminated in the blinding fashion of Beijing's. With it being well beyond Chinese dinner time, we headed to a 24-hour restaurant for a three-person feast of dumplings, dry-fried green beans and beer for a bargain £2 a head.

After handing over the pigeon spares in exchange for a pannier rack for the Giant, Holly and Matt left me to the surrounds of my mangy hotel room and thoughts of the Pigeon. I was still sulking as I got into bed. Finally I talked myself into a state of common sense and it sank in that I was still about to ride a bike across China, only now it would be on a bike that worked. With that, I put my alarm back two hours and fell fast asleep.

After fielding the first of 96,702 questions about whether or not wearing shorts meant I was cold, I attached the pannier rack, loaded up the Giant and set off through Yanqing.

A relatively small town, in 2022 Yanqing will be the lesser-mentioned third location hosting the Winter Olympics alongside Beijing and my next stop, Zhangjiakou.

Before the world's skiers and bobsledders arrive, Yanqing will continue to serve as a base for the local tourist attractions, the biggest of which is the stretch of the Great Wall at Badaling. Much-maligned by whiny foreigners, Badaling is by far the most popular stretch of the Great Wall for tourists.

I had a great time there when I visited four years ago. No, it isn't as good as all the wild bits of wall, which you can have to yourself at times, but Badaling has a place in the hearts and selfies of millions of Chinese people, who for my money are by far the world's best tourists and part of what makes Badaling great fun.

Sadly, my visit culminated in a distraught woman, who was dressed as a panda, chasing me all the way back to the train station as part of my first experience of just how seriously some Chinese people still take losing face. I had suggested, fairly I might add, that the £150 she had quoted me for a few panda hats was incredibly dishonest of her. A clash of cultures followed. I laughed at her attempt to rip me off and she comprehensively lost her shit. She then gave chase, providing me with the honour of being pursued by the world's most mobile panda. This must have looked particularly confusing to those high up on the wall above us.

As I left Yanqing that morning it wasn't the Great Wall or the Olympics that the town was fixated on, but the World Potato Congress 2015. I didn't see a single Olympic ring or panda hat but adverts for Spudfest were everywhere. One of China's greatest skills is its ability to take everything seriously, even the potato. Only China and the United Kingdom have hosted this event twice and most of our DNA is potato.

Beyond the wall-sized posters promising to grow 'a global potato family' I entered the China of small farms being worked by pensioners that is slipping from the global view of China, if not quite yet, reality. This is a rectangular world. Be they horizontal or vertical, two-dimensional or three-dimensional, four-sided shapes dominate this landscape.

After the traumas of the previous day the first hour was a joy.

Already beyond Badaling and the tourism ring of Beijing the looks of disbelief that would mark every single one of my days on this journey began in earnest. There would be a familiar pattern to these moments. A squint would precede a double take, before a motionless stare would await my smile to crack it into reciprocating. Finally, I would be met by a beaming grin that was as much equal parts disbelief and delight, as it was teeth and gaps.

Less than an hour later the smiling paused. 10km after rejoining the G110 national road[17] from my road of rural delights I reached some real, perspective-rich, trauma. I had presumed the miles-long queue of lorries I was passing was a result of the upcoming provincial border or one of the G110's infamous traffic jams (inn 2010 there was a traffic jam on this stretch of road that some people spent five days in[18]), but the crowd of more than three hundred or so that I eventually reached confirmed this was a different kind of blockage.

The middle of the junction looked like a scrap yard, fortunately the driver of the car had been removed before I arrived. The odds that this removal had taken place at a time when the individual had a pulse cannot have been better than evens. All three vehicles, the car and two lorries that had sandwiched it, were the same shade of dirty red. This somehow gave the scene a gory artistic quality as the shards of red metal and flakes of paint on the road looked like the vehicles themselves had spilled blood.

I pootled passed slowly, following a train of scooters driven by heads turned at ninety degrees. It was clear from the positions and relative weights of the vehicles that this was the car driver's

---

[17] Equivalent to an A road.

[18] http://www.nytimes.com/2010/08/28/world/asia/28china.html

own fault but it felt good to be on a stable bike with functioning brakes.

For the vast majority of the 5000km I would be traveling in the cycling-lane-cum-hard-shoulder that adorns almost every road in China. On this day more than any other I hugged the very edge of that lane. As I climbed over the Olympic ski runs in waiting, amongst the soot and filth being belched out of, and falling from, passing lorries, I did not miss the Pigeon and its 19th century stopping technology.

I stopped for lunch 40km west of Yanqing at Tumu, site of a humiliating defeat for the Ming Dynasty at the hands of the Mongols in 1449. Here, some half a million men took a pasting off only 20,000 in what should have been the military spanking to end all military spankings. It seems implausible that the Mongols won.

The defeat could have cost the Ming Dynasty Beijing and more. As it was, they lost so spectacularly that the victory shocked the Mongols into inaction. Expecting a bit more of a scrap, which is not an entirely unreasonable assumption when outnumbered 25 to 1, they waited six weeks to advance on Beijing. By the time they did so, the Ming army had regrouped and it was too late. The gargantuan Ming graveyard I had passed the day before should really have been significantly smaller. The Ming Dynasty went on to last for almost another 200 years and the Mongols never threatened China's sovereignty on the same scale again.

Tumu also marked my departure from Beijing and entry into the province of Hebei. Draped around the municipalities of Beijing and Tianjin like a wet-look, permed, mullet, Hebei is as disgusting as that sounds.

The source of much of Beijing's infamous pollution, Hebei is home to the world's third largest steel company. Unlike the largest producer, Luxembourg's – *really Jean-Claude, really?* -

Arcelor Mittal, Hebei Iron and Steel Company produce most of their 45 million tonnes of steel in their own backyard. In short, I wanted to get out of Hebei as quickly as I could. Coincidentally I felt the same way about Luxembourg, despite its clean, tax free air.

The afternoon dragged as I wheezed and slogged through the hills, amongst thousands of lorries and the appalling air. As I stopped to fix the Giant's first puncture amongst the three-inch-deep litter surrounding the side of the road, I was reminded of the strength of the sun, my genetic disposition to sunburn and the importance of sun cream. My jacket had rolled up to leave me with identical sweat-band sized sunburn on both wrists. It looked more like I'd spent the day restrained by 17th century pirate ship handcuffs than cycling around northeast China.

Unlike Yanqing, Zhangjiakou, my intended stopover for the second day, is being name-checked in the 2022 Olympic paraphernalia and as such is on its way to joining the exalted company of Lillehammer and Albertville as a wherethehellisthat? host city of the winter games.

I approached the city, which BBC sports commentators will soon be calling Zang-gee-ahh-co with the confidence in their voice audibly declining as they progress through the word, at dusk. Here I experienced my first bonk[19] of the journey. It wasn't a big bonk. It was just a quickie. My legs had gone but my mental faculties were still in working order. Despite the encouragement of a couple of local cyclists I had to stop 20km short of my hotel to consume some emergency chilli noodles and Pepsi, at the same time as fielding more questions about whether I was cold because I was wearing shorts.

---

[19] This can be as technical as you like, but basically the point where exhaustion and a lack of energy causes vital bits of you to fail.

I ate the noodles in the shadow of one of Hebei Iron and Steel Company's ginormous factories. For its many sins, heavy pollution has one redeeming feature, when it is set against the backdrop of a dimming sunset it takes on a truly artistic quality. That night the smoke was billowing in beautiful, parallel, wind-assisted diagonals before disappearing into the sky.

As mesmerizing as the sky looked, its potent metallic smell was less alluring. I strapped on my face mask and cycled through the soup as the city descended into darkness. The mask was fantastic at keeping pollution out, but also dreadful for keeping my own chilli and Pepsi scented emissions in.

Suffering from my own pollution, I ground into the city to the sound of fighter jets that were practicing take-off and landing. A sudden blast of noise I didn't particularly enjoy as I rode through the dark streets, seemingly on a tour of each of the city's potholes. I arrived at my hotel just before 9pm, plodded through the whole reservation, no reservation, no problem nonsense and made it to my room in time to shower and fall asleep to the sounds of my neighbour, her hourly visitors and their many, many showers.

Zhangjiakou, translates as Zhang (as in Mr. Zhang) family gate. Its Mongol name, Kalgan, also means gateway. Sitting upon one of the many component parts of the Great Wall and with the Mongolian plateau spreading out beyond it, Zhangjiakou is strategically important in the way gates often are. Especially when the only other way in is over a wall.

It was also the first place where my journey would meet with one of the many notable moments in the legacy of Genghis Khan. Despite being grossly outnumbered he led a Tumu-like thrashing here in 1211, which was a key victory as he made his way south to the much bigger prize of Zhongdu, the city that would become Beijing. After victory at Zhangjiakou he spent four years siesing Beijing into a state of cannibalism and eventual surrender.

This is the Genghis of school history books; the hard as nails bastard to end all bastards. Thanks in part to his innovative foreign policy of encouraging the perpetuation of rumours[20] that he was a merciless arsehole, and in part because he was a merciless arsehole, Genghis is one of history's great bad guys.

Nowadays though there exists another side to him, his academic alter ego, Chingis. Chingis is the correctly pronounced, well-researched side of the man. In his fantastic book, Jack Weatherford[21] makes an impassioned defence of Chingis' exasperating achievements, which lay beyond the violence that supported them. After all, he is the man who expanded an empire twice as far as any other. Weatherford goes as far as to credit Chingis with the making of the modern world.

In something that reads like a centre ground utopia that modern politicians could only dream of, Weatherford tells us that Chingis "smashed the feudal system of aristocratic privilege" in so doing he built a meritocratic system. At the same time he lowered taxes and abolished them entirely for key public service workers like "doctors, teachers, priests, and educational institutions".

This was just the start, as well as creating "an international law" he instituted the rule of law, under which leaders were as accountable as every other citizen. "He granted religious freedoms" and instituted the practice "of granting diplomatic immunity". His reorganisation of the Silk Road created "history's largest free-trade zone".

He was not just the statesman Chingis and the barbaric warlord

---

[20] (Weatherford, 2004)

[21] (Weatherford, 2004)

Genghis, but also, quite probably, owner of the most productive loins in history. Though it cannot be proved beyond doubt unless his body is found and DNA is allowed to be taken from it, it is believed that around 0.5% of males alive today are direct descendants of the Great Khan.

Unsurprisingly this figure rises dramatically in the lands of his former empire, where some 8% of the male population share near identical Y-chromosomes. This expansive lineage was obviously aided in its compound growth by his immediate descendants too, but somebody had to be the spark. Presumably in one thousand years' time, North London will be showing similar patterns for Russell Brand's DNA.

The research[22] that led to this discovery is comprehensively scientific, but without Genghis' DNA to prove beyond doubt that he is the daddy to end all daddies, the use of circumstantial evidence is key to the scientists' conclusions. In other words, it reads like a hyper-intellectual episode of the Jeremy Kyle Show. The thought of Kyle interviewing Genghis is a heartwarming one.

Kyle: "Aren't you going to accept that these children are all yours?"

Genghis attempts to reply but is interrupted by Kyle who wants blood.

Kyle: "Who else lived around a millennium ago, in Mongolia, leading an empire, fathering sons who followed his terrible example? Who else Genghis? Who?"

Genghis opens his mouth but Jeremy hushes him with his finger and crouches by Genghis' side.

Kyle: "Genghis, I want you to look in that camera there and admit what you've done."

---

[22] (Zerjal, 2003, p. 717)

Genghis rises from his seat, draws his sword and decapitates the poor man's Trisha.

Genghis: "I fathered them, of course I did. I'm the Great Khan, I fuck when I want. Anyway, who was that? What the fuck happened to Kilroy?"

Floor manager informs Genghis Khan about Kilroy and the whole UKIP thing. Genghis shrugs his shoulders and strides off, mumbling something about being the only immigrant Kilroy should be scared of.

Anyway, the researchers have 95% confidence that the common ancestor lived around a thousand years ago and most likely came from Mongolia. That the highest frequency of those sharing the same chromosomes live in a region that translates almost exactly to Genghis' empire, and later empires controlled by his immediate descendants supports this further. What's more, the likelihood that chance caused this is disproved with a number to the power of 237, which is the very definition of a head-fuck.

So there may even be a little bit of Genghis in you, especially if you're a Mongolian, but even more likely if you're one of the Hazaras from Pakistan. The most interesting outcome of the research isn't the unsurprising news that Genghis and his sons put it about a bit. It's one particularly intriguing pocket of their legacy. The highest frequency of the relevant genetic code was found in Pakistan. Brilliantly this confirmed that the Hazara people's centuries-old oral history that they were direct descendants of Genghis was true. Old Grandma Hazara was telling the truth all along.

Nearly a millennium after Genghis sacked the city, Zhangjiakou remains a military city today. Just as fighter jets had welcomed me to the city, ten fully loaded People's Liberation Army (PLA) trucks accompanied me out on the pot-holed and dusty road west.

As the road became smoother I made good progress until the wind started to bite 40-50km in. Reminded by the previous day's bonk and the pitfalls of not eating regularly, I pulled into a garage at midday for some noodles. With the air clean enough to forgo the mask, I also allowed myself the treat of multiple fizzy drinks that I was free to belch out into the open air.

Now well clear of the Beijing tourism ring, which stretches to the Great Wall, my ridiculous appearance, ability to speak a very modest amount of Mandarin and entirely alien ways made me the subject of great interest and excitement. One of the older men in the petrol station suggested to one of the younger girls I was a good potential boyfriend, when it became clear I understood this, she blushed and ran away, in what I would like to believe was embarrassment rather than fear.

I then had a conversation I would have hundreds of times over the next two months. Hereafter this will simply be referred to as *the conversation*[23].

"Where are you from?"

"I'm British."

If inquisitor is female - "Are you married?"

"No"

"Why not? How old are you?"

"31, but I have a girlfriend in Beijing"

"She is British too?"

"Yes."

"Then when will you marry her?"

Eventually I worked out the correct answer to this was "next

---

[23] This reads like a conversation between two very dull, simple people because that's where my level of Mandarin was (is). It is not a reflection on the poor souls who were friendly and patient enough to talk with me. It also will hopefully make you grateful I'm not documenting each of these repetitive exchanges in full.

year" and not "I don't know".

"That is good."

Gender neutral - "Where are you going?"

"Xinjiang, Kashgar."

"Ooooh. That's a very long way. Where have you come from?"

"I've come from Beijing."

"No, where have you come from today?"

Mispronounce name of town left that morning/point at tent whilst saying "I don't know, I just stayed in my tent."

"You are one person yes?"

"Yes just one person, well I had/will have two friends in Ningxia."

"They are also English?"

"Yes."

"How long will you travel today?"

Answer.

"Very good, but are you not cold?"

"No, why?

"Because you are wearing shorts."

"It's ok I cycle my bike fast so I am warm."

"You have a lot of water?"

"Yes."

"Good, water is very important."

"Have you eaten?"

"Of course, I need to eat a lot."

"OK".

If inquisitor is male - "Are you married?"

"No, but I have a girlfriend."

"You also want a girlfriend in this province[24]?"

---

[24] This, I hasten to clarify, is the search for covert prestige through the mutual understanding that we are the terrible gender. It's not that every man in China is trying to pimp somebody out.

"No, one is enough."

"True."

"OK, good luck! Bye Bye"

"Thank you, bye bye!"

Conversation ends.

As I sat down to eat my noodles I was invited to try the food that the eight (yes 8!) staff of the petrol station were having for lunch. I had some of their delicious tofu but declined the dumplings with the same modesty with which I had earlier turned down the girl. You've gone back to reread "delicious tofu" right? So yeah, it turns out that tofu, when it's not being touted as a meat substitute and has been cooked properly is actually delicious. I even order it in restaurants and everything.

Back on the road I was amongst the Great Wall and its watchtowers that sit atop the mountains like the chipped spine of a battle-scarred dragon's tail.

Right then, the Great Wall. I'll keep this short. It isn't one wall; it is many different walls built over many centuries out of many different materials. It wasn't perfect at keeping invaders out, but it did make invading harder. It probably did a better job of defining the territory within. Despite what smug pub quiz bores say, you can see it from space, there's been some tremendous progress made in satellite technology.

Now for the serious bit about the wall. It is without doubt the most impressive feat of human engineering that I have seen. There are parts of it around Beijing on mountain sides so steep that even without a massive brick to carry I wouldn't consider tackling. At times it was a Keynesian public infrastructure project over two millennia before the Treasury's most colourful and brilliant employee had started learning his times tables. At others, it was a genuine part of defence strategy. It is now believed the many constituent parts of wall could well be over 20,000km long[25] in total.

The very first stretches of the wall were built for the First Emperor over two thousand years ago, presumably on one of the day's he wasn't having his half-brothers murdered or demanding the construction of history's most elaborate grave. Since then other dynasties have added more walls. Unsurprisingly the peak in building came just before and just after the height of Mongol dominance of the region.

The image, if any, that you have in your head is probably the stone walls built by the Ming dynasty north of Beijing around 400-500 years ago, but many of the earlier incarnations were merely mud ramparts. If anything, its inconsistency and piecemeal formation, makes it all the more fascinating.

In great contrast to the Wall's magnificence, an hour after lunch I passed through a ghost town in its shadow that was completely empty.

Just outside of Coventry I stopped for another glug of sickly, sugary, shit and the inevitable burping that followed. I watched as aging trucks, piled dangerously high and wide with messy, straw-coloured, afros - which I named Carlos Vanderammas - battled with speeding Range Rovers for dominance of the road. All in the shadow of the latest extension of the high speed rail network and a thousand other contradictions modern China provides.

My final 40km were to be very, very hilly but I was determined to arrive before darkness. I stopped to refuel at Xiyanghecun and participated in what was to become the obligatory thrice-daily photo with petrol station attendants. These events often involved a very small twenty-something woman climbing under my stinking

---

[25]   http://www.cbc.ca/news/world/great-wall-of-china-even-longer-than-previously-thought-1.1263111

rotten armpit, making a peace sign and, depending on the confidence of the individual in question, either giggling uncontrollably or pouting with a disconcerting amount of control.

The first mountain of the day was a joy. A huge cycle lane and very little traffic was accompanied by close up views of many watch towers. Once over that and into the next province, Inner Mongolia, the land undulated like the hills of my homeland, Shropshire. By late afternoon, the sandy coloured knolls began to turn golden in the dimming sun, which was a nice distraction from the suffering they were causing.

The constant ups and downs took their toll. As I tired, I resorted to pushing up the steeper climbs. Just as I reached the final climb before my destination, a man in a three-wheeled truck pulled alongside to offer me a race. I accepted but he would not let us start before I finally agreed that he was the "Watermelon King of this town". He won the race, but I made it to the flashiest hotel in town just before the sky had lost its light smoky, grey tinge.

My third overnight stop was in Xinghe, a town nestled just inside Inner Mongolia on the border with Hebei and Shanxi provinces. Xinghe's name could mean Desire for Peace; pretty understandable when you're a town sat so close to many Mongol routs.

Much to the confusion of the security guards, I pulled the Giant up next to the numerous black Audis that marked my hotel out as the place for Xinghe's great and good to do business, party business, and party.

I strolled in with my bags and stench, proudly proclaimed I had a reservation and went through the formalities with three visibly shocked receptionists. After my room key was handed over I asked if they had a restaurant. One girl began to say yes before another interrupted to say "you must go to your room and wash first".

Fortunately for me 'blacking up' is not part of most Chinese people's knowledge of some British people's most appalling habits. As I looked in the mirror it became apparent the shocked faces were not merely a result of seeing and smelling a filthy alien but seeing one who had applied his mid-afternoon sun cream with oil covered hands and then ridden through soot, producing the black yet somehow ghostly appearance of a dead racist.

Freshly washed I made an effort to show my clean, and definitely not racist, face to as many people as possible before I entered 'Zero Restaurant'. Inside I unintentionally went full Mr. Bean, much to the amusement of the three other guests. With all four of the waitresses absent I started to look under the empty buffet lids until I reached the last one and a fellow diner finally decided to inform me that there was a menu, I just needed to wait for a waitress to return.

I ordered, and consumed at speed, the holy trinity of a mixed vegetables, rice and a meat dish for the extortionate price of £11, almost twice what the meal for Holly, Matt and I had cost in Yanqing. As I shoveled the food into my chomping mouth the only remaining diners paid me the compliment of remarking behind my back "the foreigner eats his chicken with his fingers but he is very good at eating rice with chopsticks" before pausing to consider further, then continuing with "for a foreigner".

4.1 PUNCTURES, BLOODY PUNCTURES

On this journey, there were many, many punctures. Rather than whine about each and every one of them, I've done my very best to mention only those with a significant effect on the journey. For example, those punctures leading up to and including the explosion that led me to give up on the Pigeon; and those that had a greater effect on my day than a mere ten minutes of irritation.

That said, there was almost an average of one puncture a day, so it would be remiss of me not to spend a very short while sharing what the trip taught me about punctures and whining on a bit.

Punctures come in several forms. First, the big ones, which consist of an audible pop, followed by a complete loss of control and the feeling of being sat on a contraption with at least one wooden wheel. These are my favourite. They're honest, easy to find, and generally easy to fix.

Second, the silent, yet audacious, show offs. These are the punctures that announce themselves with a slight change in handling and a squishy tyre when you dismount and give it a squeeze. A rudimentary check then reveals a sharp object that, in the style of a step-father in a disappearance-soon-to-be-murder case, is still at the scene of the crime. I also like this form of puncture because the problem area is immediately identifiable and easy to fix. When you pull the offensive object out, the tyre lets out a pathetic pfff of air, reminiscent of a sly fart in the early days of a relationship.

Third is the troublesome cousin of the second variant, when the object that has pierced the inner tube hasn't stayed around for the autopsy. Leaving you with the irritating task of finding a tiny hole by the side of the road. These are the worst punctures.

Finally, the mystery slow puncture, of which this trip experienced many. The kind of irritating slow depreciation in pressure, which can be remedied by one full inflation per hour. My response to these was to always make-do with the hourly inflations until I reached a hotel, where I could identify the leakage using a sink of water or, on one boundary-crossing occasion, the very same bath in which I was soaking.

Finally, if I could give you one piece of genuine advice, it would be this: old style sandpaper, glue and patches repair kits are vastly superior to the self-adhesive circles of Sellotape that some plonker has decided are a good idea. Take the extra five minutes to use the old puncture repair kits that your dad taught you how to use and save yourself hours in the long run. Let's bankrupt that sadist's solution together. Then afterwards we can burn the factories producing Presta valves to the ground.

5. INNER MONGOLIAN

If it is possible to have a spiritual home without ever visiting the place in question, then Mongolia is my Graceland. My Chinese name, Xi Meng, translates as Western Mongolian. Something I wanted to extend to be Very Western Mongolian but was dissuaded by one of my teachers in Beijing who gave clear advice on the matter - "no, this is not a good idea, you will sound stupid".

Though I only have this name due to its close phonetical proximity to Simon, rather than any link to Mongolia, I also spent a year of my life working in a Mongolian Barbeque restaurant, in that most likely of locations, Shrewsbury, the county town of the middle of nowhere. A place in which no Mongolian had ever stepped and modelled on a Taiwanese invention from the latter half of the 20th century. In quite possibly my favourite Wikipedia entry ever, we learn that Mongolian Barbeque is "not Mongolian and is only very loosely related to barbecue." Three nights a week I would unwittingly peddle the bullshit that the two huge sticks I used to flip a customer's food would have been swords in Genghis' day and the huge hot plate on which it was cooking would have been an upturned shield. If you want to eat Taiwanese food in Shropshire today you can still visit Jenko's, but you probably don't want to because it's moved to Telford. The only authentic aspect of Jenko's Mongolian Barbecue was the large number of Chinese people working next door in the China Rose restaurant.

This deeply inauthentic experience and misleading Chinese name has left me with an affection for Mongolia that is as pointless as it is ill-informed. As a result, I was excited about cycling through the Chinese chunk of this vast region.

This enormous region is split between the eponymous nation state and a province in the world's most populous country as a result of historic shifts and surprisingly recent developments. Mongolia the independent nation is beguiling in its youthfulness. Thanks to Genghis and co, the fact that present day Mongolia is not yet one hundred years old has the same effect on my brain as a Calippo that is slightly too cold. How can the land of Genghis be so young?

In Chinese history the Mongols are not viewed as foreign invaders, instead, they are part of the country's dynastic history. Under Genghis' grandson Kublai, the Mongols took control of China and became known as the Yuan dynasty in the final third of the 13th century. After they were supplanted by the Ming dynasty just shy of a hundred years later, the Mongols retreated to an area of land that largely traces over the modern day boundaries of Mongolia and Inner Mongolia.

For a further two centuries, the Mongols reverted to a similar existence like that which preceded Genghis. They fractured into warring tribes and occasionally raided Ming China; sometimes to the extent that led to the crushing victory at Tumu but never to the magnitude that they once again became part of Chinese history lessons.

The Ming's successors, and China's final imperial dynasty, the Qing, conquered the Mongols in the first half of the 17th century. It was the Qing's administrative borders, which provided the boundaries for Inner Mongolia in China and independent Mongolia today.

When the Qing dynasty fell in 1911, the region then known as Outer Mongolia declared independence but Inner Mongolia remained part of China. The reasons – there is always more than one – are part of a historical debate that far outstrips the confines of a single paragraph, but I'll do my best.

The motivation for independence arose from economic troubles and resentment towards Qing assimilation policies, something the Qing dynasty had itself opposed for most of their rule. In classic international relations style, the regional and global powers intervened in such a manner that Russian support for *only* Outer Mongolia becoming independent seems to have been the most significant influence on the outcome. Though, disunity amongst Inner Mongolia's power brokers and the frailty of China at the time were also factors, Russia's position was telling. You can find out more about this by searching the internet, following a chain of reference points to relevant books, then searching the reference points of those books, and so on and so on. We're all academics now.

Independence was formally declared in 1924 and the People's Republic of Mongolia was born, making the country younger than some human inhabitants of the earth, which as I said, feels wildly at odds with my perception of Mongolia. Interestingly, the Government of Taiwan still views all of Mongolia as part of their territorial claim, as part of a dispute that I am no way going to try and explain in a single paragraph.

At least the designation is simple. Like the vast majority of Chinese provinces, Inner Mongolia doesn't leave you guessing with a mystical or exotic name. Like Hebei, which means North (of the) River, it gets straight to the point. Unlike Hebei, Inner Mongolia is ginormous; it stretches around two-thirds of China's border with Mongolia and a decent chunk of the border with Russia too. Partly due to its size and the disparate distribution of hotels, I had decided to try and cover as much of this vast province with the same speed I'd chosen to clear Hebei with. So my excitement was tempered by the knowledge that my second week would cover a greater number of kilometres than any other; 731 of the metric bastards.

First, though, I had – in theory at least – a gentle introduction to Inner Mongolia. Every so often the regularity of cities and towns big enough to host a hotel where a foreigner could stay would grant me a shorter day in the saddle. My fourth day was the first such an occasion. It was just 61km from Xinghe to Jining through the frozen farmland and dusty scrubland, where Genghis first trampled over 800 years earlier.

Despite this short distance, my first day in Graceland was a chore. It started with a morning of yo-yoing over more undulating hills, but this first half of the day was an enjoyable slog that ended with me sat in glorious sunshine at the top of the final hill. I sat stuffing my face full of Oreos, looking down to the plains and the cardboard cut-out silhouette of the industrial city I was aiming for.

Better still, on the way up to this vantage point, a young couple driving a new Mercedes 4x4 down the wrong side of the motorway stopped to give me a Mongolian gift. I understood the following: it was Mongolian; I shouldn't eat it; and it should go in a place. I didn't understand what place or its purpose but was heartbroken it wasn't a massive biscuit as it first appeared. My best guess is that it is something you use to fragrance your clothes by leaving it in a wardrobe - like cedar wood, as heavily advocated by my Nan Maureen.

Inner Mongolia formally announced its arrival in cliché form through the appearance of yurts; both fabric and concrete - for the less nomadic, more modern, Mongolian. The ancestral tombs of this region also take the form of yurts and dot the landscape like the miniature encampments of spirits on earth.

Already, the colour pallet for my journey was well established. Everything had a dusty yellow-brown hue. No other colour, be it the red of a petrol station or the green shades of the foliage, escaped Northern China's dusty tinge. Only the occasional golden sands of the Taklamakan and Gobi deserts or the oases that would briefly disrupt them got close to breaking these subdued tones. At this point though, those changes were over a month away.

Road signs also began to contain the vertical cursive of Mongolian script; a form of writing so alien to me it seemed implausible that it could ever be deciphered. Mandarin is at least a serious of shapes that are recognisably different, some of which are even obvious in their meaning; Mongolian on the other hand looks like Arabic that has been simplified to the point of alarming uniformity and then rotated 90 degrees.

The wind had been bad on the hills, often stopping me on the descents if I stopped peddling, but on the final flat 20km into Jining the task was tortuous. Trying to get through the wind was like trying to clean a garlic press with cold water, no washing up liquid, whilst had-cuffed, blindfolded and being a newt.

I had to learn how to ride the wind. My preferred method was to give up and sit by the side of the road. Failing that I would stay in the easiest gear for the impossible gusts and crawl at about twice walking pace, before pressing on whenever it dropped. This final short stint took three energy-sapping hours.

As time dragged, I also began to worry about having no sensation in both sets of fourth and little fingers. Like any good male does with a physical problem I chose to ignore it, moan about it and ultimately take no action. Months later I learned it was a relatively common thing known as handlebar palsy or ulnar neuropathy if you want to show off. Essentially, the near permanent compression of the ulnar nerve near the base of my palm was causing the two fingers I can't swear with to go numb on both hands. Only three weeks after the end of the trip – spoiler alert, I make it – did the feeling fully return to my four politest digits.

I had now ventured deep into the China that sees almost no

foreigners. This was especially noticeable upon arrival at the few hotels who did manage process my reservation, where sometimes the staff would eagerly await my arrival. After the torture of the wind I arrived at the best hotel in Jining in my usual dishevelled state and as I approached the desk I was greeted in English with "you must be Simon".

The best treat of all was the room itself. It was genuinely non-smoking, a real rarity in China. I was also brought some fruit and in a sweet display of stereotyping, some extra coffee for free – "because you are a foreigner, so you like coffee". I even managed to order room service in Mandarin. I tried to order a burger but as the hotel didn't have any beef burgers or buns in stock I agreed to have steak with a club sandwich because, as the concierge advised, "it's all the same bits, just in different places".

Wikitravel provided the following, damning review of my home for the evening *"Jining's main point of interest for tourist is Jining South Railway Station, which is your interchange point if you are heading from Beijing to Ulaanbaatar by local train"*. With this confirming all of my prejudices about Jining's cultural sights and delights, I made eating my last activity of the night and went to bed. I'm sure a Chinese cyclist would do the same if faced with the prospect of spending the night in Crewe.

With the fear of another day of fierce winds waking me at 4.20am, I checked the forecast. It was not good. The wind mirrored my direction of travel with an exacting attention to detail. It was as if the little arrow knew at what time, and to the very degree, I'd be altering my direction of travel.

By now my morning routine was already well established. On the way to the bathroom, I would flick the kettle on before beginning the very necessary, petrol-station-toilet-avoiding, process of expelling the previous 24 hours' food. The energy I was expending on the road often meant that this would amount to very little end product. Put it this way, if I deposited it in your kitchen, you'd think you had a rat problem.

As soon as this moment had quite literally passed, I would shower to make up for the failings of the cleansing efforts made by the previous day's exhausted arms. Next, I would assemble the pot noodle's constituent bits into an increasingly tedious feast of mundane necessity.

Whilst the beige worms were busily soaking up the water and artificial flavourings, I would begin the creaming process. Starting with sun cream on my face, then arms, then legs, before applying some disappointingly neutral lip-salve and finally ending with Graham's tingly treat.

I would then eat the noodles, paired with a 3-in1 coffee drink, whilst simultaneously dressing in clothes so awful that they provided an extra incentive to ride safely each day through the fear of being found dead in them.

Due to the simplicity of my route, I would only be forced to resort to Google Maps' spoken directions when entering or leaving the bigger cities. That morning, Mrs Google Maps interrupted my podcasts to tell me what to do in her half-hearted dominatrix voice. Following her demands, we went on a very disappointing detour through a building site on a road not yet built. No wonder Google is blocked by the Great Firewall of China if they're going to go around knowing the future.

The Great Firewall, with its restrictions on information and doctored pictures of political leaders being replaced by Winnie the Pooh, is much like its brick based relative. It's as much about defining what's inside it as keeping the outside out. There are ways around this in the shape of VPNs, which are also necessary for procrastinating and accessing news that only suffers from the editorial interference of billionaire owners.

Despite the inevitable arrival of the wind, which was at times accompanied by its house band Sleet and Snow, out on the road, I had a glorious day thanks to gravity. Hohhot, capital of Inner Mongolia, which was 151km away, has few lovable features, but being a whole 300m closer to sea level than Jining was certainly one of them.

Over the first week, especially in the aftermath of the first bonk, I began to treat myself like a little donkey. I would stop hourly for five minutes to rest, consume one item of food, have a swig of water, and then return to plodding on down the dusty road.

On the second of these rest stops on the way towards Hohhot, a man with a dialect I couldn't understand resorted to writing in characters in the dirt that I couldn't read, as he attempted to communicate with me. I told him I was stupid and so couldn't understand. Something he clearly found believable thanks to my extra special 'nobody told me it would be below zero' outfit. Perhaps he was asking me why I was wearing all of my clothes or why I was wearing them in the wrong order.

At my first break, it was very difficult to retrieve my penis from my shorts following the wind chill's aggressive attack on both the organ in question and the remaining fingers I still had any sensation in. Honestly, it was like trying to pick up an oily peanut with chopsticks, eight broken fingers and a hangover.

To correct this problem, I had taken drastic action. By the time I met the man now stood scraping characters into the icy dirt below me with his bare hands, I was wearing every item of clothing I possessed. With my windproof shorts now on the outside of a pair of Uniqlo chinos and at least seven layers on my top half, I looked like a toddler who'd decided to wear everything in the fancy dress box. Though I couldn't understand him, perhaps thanks to my outfit, he appeared to find my stupid argument convincing. Needless to say, regardless of the sartorial crime I was committing and the impression it gave others, it was tremendous to be able to find my penis at toilet stops without the need for a search party.

The G110 on the stretch between Ulanqab and Hohhot was freshly tarmacked, lined with bright green barriers, set amongst manageable hills and at times surrounded by seemingly endless grasslands. After the first set of hills, I stopped for noodles in Zhuozi, a town that had an end of the world feel as a huge, dark, cloud-topped, mountain loomed beyond the road leading out of it. Fortunately, the G110, the road I would use for most of the first 1300km or so, went around and not over the mountain like the new G6 motorway does. On my way around all but one lorry driver was courteous enough to pass me with a full lane sized gap and I flew into the very edge of Hohhot's future urban sprawl in good time.

As I passed more and more of the yurt-shaped tombs that dressed the landscape, I began to imagine what my equivalent would be. I concluded that I had no interest in being sprinkled into a mock-up of a two-bed flat, stacked with three hundred others, from which my ashes would be hoovered up once the inheritance ran out.

In these early days of the journey, I found it was important to make hay whilst the sun shines (though I'm sure you need rain to make hay). The more progress I made, the more positive I was. The closer to my destination I got, the easier it would have been to solve any problems. It was great for morale. Conserving energy is for racers, not idiots. To illustrate this point, I only caught the beginning of a blizzard for my final 5km instead of my final 30km because I had got into top gear on the downhills and pedalled like mad as any good idiot would do.

I also had company awaiting me in Hohhot, in the shape of my saviours from the first day, Holly and Matt. Once I had finished scrubbing the layer of detritus, which had adhered itself to my body thanks to the sun cream covering it, we set off for hotpot.

Not to be confused with anything that has been served in the North of England, hotpot is one of Mongolia's great gifts to the world. It comprehensively beats Mongolian Barbecue in the authenticity stakes by being Mongolian and utilising the cooking utensil it claims to employ. Hotpot is, unsurprisingly, cooked in a hot pot. The pot sits in the centre of the table bubbling away and nowadays is often powered by a frighteningly large gas canister, which sits under the table within inches of the diner's lower limbs. Frequently these are big enough to blow up the whole restaurant, never mind the table. Diners cook their own meat, fish and vegetables, which arrive raw, by dipping or drowning them it in the boiling stock. As a warning, the raw meat often looks incredibly seductive, often like a giant plate of sliced ham. It once took Holly several goes to convince her hungry mother that she should not to eat the raw slices of mutton in front of her.

There are many variations of hotpot across Asia. The Mongolian hot in the pot is a milky coloured chicken stock. The other variant of hotpot prevalent in China is Sichuan hotpot, which is blisteringly spicy. Filled with chillies, the eponymous peppercorn and an oily chilli paste, this variety ensures that diners have a mouth of fire. Crucially, because it's in liquid form, those eating Sichuan Hotpot often imbibe far more Chilli than they first realise. The unintentionally large quantities of chilli are a test for even the most stellar of stomachs. Sichuan hotpot is like a bullet. The real damage is not done on the way in, but on the way out.

Perhaps because the Mongolian stock is a little bland and the Sichuan stock is a hosepipe-free enema waiting to happen, most people opt for half and half. As did we on this occasion. Creatively, this is often delivered in a pot containing a yin-yang wiggly line that separates the light stock from the dark one. Thanks to balancing out our yin with some yang, neither Matt,

Holly, nor I suffered from Hohhot hotpot hot-bot the following morning.

My companions continued to be great company until midnight. At which point they began to beat what remained of my exhausted and drained carcass at cards. An event that took place, without explanation, in a Christmas-themed bar where the locals were drinking 16% super strength lager. Yet neither the kitsch, nor the kids on super-booze, could stop me from nodding off like a grandmother in the sherry-tinged haze that follows Christmas dinner.

Though it was a relief for our Graham to have a day away from the saddle and fun to have conversations that expanded beyond how cold my legs were, Hohhot was a disappointment. Delightful as it was to leave the drain-influenced stench of the hotel room behind, the sights of Inner Mongolia's capital did an equally good job of stinking the place out. One of the temples was blockaded by a bouncy castle, the much vaunted central mosque had neon-emitting TV screens built into the façade, and the museum had taxidermy so bad the camera on my phone was unable to focus on the beady-eyed animals before me. One vaguely stoat-like creature looked in worse condition than much of the roadkill I had already passed.

The city was at least sat under the never ending blue skies after which it was named. Altan Khan, descendant of Genghis a few generations down the line, named it Koke Kotha – The Blue City[26]. Clearly a man with a talent for naming things, he is also the man who gave the world the title Dalai Lama[27].

---

[26] (Man, 2008)

[27] (McKay, 2003)

Once Matt had been despatched to the train station in a taxi, I enforced a trip to Pizza Hut upon Holly to stock up on calories. Despite people queueing outside in the freezing air to get in, not a single table within sight of us was eating pizza. I could see chicken wings, noodles and even prawns being eaten thousands of kilometres from the sea, but nobody was having pizza. The power of brands is limitless, but at least it has a sense of humour.

The elation of being one large pizza and the crust from Holly's richer lasted only as long as it took us to traverse the busy road bridge back to the hotel. Upon returning, one of my worst fears was realised. The locked bike had gone from outside the hotel.

With panic improving my Mandarin by anything up to 20% I asked loudly, often, and repetitively where it had gone. Eventually, I managed to establish that two men had put it in the staff quarters for safekeeping. Relieved, I said goodbye to Holly who had to fly back to Beijing and settled down to sleep in the stinky room.

After retrieving the Giant from the staff quarters and hauling it up four floors I began my flattest day yet. The almost immediate gear change down three cogs with a single push of the thumb saw me find the one gear I would use for the entire day. Realising an economics podcast on healthcare statistics was not productive for generating rhythm in my legs, I switched to terrible late 90s pop punk. I cracked on with my most proficient performance to date, to the sound of inspired lyrics such as the wonderfully sarcastic "The old folks are losers, they can't work computers" whilst gleefully imagining the protagonists themselves now having to ask their own teenagers how to sync the laptop and television.

By the end of my third and fifth days, my right knee had started to protest about the number of rotations the longer days were requiring. I eventually worked out that turning a bigger gear through less rotations was the answer to this problem, but until that enlightenment I would resort to what I now call a Paracetamol Power Hour.

Numb-kneed, I covered the 145km on a stretch of road that was bordered on one side by the Great Blue Mountains and the glimmering Hasuhai Wetlands on the other, in under 12 hours. More impressively, this was inclusive of the time lost through being a point of curiosity for everyone I met.

From here until I arrived at the tourist sites of Zhangye two weeks later, more often than not I was the first foreigner people had spoken to in their lives. On this day, in particular, I lost time by becoming the novelty item in everybody's day. In return I was rewarded with the chance to make my first joke in Mandarin - a big breakthrough - whilst having my photo taken with three women I exclaimed "Look! I have three wives!" a remark that received a rapturous response from their actual husbands. More Jim Davidson than Ross Noble, but you have to work with what you've got, which in my case was about 1000 not particularly hilarious words.

Hunger on the road was becoming more of an issue, I adapted my approach from the donkey diet to treating myself as a steam train, by taking on smaller, dirtier, fuel, more often. In this case, my coal was strawberry flavoured muffins, which were neither muffins nor strawberry flavoured. Their identity crisis was of no interest for me, though, they had what I wanted – calories - in an abundance that shouldn't really fit into such a small packet. I was shovelling my coal in at regular intervals, however, by now my metabolism had finally clocked what was going on to such an extent that it began to feel like the muffins would just disintegrate upon hitting the floor of my empty stomach. In just over a week my concerns over needing to become a Wiggins-like whippet had subsided. Instead, I started to worry how I would find enough calories each day once I reached the deserts and the frequency of petrol stations and shops dissipated.

Talking of coal, it was everywhere. Inner Mongolia is mining country and by the time I stumbled into my latest hotel, I was wearing the face of a man who had done a real day's work. It was clear that I would not be alone in this appearance, even the otherwise demure hotel receptionist's immaculate skin and brightly coloured chain-hotel polo shirt had a sooty tinge to it.

I had decided to stay in Donghe, an industrial suburb of Baotou, a place Lonely Planet bludgeons with the following review - *"unless you have a particular interest in steel production there is little reason to stop"*. Lonely Planet clearly hadn't envisioned anyone cycling for 150km before arriving. If anyone had a reason to stop there, it was me.

After checking in, I took a miserably weak shower before carrying out some 21st century administration in the heavily smoke damaged room. Not fancying the culinary delights of a town coated in soot I forced in a fourth pot noodle of the day before falling asleep to the sounds of a prostitute who couldn't even be bothered to keep the false screams of pleasure in time with the beat of the bed hitting the wall. Fortunately, this was the penultimate night I was in close enough proximity to the world's oldest profession's operatic output to have my sleep disrupted. Though I will say this for the prostitutes of China's lowly-starred hotels - they get their work done by midnight.

After much confusion as to why I had asked for a knife at breakfast, I was presented with a spoon with a spoon to spread the butter on my self-assembled toasted egg sandwich. Still, some wonderful beige carbs and protein got me through the Baotou rush hour and back out onto the G110. Baotou was clearly a town proud of its steel industry as a grand soviet style statue of a steel worker, hammer in hand, confirmed on the outskirts of the city. Yet in the centre I had ridden along a mauve bicycle lane through a park, reminiscent of the Mall in London. I had also passed the symbolic 'Victory Mall' where Hugo Boss and friends were fronted by a classic white statue of Chairman Mao saluting the switch from an export-driven economy to one of unrelenting materialistic consumption.

My eighth day also marked the move in temperature I'd been anticipating a week earlier. It was the beginning of regular mid-morning stops to shift from five layers to one when the temperature would rise to around 20 whatsitmajiggies around 10am. Unsurprisingly this increase in heat came in partnership with the exotic first smatterings of scrubby desert. Ominously for the camping to come, it also came with the sight of a dead wolf. Yet for this day at least, the temperature was pleasant and the predators were dead.

Late in the afternoon, I participated in a mobile interview as a passenger in a Porsche 4x4 filmed the driver asking me the usual questions. It was like a medical tow in the Tour de France, only this one finished with the doctor offering the suffering rider a cigarette. The offer of a cigarette was more often than not how *the conversation* would end. Being male it was always assumed that I smoked. It made no difference that I would almost always have a burgundy, sweat covered, face and would be gasping as the offer was made. My response of "no thank you" was always met with confusion. Only when I explained the distance I had cycled, mimicked the turning of pedals, whilst panting out something like "so, you know, I am very tired", would the confused frown morph into that most brilliant of Chinese faces. The one that looks as sage as Confucius himself as the head tips back and eyes close, before the face returns back down with pursed lips and a serious stare, to give the recipient confirmation of complete understanding.

If I hadn't had another knee break-down, which stretched the final thirty kilometres into a four-hour odyssey through yet more edge-of-town heavy industry, this day would have been a great success.

As it was, my knackered knee delay meant it was dark by the time I'd finished dismantling my bike outside the hotel. As I had been pulling various bags and wheels off the bike I watched as all of the hotel's staff gathered to meet me for the obligatory photos. With previous entrances to hotels being marked by increasingly horrified faces, I decided the best course of action was to immediately apologise for my appearance as I bundled through the door. On this occasion, my general filth didn't dissuade the girls from the restaurant who wanted a photo, so I upped my warning to "I'm sorry, I'm a very dirty man". It didn't work, though. In arguably my most dishevelled state ever, I had my photo taken with a beautiful waitress of 20 who was dressed in a pristine red silk dress. The contrast, at least, must have bordered on artistic.

Once the all-important photos had been taken, I checked in. As the hotel had already sent on their guest's details for the night to the local police, I had a visit from a very nice policewoman and her young son. After it was established I was alone, on a bicycle, had a reservation for tomorrow night elsewhere, was only taking photos of mountains and clearly a danger to nothing but myself or fashion, I was left alone to try and locate my increasingly irritating slow puncture in peace.

I knew there would be testing days. I knew there would be dark days. I knew there would be days where I wanted to get on a train back to Beijing, then take a flight back to Europe where I would find some kind of small coastal town in Croatia full of fresh seafood and even fresher air and any mention of China or bicycles would be ignored. The ninth day of my journey was the first of four days that would fall into this final category of absolute screaming misery.

The same warm faces that had greeted me the night before helped me reassemble the bike before I headed out into to an orange-tinged scene of urban grey. For many hundreds of kilometres, the G110 road on which I was cycling was shadowed by the new G6 motorway, but here at Urad Qianqi the G110 took an inexplicable detour north. On this day that detour happened to be heading straight into a sandstorm.

I was to learn later of the very many different types of sandstorm a man can fail to cycle through, but I retain a particularly strong hatred for my first; the all-engulfing, slow-moving, city-shrouder. I managed to cycle the first 15km or so before I was forced to alternate between riding and walking the bike into a face-stinging headwind. I pushed on for 45 more kilometres until I reached the town of Longxinchang some seven, miserable, hours later.

From what I could establish on my phone, there was only one hotel I could stay in as a foreigner (more on this fun regulation later). After a few detours, I turned up at what seemed to be a bar, restaurant, karaoke joint, brothel and hotel all-in-one. Worse still, this multi-purpose venue already contained enough comprehensively shit-faced, middle-aged, men grabbing me for photos that heading back into the sandstorm for the night seemed a more appealing option. Eventually, my hero arrived in the shape of a slight, attractive woman in her late twenties. In a manner completely at odds with her delicate appearance and small stature, she loudly told the drunks to stop being "stupid cunts" before checking me in with an efficiency I would never again see on my journey.

With a heady mix of free-time and residual anger, I headed out for a stroll around the town square. The square was inexplicably filled with giant statues of various cacti. Having seen all of the sights in three minutes, I headed to buy some much-needed beer and sunflower seeds. On my return, I ran through reception to avoid the drunks that threatened to impede my access to the sanctity of my room. Once more the police came to see me, again seemingly out of curiosity rather than any genuine security concerns. I quickly realised that the most effective way to bring these polite interrogations to a close was to make clear I would be leaving town the next day, thus removing myself from that police officer's area of responsibility. No foreigner, no problem.

Seen as it was 95% of my entertainment on that longest of evenings in Longxinchang, this seems as good a time as any to talk about beer. It may seem over the coming pages that I am drinking more beer than it would be possible for someone cycling across the third largest country on earth to consume. However, once I was beyond Beijing's third ring road and the temptations of its many excellent craft breweries, with the exception of Santa's bar in Hohhot, I was in a world where no beer was stronger than 4%. More often than not my choice was limited to 3.1% or the pointless 2.5% beers that allow China to be both the world's largest consumer of beer and a highly productive economy at the same time.

Perhaps this isn't a coincidence. Though they won't win any awards for taste, these beers feel like they provide a public service. Perfectly matched to the spicy food and scorching temperatures of summer they are a product meeting a specific set of demands. These same criteria also mean it's perfectly suited to refreshing a thirsty cyclist who is bored to the back teeth of water, citrus hydration tablets and strawberry protein shakes. Crucially, nobody has ever had a hangover from 2.5% beer.

The perfect accompaniment is sunflower seeds. I had a bag with me for most of the trip. Just the distraction of splitting the shells open was, at times, reward enough, never mind the nutritional benefits. There's a rhythmic addiction to eating them. Covered in their scruffy black and white husks, I slept soundly for eight perfect hours.

The one redeeming feature of sandstorms is that they don't last forever. By the next morning, my quarry from the day before already had passed Beijing, which was already over 800km away. I left under a sky that looked as though somebody had deep-cleaned it overnight.

You may notice that I find it very easy to measure distances throughout this journey. This is not because I had a £500 GPS device, or even that I went to such radical extremes as using my phone. Instead, I would simply look down at the road. On the roads of China every kilometre had its own stone, a kilometrestone if you will.

Yet the measurements don't stop there. The Chinese have a fearsome commitment to numerical facts. This isn't just because they know they have the biggest of everything, it runs far deeper than that. As anyone who's been present at a meeting with a Chinese government official will confirm, you must brace yourself for a set of key facts about anything from GDP to productivity stats or even the size of a province in square kilometres, before you begin discussing whatever it was you actually arrived to talk about.

In a more recreational environment, there is no less of a belief in the sanctity of measurements and numbers. At any tourist site you must wade through the height of the statue, the size in square metres of the temple floor, the year it was built and numerous other numerals, before you find out the who, what, and why of how this thing of historical importance came to be. Even with locations that fit harmoniously with the CCP's bigger picture of China, this is the order. It is just the way things are.

To underline this point, let us return to the road, where not only are kilometres marked, but on the national highways I was using, every one hundred metres was marked. More often than not they were rewarded with their own mini-stone, at other times a simple line on the road would denote my location in amazing detail.

This was helpful in terms of measuring my stints on the bike. Ten kilometres on, ten minutes off. Ride on, ride off. Ten on, ten off. Ride on, ride off. They were also very much a double-edged sword for morale. In the high winds, like those I experienced on the previous day, knowing how many minutes it had taken to cover such a short distance was crushing. On the good days, watching them buzz by was a real boost.

The kilometre stones themselves also became a key part of my daily routine. I would sit on whichever multiple of ten, or five on a very bad day, I had stopped at for my rest breaks. They provided the perfect height to rest my legs, the perfect surface area to give Graham and his mates some contactless time and limited the stupid noises I would have made if I was getting up from the floor after 150km and 14 hours of cycling.

This was a day where the minutiae of measurements were a welcome minute-by-minute update of good progress. Under the endless, bright blue, ceiling, it was another great day for camaraderie out on the road as the frequent breakdowns of two men transporting bricks on antiquated tractors matched perfectly with my rest breaks. This created a faux race where we overtook each other persistently for 50km. It was like having a five-minute conversation spread over three hours:

"Hello, how are you?"

"Good thanks, how are you?"

"Good also! Bye"

Twenty minutes later.

"Where are you going?"

"Linhe."

Twenty-five minutes later.

"Where are you going friend?"

"The next town, if the vehicle can be fixed!"

And so on and so on.

Shortly after we parted, I was flagged down by a young couple proffering two cans of Red Bull as a gift. I tried to only accept one but turning down a gift from a Chinese person is harder than extracting one from a Yorkshireman. My teeth won't thank them, but my blood sugars were delighted.

Linhe, my destination for the evening, was the first city I'd arrived in where I wished I'd had a bit more time to linger. Not least because my hotel room possessed a bath, in which I could have happily stayed for one whole week. There was just something warm and forgiving about Linhe, which the unrelenting industrial scenery of the province's eastern half seemed to have scrubbed out.

The following day picked up where the previous one had left my mood and general well-being. Following the longest check out yet - 18 minutes - I joined Linhe's pensioners for their morning turn about the square before hitting the 6.20am rush hour to school. Yes, that's right, six and twenty. Never complain about school starting at 9am again.

Out on the road, it was a day of monuments and landmarks. I passed the 1000km mark, the G110 passed its own 1000km mark and I crossed one of China's great rivers; the Yellow one. The Yellow River is the sixth longest in the world, after all the ones you know about and the Yenesei, which you don't.

In human development terms, the Yellow River is China's Mediterranean, the life-giving water from which its civilisation grew. Yet if ever there was a piece of nature that takes as much with one hand as it gives with the other it could be this river. It is the source of the only natural disasters to kill more than a million people; something it's done three times with its devastating ability to massacre through flooding[28].

On this day it was flowing calmly enough for people to fish whilst wading waist high into its murky waters. I sat and watched it for a while trying to force the importance of what was in front of me into some kind of symbolic memory. As it was I needn't have tried. I will now forever remember the moment I crossed the Yellow River as the time I sat in the shadow of a statue of three 50ft tall padlocks. You might assume that they are symbolic of some kind of unbreakable bond between the Chinese and this great river, but it's just as likely that their presence is due to the nearest town manufacturing 78% of the world's padlocks[29].

I made more new friends on the road. I promised I'd have lunch the next day in the home town of two delivery drivers who passed me five or six times as they shuttled up and down the same stretch of tarmac.

The smatterings of desert that had appeared in the preceding days increased gradually throughout the day, until on my left-hand side was the Ordos Desert and on my right-hand side, lined first with barren scrubland and then in the distance golden dunes, was the Gobi Desert. In contrast to the Yellow River, which in truth had been upstaged by the padlocks, this was a genuinely exciting moment. Not least because both deserts sound like far-flung places in Star Wars.

Comparatively unknown, the Ordos now has the added ignominy of Ordos City, which is the place routinely visited for foreign news features on Chinese ghost towns. Despite no one living there,

---

[28] (White, 2012, p. 47)

[29] A total guess on my part, this is almost certainly not true. It's probably something like 98%

Ordos city (population: 1.2 million and counting) hosted Miss World in 2012. You will never guess the nationality of the winner in that year. OK, you will, China, but you'll never guess the nationality of the runner-up. So I'll tell you, she was Welsh. If that hasn't surprised you, wait until you hear this; a native of a country with places like Rhyl won the beachwear round.

Anyway the Ordos; big desert, terrible for agriculture, but also quite probably the etymological mother of the English word "horde". According to Gustav John Ramstedt, a Finnish diplomat and linguist specialising in Asian languages, "horde" has its roots in Ordos. It doesn't take a great leap of imagination to believe this but it is quite literally, literally pleasing that the word horde came from the land of rampaging hordes, rather than a large gathering of British peasants denouncing witchcraft or something similar.

At a time when diplomats could have a huge influence of geopolitics, rather than nudging things in the right direction or working to make things deteriorate less rapidly, Ramstedt wasn't just busy being a linguistic genius. He was also the man that the soon to be independent Mongolians asked to mediate with Russia in 1911 in the negotiations that secured support for their independence. With less success, he was again the man they turned to in 1912 to encourage Russia to let Inner Mongolia come along for the ride too.

Despite not yet hosting a global beauty pageant or giving birth to a synonym of "\mob, the Gobi needs less of an introduction. It is Asia's largest desert and the fifth biggest on earth. It's also getting bigger by an average of around ten square kilometres a day. A rate of expansion that means in just 40,000 years that the Gobi will have inherited the earth. If, of course, that wasn't totally impossible thanks to the oceans and many other ecological factors.

In my first stretch of desert, the search for calories and

particularly protein took me to my darkest place yet, as I began eating the many and varied pickled eggs intended for pot noodles. Cold and in triplet. This day though, became all about one moment where, as I cruised at a wind assisted 50kph, singing along to Idlewild from a playlist so narrow that carbon dating my bones would be a less accurate indicator of my age, I gazed over to a twinkling Yellow River and the golden dunes of the Gobi beyond it. By then heavy industry on the outskirts of Wuhai had arrived to scar the Ordos side of the road, but regardless it was a special moment.

I was in Wuhai! and I could smell heavy metals.

My last full day in Inner Mongolia started by battling the metabolism enabling virtues of the previous night's chilli. I was called to the toilet four times before leaving. There's a reason you don't go for Sichuanese on a school night. With extra heat in the lycra, I waddled to the bike before wading out into a rainy and flooded Wuhai. At my breakfast stop it became apparent that in washing the industrial haze from the sky, the rain had brought more than just water down to ground level. As I strode from the bike into a petrol station, my sodden left trainer began to foam like a washing up bowl.

Another debacle with Google Maps followed. They really must change the software they use for identifying roads in countries they're banned from. On a related note, I went on a surprise visit to a coal mine. Lost amongst the soot-slush, my misery was compounded by two punctures. The first of which occurred in front of a factory belching out some indistinguishable rancid substance, which left me with a stinking headache and six fewer months at the end of my life to endure living through.

Eventually, I was out of the industrial horrors and into the small farms and quaint mosques of rural Ningxia province. Just like Inner Mongolia, Ningxia is an autonomous region of the People's

Republic of China. In a country where power is so centralised, the autonomous tag feels largely token. In Inner Mongolia only 17% of the population are Mongols. Ningxia is formally the Ningxia Hui Autonomous Region. Yet even with double the Mongol's presence, at 34% the Hui are a minority in Ningxia.

The Mongols and Hui are two of the biggest of the 56 ethnic groups in China who are officially recognised. Along with the Tibetan, Uyghur, and Zhuang peoples, they are the only ethnic groups with a declared autonomous region. Like the Mongols and the Zhuang, the Hui are not the biggest ethnic grouping in the associated autonomous region. Unsurprisingly, in these three provinces the Han, who constitute 92% of the general population, are the largest group. Unlike the Mongols though, more Hui people live outside of Ningxia than inside it.

The vast majority of Hui are Muslims. Thanks to the Silk Road, 6.7% of the Hui's genetic makeup is of Western Eurasian origin[30], but from sight alone it is frequently only their dress that distinguishes them from Han Chinese. More often than not this distinguishing feature is the gleaming white caps worn by Hui men. These pieces of headwear must be the cleanest things I've seen in China. Without fail, and in spite of the desert's dust and detritus that is so prevalent in their home province, the caps would still all gleam bright white atop the heads on which they sat.

Ningxia, in Chinese province terms, is titchy. Meaning tranquil Xia, it takes its name from the Western Xia people who occupied it for a couple of centuries before the Mongols disturbed their tranquillity. With the exception of the municipalities based around Beijing, Tianjin and Shanghai; the Special Administrative

---

[30] (YongGang Yao, 2004, p. 2265)

playgrounds for bankers and gamblers of Hong Kong and Macau; and the tropical island of Hainan, Ningxia is the smallest administrative region in China. This is magnified by neighbouring giant Inner Mongolia and amplified further still by sitting in the West of China; where all of the largest provinces are.

Perhaps because of its comprehensible size, Ningxia felt as though it had a definitive character to it. A character I really liked. Inner Mongolia's send-off had been pollution and punctures in the pissing rain. I even had what I suspect was my first, and probably only, tail by a bored official who couldn't have been less covert if he'd shouted "Hey Simon Clode, Passport Number 504611111, how did you get such a fictitious passport number?" as he followed me and observed me in his wing mirrors in three separate lay-bys. I waved at him each time but he didn't reciprocate once. Perhaps he was just shy.

In stark contrast, Ningxia's welcome was one of friendship, food, and fine weather. Despite losing time in the morning, thanks to the punctures and my site visit to the coal mine, I took up the dinner invite from the day before. I had thought that dinner would be with both drivers from the van but it turned out on arrival that it would actually be with one of them, Mr Ma, his wife and some other friends.

After I washed as much filth off my limbs and face in the Ma's shower as I could manage, our steadily growing party headed to Pingluo County's premier hotpot restaurant.

We were joined by another of their friends at the restaurant who was wearing a t-shirt that read 'Normal Size Go Away' with no sense of coincidence as his humungous belly stretched the material to bursting point.

The food, as ever in modern day China, was plentiful. As was the piss-weak beer. By the time the third bottle arrived, I'd accepted the offer of a lift with the Ma's for the final 60km of the day. It wasn't the fact I was drunk – we were on the 2.5% stuff - it was the fact I knew that I had at least three more hours of hospitality to come. I'd be damned if I was going to trade that off for the integrity of a bicycle journey that had lost its virginity on its own doorstep before lunchtime.

After *the conversation,* we discussed money, primarily the cost of houses in Beijing and London, and the price of iPhones and Range Rovers. We agreed, using each other's evidence that Range Rovers[31] were at least twice the price in China and iPhones were also slightly more expensive.

Stuffed beyond belief, we began the inevitable procession of photographs. Something that culminated with me having my photo with the army of waitresses who had just arrived to begin their evening shift.

Another of my favourite things about China today is the motivational speech, and sometimes dance, that precedes the working day at many businesses. The format is simple, the staff assemble in military formation to receive words of wisdom and inspiration from their bosses and then everyone sings and/or performs an energising dance. In the busy world of food service, this makes some sense to me but I will never stop finding it funny to see rows of estate agents doing the Chinese Macarena in preparation for a hard day's lying.

On this occasion, I stepped out of the restaurant just as the motivational speech was finishing. Sadly, there was no dance and instead a photo of me towering over everyone by at least six inches at my monstrous five-foot *nineish* became the order of the day.

The Mas and their friends were desperate to show me some

---

[31] Or LuHu (Land Tiger) as they're called in China.

sites of Pingluo County. I insisted I needed to be in Yinchuan by 7 o'clock, because my less than capable friends would be arriving from Britain to join me. As such we made a hastily arranged trip to a beautiful Taoist temple in the centre of town, rather than a three-hour odyssey as they first suggested.

After we returned to the Mas' flat, they showed me their wedding photo album, a deep source of pride for them and many other young Chinese couples. The wedding photo industry of China must be worth roughly the same as the Spanish economy. Rarely a day goes by without seeing two people in their early twenties, dressed in various outfits, posing affectionately to build their wedding album. It doesn't matter where either, as well as all the photos under blossom coated trees, I've seen couples stood by an empty reservoir in Yunnan and wading together in the polluted sea of Qingdao. Most confusingly of all, I've seen more than one photo shoot taking place outside a supermarket.

The Mas' album didn't contain any scenes as confusing as those I've just mentioned but it did involve at least twenty costume changes. I'm sure, given that these photos are always taken before the wedding takes place, that this is just a test of worthiness for the groom. He really must love you if he's going to put a sky blue pink suit on and pretend to lick a plastic ice cream in a moment that will be captured for eternity.

After I read one of the French poems in the album aloud, we headed out into the street and awaited delivery of a huge truck to throw the bike on the back of and head down the road to Yinchuan. I felt a little guilty about breaching the integrity of the trip, but the fact I could have cycled if I'd wanted to but had more fun meeting people, quickly erased any remorse.

In a sign of the tardiness to come, when we arrived at the hotel my two friends Jon and Tom were not waiting outside with the hastily arranged gift for the Mas as I had instructed them to buy.

After retrieving them from the sofa, I said my farewells to the Mas and eventually got down to the business of hugging and insulting my old friends.

It was not just the Mas I was saying goodbye to, but the road too. China National Highway 110, or G110 to her friends, had carried me almost all the way to its end point in Yinchuan from Beijing, over and along the Great Wall, through the filth and the fury.

It was, however, time for a new road and also time for a new chapter.

Chapter 5.1 to be precise.

5.1 MEALS ON WHEELS

Despite being a man whose favourite apple is, in fact, a ball of mozzarella, concerns about being too fat for this journey very quickly switched to panic over sourcing enough energy each day. I had always known that a big part of my diet would be pot noodles, or as they're known in China 'convenient noodles'. Mentally prepared or not, this didn't delay the near immediate boredom I would experience consuming them. When you speak with Chinese people about convenient noodles, you get a sense they'd rather the noodles were called only-when-absolutely-fucking-necessary noodles, and with total justification too.

Costing an average of 50p they represented great value in providing around 400 calories, but even doubling the quantity meant I was fighting a losing battle. They did, however, form a good base to supplement with snacks from petrol stations.

Though the theory is that they come in many flavours, the truth is that only-when-absolutely-fucking-necessary noodles basically all taste the same. For the most part, they come with the same vinegar sachet, miniature dehydrated bits of meat and veg, and seasoning. They also come with a thick paste, which looks like playdoh and simply cannot be made of any natural substances. The only good thing about convenient noodles and their additives is that they make one's excrement comically long.

This work to layer my stomach was shared out with naan bread as soon as I was far enough west that bread became plentiful. The best meals on the road were where I had both noodles and the naan to dip in their spicy playdoh gravy.

The best days were ones where real home-style cooking was available with delicious meat and vegetable dishes. Normally I would eat at least two or three people's portions with rice too. I could feel my body actively craving protein. Equally, I was desperate for nutrients from vegetables and fruit. During my kebab marathons later on in the ride, I would balance out two portions of kebab with two portions of fruit and veg.

Even on a day where I had noodles for breakfast, real food for lunch and managed to get an evening meal, I would still need to constantly eat. Once outside of Beijing, I was not in the land of supermarkets stocking high energy nut bars. This meant I was at the mercy of the petrol station's supplies of Oreos (strawberry, vanilla or preferably double chocolate), Muffins (strawberry, chocolate, and particularly exotic for the middle of China, tiramisu), Snickers, and pickled eggs. I would eat one of these things on each of my five-minute breaks.

I was consuming around 8-10 litres of liquid a day. The vast majority of which was obviously water, but where I had access I would dramatically heighten the likelihood of false teeth before retirement with Red Bull, full-fat Coca Cola and Sprite. Sometimes I'd even get hold of a cold coffee, a short-lived delight that would rapidly turn to regret and self-loathing.

The hydration tablets stopped me from getting cramp and the protein shakes clearly helped with my recovery as not once did I feel stiff. Maybe they're a placebo thanks to powerful marketing, but I found them great. One oversight was to not take multi-vitamin supplements. Even on days with plenty of veg and fruit I was burning through the goodness as quickly as the energy and protein.

Not quite Grandma Wang's secret recipe you were hoping for right?

6. Mirage a Trois

At times, what follows may read like the character assassination of Jonathon Tostevin and Thomas Wintle. So before we get to that point I should make two things clear. First, they are both very clever people. One of them was running a charity and studying for a masters on top of having a middle-management job until he became clever enough to stop doing the first two of these things. The other recently had the job objective to 'stabilise world oil markets', which admittedly is a stupid objective, but hopefully highlights the faith his intelligence leads others to have in him. Secondly, I do genuinely like them both.

Their participation in the ride came about by chance. Jon was coming to the end of a stint sorting out Ebola – told you he was clever[32] – and was looking into taking a holiday before going to Sierra Leone to check the Ebola had all gone. He sent me an e-mail to see if it was a good time to visit me in Beijing and ended up agreeing to cycle 1000km across China. Tom heard about this and decided he also wanted in on it.

In the months before they arrived, I sent them a series of strong *suggestions* about training, highlighted the importance of cream for their Grahams and told them to buy padded shorts. The last of these they both achieved. One of them brought proper Graham cream, the other – the scientist – brought Sudocreme. One of them went for a two-hour ride on a Boris bike and the other went camping.

Boris bike, camping, Sudocreme.

It was a poor start that only got worse when Tom made clear he intended to cover his head with fashion's greatest crime – the

---

[32] Well, you haven't got Ebola have you?

bandanna. Something he would pair with lycra without the decency for some modesty shorts, meaning I spent a week on tour with Hampshire's answer to Mr Motivator.

Overjoyed by the genuine luxury of my five-star hotel bed, I was in no great rush to get on with purchasing the Unprepared Brothers' bicycles. When I did eventually prise myself away from the first pillows I had slept on in two weeks that seemed not contain ball bearings, I discovered a loveable city. Yinchuan appeared to have dodged some, if not all, of the architectural bullets befalling the majority of its provincial capital compatriots. Visit Ningxia, it's bloody lovely.

With varying levels of exhaustion, jet-lag and laziness permeating our group, we got lost in Yinchuan's laid back nature. Almost immediately a trip to the historical Western Xia tombs was written off. Instead, we strolled, tofu sticks in hand, to the bike shop.

In stark contrast to the Sudocreme and Boris bike regime employed by the others, I had done some real preparation and arranged to meet Wang Kai, a man who loves cycling and crucially for our needs, owned a bike shop. Kai set up different bits of the Merida bikes, whilst Jon and Tom hopelessly wobbled around the shop and all variations of our bank cards failed to work. Eventually, I managed to bleed enough cash from an ATM to buy the bikes. After Kai had chucked in some freebies and pulled one of the best faces I've ever seen in a photograph, we were on a way.

With the bikes finally purchased, our tragic laziness peaked as we indulged in that greatest of British traditions by sitting in a dark, windowless bar, seeing out much of the remaining daylight when it was lovely outside. We got what we deserved with the worst food I would eat in my 60 days outside of Beijing and the most watered down beer I've ever drunk. However, it did provide us with the necessary seven minutes to catch up on two years of each other's lives, which meant we could spend the next eight days with our headphones in and sit in long, comfortable, exhausted silences.

Once out of the bar we went in search of some gas canisters for my camping stove and some shorts for Tom because he'd come on a cycling holiday without any. After much misdirection from locals and search engines, we fluked upon two camping shops that were rich with things we needed like gas, but also things we didn't, like a second bandanna.

Our first ride as a trio passed without any major incidents and by sunset we were being chased out of the hotel pool for not wearing swimming caps. I hate the rule that bathers must wear a swimming cap. I always forget it exists, then end up with my spine shuddering as I pull on a wet and cold communal number that a lifeguard has found rotting at the bottom of a basket. After a brief discussion, we all begrudgingly squeezed our fat, western, heads into some damp, second-hand, head-condoms, and were free to swim against a backdrop of golden mountains, which only seemed marginally taller than the floor hosting the pool.

To plagiarise Sue Townsend, our first day on the road together began like this.

09.00 – Leave hotel.

09.30 – Stop for noodles.

10.00 –– Toilet stop.

10.30 – First breakage; a snapped pannier on Jon's bike.

11.00 – Reach 1km.

It was not an auspicious start to our first day as a team. Worse still, when my back was turned, the least prepared one had put on a second, unrequired, bandanna just to annoy me. Being more vulture than culture, we were unable to pass Yinchuan's botanical gardens without visiting the intellectual property thieving dinosaur park attached to it. The immensely cheerful young woman at reception successfully upsold us tickets to the gardens too. Clever girl.

When we eventually left the city area an hour later, we discovered ideal conditions for the newcomers to be introduced to long distance cycling with a tailwind pushing us south for much of our relatively short journey of 90km. A brief rain shower early on in the ride was dealt with badly. Tom had brought a poncho, which was little more than a green bin bag with a piece of string. He finally managed to attach just as it stopped raining.

We stopped in a small town to avoid the next shower and eat some lunch. On our approach to the restaurant, we were waved in by some of the existing patrons but walked through the wrong door. Nobody in the room we entered acknowledged our presence, which given our alien appearance seemed unusual. Eventually, I wandered over to ask for a menu from two young women sat at the far end of the room, but I was energetically waved back to the booth at which we had all taken a seat. Eventually, an older woman, who was squeezed into some shorts not particularly suited to the day's weather or the girth of her thighs, came down the stairs and approached our table. I again asked for a menu whilst miming the opening of a book, the woman was unmoved, only saying there was no menu. So I moved the mime act up a notch to mimic spooning food into my mouth whilst saying we wanted to eat. At which point she and the younger girls, who had earlier waved us away, began to smirk. "This is a place for massages" she explained, in more words than I could understand. I would suggest the additional words and phrases, which lay beyond the grasp of my knowledge, gave more than one meaning to her oral menu.

Relieved I didn't choose to mime eating a hot dog, we made a polite exit and entered the adjacent restaurant. In truth, this was an establishment we should probably have thought twice about eating in given the neighbours. Though since my favourite baguette shop at university was called Ab-Fab and backed onto a brothel called Abigail's[33] it's a bit late for me to be concerned about any kind of coincidentally[34] close proximity between the food I eat and the sex trade.

Once inside the restaurant, I was able to enjoy one of the great pleasures of hosting guests in China as our first real Chinese meal was placed on the table. The one guidebook cliché about China that is not overplayed is just how much better Chinese food is inside the Middle Kingdom than it is outside. I can't tell you for sure what we consumed because the only photo I have is one of the decimated table that we left behind. But I'll do my best to reimagine the feast.

One thing that Britain and a select few other countries have got drastically wrong in their cultural evolution is the individualisation of food. The best way to eat, at all times, is in a communal environment where everybody gets a bit of everything. At lunch we each had two different types of meat and at least eight different vegetables; some of it in a curry sauce, some of it with Sichuan peppercorns, another dish was flavoured with fresh red chillies and something else was in a sweeter gravy. There was lotus root, aubergine, beans, tomatoes, broccoli, cauliflower, potato, cabbage, peppers, chillies, ginger, garlic, beef and as we learned afterwards, donkey meat.

As a group, we had been amazed by the size of the pork ribs. After a local, who was intrigued by our presence in his favourite

---

[33] Previously operating under the much funnier name of 'A Touch of Class'.

[34] I'm sure that language is legally water tight. I do genuinely think they had different owners.

restaurant, finished running through *the conversation,* I enquired just how big the pigs of Ningxia were.

The man looked down at the bones and has face immediately creased. As he raised his head to make eye contact with me I was convinced I heard him say "This is not pork, this is road meat".

"Meat from the road?!" I exclaimed. The other two remained blissfully unaware, smiling like a couple of retirement home residents who both believed they had won a game of bridge with the Snap cards on the table.

"No!" The man exclaimed, before repeating what sounded like road meat again. Faced with my crinkled brow and the two innocent beaming gurns behind me, he expanded further "You know, like a small horse."

And then – after thirty seconds of desperately searching through a translation app - it clicked, it was donkey, the word for which is very similar to the word for road. We'd been eating donkey ribs and they had been delicious.

At that point, Chinese hospitality and excitement kicked in and we were invited to join the man and his friends at their table in the adjacent room. Despite seeing that, at that very instant, we had just finished eating a small horse, he persistently offered us food. We declined the food politely, however, to turn down the huge shots of Baijiu being poured for us would have been rude. Particularly as they were being delivered with giddy messages of welcome and friendship.

Baijiu, literally white alcohol, is the 40-60% strength dancing juice of China. At its worst, it has an aftertaste of burning plastic. At its best, it is a barely palatable way of falling over. The bottle on our new table was closer to the better and stronger end of the scale. As it was lunchtime we were instructed to sip at each toast, rather than down the giant portions. The was toasts to friendship (it had been all of five minutes now after all); health, which seemed ironic given the lighter fluid we were all consuming with a side of second-hand smoke; and confusingly, to them being in their 40s and us being in our 30s (I could have misunderstood the true meaning of this one).

Baijiu despatched, the procession of photos began as another bottle appeared. Having already imbibed the equivalent of five shots of vodka each, I started out on a speech of thanks. I praised China, Ningxia and finally thanked our new friends, in the vain hope it would get us out of there before all seven of us woke up the next morning on and under various tables there and next door. Miraculously, my sickly sweet speech worked and we were waved on our increasingly boisterous and wobbly way out of town.

By late afternoon we reached the romantically named 108 Pagoda, which sits on the opposite bank of the Yellow River from the small town of Qingtongxia. We arrived gloriously out of season to find an army of workers building a selection of grand gateways and bridges the complex doesn't need. From a distance the 108 brick stupas, which are much wider at the bottom but also have a – ahem – bulbous tip, made it appear as if we'd stumbled upon Buddha's backyard bowling alley.

The 108 stupas represent life's troubles and afflictions. In order to ward these off, Buddhists pray 108 times. We didn't pray once. Instead, we climbed back up the hill towards the main road, where I left Tom and Jon to set up camp whilst I went to pick up supplies from a petrol station a few kilometres back up the road. I know that you've been thinking this for a while, but I'm using kilometres because that's how roads are measured here. For consistency, I'm using them to describe indeterminate distances too. Just be grateful I'm not saying 'a couple of clicks'.

After a brief scare from the first of many angry petrol station guard dogs, I would meet on my journey, I bought some wine, brandy, and pot noodles to cover off the main necessities for wild camping in China. I was even handed a bag of sweets free of charge from the cheery manager. Sadly, I had accrued a double puncture on my way there. Still, only 106 afflictions to go I supposed as I pushed all the way back up to find the boys and the puncture repair kit.

The light was dimming and intimate cleaning procedures were in full swing by the time I arrived at Camp Baby Wipe. After consuming all the petrol station had to offer, we settled down to some modern camping entertainment by watching last week's Have I Got News for You, presented by Victoria Coren.

Having spent 48 hours mocking their lack of preparation it was time for the tables to be turned. Thinking that I'd be camping in the baking hot desert much more often than not, instead of buying a sleeping bag, I had brought something that shared more DNA with a moth's wing than a quilt. This was compounded by buying a basic groundsheet that offered all the benefits of, well, a basic groundsheet. As Tom settled down inside his private tent, I had my poor decision making rubbed in my face – at times literally – as Jon cosily slept and rolled around in his thick sleeping bag atop his inflated mattress. As I stared at his warm, beardy, sleeping face I consoled myself that at least I *only had 105 more afflictions to go.*

I awoke the next morning freezing cold and disappointed to find I was next to a bearded man and not Victoria Coren. A bearded man who had become so warm during the night that he had removed more layers than I was wearing.

After a few thorny punctures – one of the apparently unforeseeable side effects of dragging bikes through a field of thorns – we got on our way. It was a disjointed start as punctures persisted and bodies slowly awoke from a night in the tent.

Jon entertained everyone, not least the petrol station attendant, by mistakenly trying to buy panty liners instead of wet wipes at our breakfast stop. After this and our stop-start beginning, I finally lost patience with my many thorny punctures and replaced both inner tubes.

Then with tyres full and bodies, finally awake, out of nowhere we found form and worked like a team pursuit unit. We flew through the tree lined avenues in what feels like the only province in China where people don't litter. It was brilliant. As the journey progressed I would learn that everything you've ever heard about cycling is true. Being third in line really did provide a chance to recuperate and our speed improved as we settled into a rotation of one kilometre at a time, followed by a break after two turns in each position. Being three British civil servants and never needing an excuse to give everything a cricket analogy, these stints became known as *overs*. Please don't hate us.

With roadside villages and towns aplenty, staying fed was a joy. We stopped for fruit in a village that I'm almost certain translates, appetisingly, as Second Squatting Ditch. Then an hour later we stopped for baozi, the big soft steamed dumplings, which were made by a husband and wife team in the kind of bare minimum establishment it's impossible not to fall in love with.

China is an explosion on the senses. Even here within the bare walls and amongst the bare minimum, the sight of steam, the smell of chilli, the noise of chattering and clattering, tickled every sense. With soy in small dipping pots and tired hands at the helm of chopsticks, even the mess we made couldn't distract from the pure, simple, sensory, explosion we were having in a roadside café.

As we prepared for the long afternoon stint at a petrol station – where else? – we were overwhelmed by photo requests; most notably by a group of young petrol station employees about half the size of us.

The day's sensory overload continued with a rich and varied feast for the eyes. There were watchtowers, glimpses of Gobi dunes and beautiful blossom. The kind of scenery that made smearing cold cream all over Graham at 6am worth it. However, this sensory overload started to take its toll just before the 100km mark as the adrenalin evidently drained from our bodies and we started to fall apart. Tom probably felt it hardest and decided to lie down and stretch his many ailments out in the centre of the petrol station forecourt much to the amusement of the attendants.

Despite our crumbling bodies, Zhongwei made for a magnificent penultimate stop. It was a friendly, wave-heavy, joy of a town where the school children have done their English homework. It's these moments of fun that drag you over the last 20km. On our final break of the day I went in search of additional puncture repair kits. Despite the bike shop I found not having any in stock, the lovely owner went on a search for some and gave them to us for free once she had located them.

Thanks to the spirit and enthusiasm of Zhongwei we made it through the last 20km as the sky was turning the shade of red that so delights shepherds. Our destination was Shapotou, a town dedicated to desert tourism.

Once inside the hotel, I made the mistake of trying to celebrate with a baijiu and protein shake cocktail aperitif, which not only tasted horrible but left me with the taste of baijiu in my larger water bottle until I eventually capitulated and threw it away three weeks later. Other than a game of illiteracy-inspired menu roulette the evening passed without incident.

This was in marked contrast to the following morning. As a result of the early night, I awoke at sunrise. I decided to show Jon the courtesy he deserves by locking the door to our bathroom. Sadly, the lock threaded and I was trapped in the bathroom. I gently tapped on the bathroom window, until Jon rolled over to face the direction of the bathroom. He squinted, frowned, before finding focus and laughing at me. With not a word of the CCP's Chinese he managed to attract the attention of one member of staff, who failed to release me but who themselves found a second member, who also failed, who in turn found a third, who failed as well. Eventually, the fourth member of staff to attend the scene managed to free me.

With three hard days ahead and an early sign from the hotel maintenance gods that the day wouldn't be a breeze, we eschewed the usual practice of making progress and went sand tobogganing instead.

Shapotou Cultural Tourism Scenic Happy Place Economic Development Zone[35] is a bit rubbish. What it does have, though, is China's longest sand toboggan hill, so we spent all of fifteen seconds plummeting 200 metres down a giant sand dune. You don't need me to tell you how much fun that is. What wasn't great fun, after a morning of messing about in a theme park dedicated to sand, was fixing a puncture in the heat of the day, just moments after heading off at 2pm.

We also added a fourth team member, Cynthia, Tom's toy camel. Who would sit proudly on his handlebars, secured by zip-ties, in a deeply unsettling manner.

The day had an almost exclusively uphill profile and as is the way with such routes, was really hard work. Yet by the end of the day we were camping with glorious, rugged mountains to our south and the golden, rolling sand dunes of the Gobi Desert to our north. As we settled down at sunset, to a meal of pot noodles and some astonishingly acceptable wine from the nearest roadside

---

[35] This may not be the offciail title.

shack, the afternoon's suffering became a distant memory.

Having worn almost all of my clothes to sleep in, I made it to such a high temperature that the morning air felt genuinely cold as I emerged from the tent to begin the process of undressing, creaming and redressing as quickly as possible.

We ventured back to the small village we had passed the evening before, which, like many others, existed exclusively to support the vehicles using the road that it sat beside. Shunning the regular visit to the petrol station forecourt, for a change of scenery we went to one of the small huts in such villages that serve both as a business and home for thousands of families across China.

There was barely room for the three of us and the sixty-something lady busying herself running through the various pot noodles she had in store. The remainder of the space was taken up by the couple's bed. The bed's built-in heating, provided by a wood fire underneath it, was emitting so much heat it was possible to feel the warmth several feet away. Once the familiar sounds of a squealing kettle and tearing of additives had finished, we slurped up the noodles on the bench outside the hut. As we did so the air began to warm in the early morning sun.

The day started well; the first 50km came easily as we worked together to beat the wind and pass into Gansu province. Ningxia was over far too quickly; it was the cleanest part of China I would experience and it felt like a province that had managed most successfully to maintain its own personality despite still being part of the thundering, homogeneous development that runs through the country.

Moving swiftly on from meaningless, half-baked, sweeping statements…. A cycling career highlight for all of us was achieved when we each successfully took a beer on the move from some delivery guys' van, whilst we were descending at a speed that will displease my maternal parent.

We had lunch at a venue selected by Jon solely on the basis of it having a slightly better picture of sheep on the sign than its competitors. I wandered in and asked the proprietor what his best dish was, a question that entertained him immensely. He pointed at the character for sheep, mimed shaving the character and said noodles; which all sounded perfect. Twenty minutes later we were eating shaved bits of lamb – imagine a doner kebab if it was made of actual meat – and thick noodles, in a rich, spicy sauce, alongside a huge bowl of mixed veg and rice.

Full of food and a single beer each, we unexpectedly hit the mountain we'd cheerfully been referring to as Old Snowy all morning. Mistress Google Maps missed this one. It was nearly May and we were heading up to the snow. Old Snowy really taught us a lesson.

It was particularly cruel on Jon, the tallest and strongest of us. Another chapter of 'All You Ever Heard about Cycling is True' proved itself to be correct. This stuff about weight and power ratios that colours too much of conversations about cycling in the modern age? Turns out that it's all true. If you're a real man, dragging a bicycle over a mountain is much more of a chore than it is for the whippets of this world.

To compound the misery there was also a lack of petrol stations and small shops, which cut off our supply of sugar, caffeine, and liquids. It wasn't long before anything in the distance that looked slightly red became a mirage of a forecourt shop promising us Oreos, water, and warm fizzy drinks.

These issues were made even less enjoyable by each of us suffering stomach troubles of varying degrees. Weakened and punished, I introduced my favoured method of pushing every so often to break the agony of using the same muscles minute after minute, hour after hour, and eventually we made it to the top. To celebrate we drank one of the three beers, which had been gifted to us earlier and had been making the whole experience precisely 1.5 litres harder ever since.

These subdued celebrations were followed by a merciful 30km downhill, through mountains, watchtowers, some ancient mud and sandstone Great Wall, and mud brick villages; all with the Gobi in the distance. It had begun to look as though the day had swung back in our favour.

It hadn't. We should have set up camp amongst the Wall and its watchtowers. Instead, with an hour of daylight to go, we pressed on to try and reach the Wall on the other side of the town we could see below us. This was good for supplies and gaining kilometres but very bad for camping locations.

We eventually made it to the Great Wall's watchtower we had been aiming for all day, it was even signposted by a brown sign denoting a tourist location. At sunset, in the shadow of snow-capped peaks, which were even taller and grander than Old Snowy, we set up camp. However, pristine national park this was not. We ended up camping on a hybrid of a graveyard and rubbish dump[36].

I'll let you decide whether we decided to sleep closer to the dead or the dirt on our first night in Gansu.

---

[36] I do know the name of this town but I'm not in the business of shaming whole towns. In addition, a brand new ghost town was awaiting the displacement of the residents on the other side of the highway. Clearly, what we were riding through was just the mass scale equivalent of writing off a rental deposit by having one last house party.

6.1 MADE IN TAIWAN

Unsurprisingly China produces more bicycles than any other country on earth, but the two biggest bicycle companies are both Taiwanese, or they are both based in Chinese Taipei if you want to use a name both the People's Republic of China and the Republic of China agree to use in some international arenas. Giant and Merida, the Taiwanese manufacturers of the bikes Jon, Tom and I used, are the two brands in question.

Both my beloved and begrudged Bianchis were made on the same island. As was my Kona and my post-university indulgence GT. The history of Raleigh makes it likely that at least the final of my three bikes from the Nottingham manufacturer came from Taiwan. Only my very first bike and my Spooky Bandwagon, which was made in the US, were definitely not made in Taiwan.

The Meridas we bought at Wang Kai's shop cost around the same as my Giant, one of them may have even just crept over the £200 mark. Like the ATX whatever-it-was, the Meridas were unmemorable in model name and number terms. Equally, though, they were indestructible and reliable. We carried out no maintenance or tuning during their eight days of intensive service.

These bikes just work. It's what they do. It's not hard to see how Taiwan became a world leader in bicycle production. The two companies brief online corporate histories have a striking similarity. Merida[37] was launched in 1972 by Ike Tseng after he had been so irritated by a sign besmirching Taiwanese bikes in a US bike shop that he decided to start engineering bikes. Initially, Merida made bikes for other firms, including Raleigh, before launching their own brand in 1988. Giant was founded in the very

---

[37] http://www.merida-bikes.com/en_gb/about-us-647.html

same year as Merida, following the destruction of an Eel farm by a typhoon[38] Giant was created by one of history's most inventive jumps in business diversification. "Well lads, that's the eel farm fucked by a typhoon, shall we make some bicycles?".

Early on its history, Giant also produced bikes for big western bike brands, including Schwinn. Recently Giant's founder, the brilliantly named King Liu, also took on marathon bike rides but did so in his seventies. The first was around Taiwan at the age of 73[39] and then two years later he cycled from Beijing to Shanghai. Now in his eighties, King is still serving as Chairman of Giant.

This hard work and vision have seen them rise to the very top. Giant is comprehensively the largest bicycle company in the world, Merida is the second. Giant's market capitalisation in the bear market of January 2016 was just over £1.5 billion. At the same time, Merida was valued at £850 million. When I started my bike ride Giant and Merida were worth 25% and 40% more than this respectively. Giant is worth around the same as Virgin Money or Atkins. Merida is worth as much as Debenhams or Wetherspoons. They are huge companies. Merida also owns 49% of Specialized, one of America's most well-known bike companies.

However, it is not purely quantitative measures that set them apart. The companies both make bikes of a quality superior enough to have Tour de France teams. Ironically, given the follicle well-being divide between Jonathon, Tom and I; Giant and Aplecin, makers of shampoo for baldies, have the Giant-Alpecin Team. Merida sponsors the Italian team Merida-Lampre. Lampre just make sheet metal, thus robbing this sentence of any point. Within 30 years of rising from the remnants of a destroyed eel

---

[38] (Ramzy, 2013)

[39] (Ramzy, 2013)

farm, Giant had won world championships. This incredible journey is synonymous with the rise of the very best companies from both Taiwan and the mainland. The growth may have been powered by economies of scale production techniques and cheap labour but you'd be a fool to think this region doesn't do innovation better than most too. More importantly, it also shows anyone can do anything if they really want to. Even with this in mind, the speed of this region's change and growth happens on a different level.

China is a country where I once returned from a night out at 4am and noticed a huge curtain in reception, and by the time I left the flat at lunchtime on the following day the curtain had gone to reveal a brand new coffee shop. I wasn't even living on an eel farm at the time either.

7. THE LOST LEGION

With no desire to sleep with the dead and their descendants' waste any longer than necessary, we were gone by dawn. On the edge of town, the shit hole we had been calling home for nine hours gave us a fitting send off. As we finally fixed the slow puncture on Jon's bike, which had been the least of many problems on the previous day, Tom peered over the bridge we had stopped on and saw three rotting sheep carcasses and a dead dog. It certainly didn't look like the most inspiring town but was throwing dead animals off bridges really the most fun thing to do here?

Probably, yes.

As we took part in the now customary buttock-baring change from pre-sunshine clothes to sunshine clothes, a man tried to sell us 500g of bread for £5. Hilarious, but not nearly as funny as the next five hours of our most successful day to date.

Though productive, the day had a slapstick feel to it. I was first on stage at Idiot Cyclist of the Year. As we entered an almost entirely abandoned town, my reading age of five in Chinese saw me still reading the name of a shop as my front wheel hit a lump of concrete, catapulting me over the handlebars. Fortunately, having spent the majority of my teens being dreadful at mountain biking, as I flew over the bars some form of muscle memory kicked in. After flying through the air with all the grace of monkey shit heading for a tourist's head, I rolled flamboyantly out of trouble and back up onto my feet in one movement. All before realising I was 31 and that I would sit down and take a moment after all. As I looked up to the laughing faces of my compatriots, I was relieved to see nothing serious had happened to the bike.

Not to be outdone by my slapstick exploits Tom strolled on the stage and asked if it was ok to drop rubbish into a bin without a bottom. I assumed he meant no bag and so said yes, as bins in China are often unburdened by something as glitzy as a bag. He didn't, he meant literally no bottom. And so we looked on as a man with a Masters in Science from a University called Cambridge, dropped his litter straight onto the floor and looked surprised that this was the outcome.

Through no fault of his own, he topped this hilarity by some margin about an hour later, when a toll bridge barrier closed right on top of the head he was only protecting with a bandanna.

Unfortunately, this huge clunk didn't drive him to anything so rash as covering the offensive garment with a helmet, but at least he didn't die and we made it to Wuwei in great time, averaging over 20kph for the day. This was the end of their tardiness and my frustrations, from here on in I was a very proud mother of two fully fledged cyclists.

In Wuwei we reached a new level of being very, very foreign. We graduated from just stares and nervous "hellos" to children screaming "foreigners" and gasping at us. The shock we provided peaked as we entered a cheap noodle restaurant. The poor waitress was literally lost for words and had to fetch someone else to speak on her behalf, such was her surprise at our patronage, or possibly, scent.

Though we had time on our side we were unable to see Wuwei's greatest claim to fame; the statue with many names. My favourite of its many names is the catchy *Galloping Horse Treading on a Flying Swallow*. From images, I can confirm that though the horse is treading and possibly galloping, the swallow definitely isn't flying. Unfortunately, this piece now sits in Lanzhou, the provincial capital of Gansu, leaving us with little else to do in the afternoon and evening but read and continually eat.

In the early evening, we went to a Hui restaurant and kept

ordering food until the waitress insisted we stop. As we devoured the many, many dishes in front of us we became the subject of multiple unsubtle attempts to include us in the background of a selfie. At least Tom wasn't wearing a bandanna by this point.

Wuwei marked our arrival at the Hexi Corridor stretch of the Silk Road. The corridor runs almost the entire length of Gansu from Lanzhou in the southeast to the border with Xinjiang near the northwest corner of the province. Gansu, like Ningxia, is one of the few provinces to have a slightly more inventive title; taking its name from two historical prefectures, Gan and Su.

In truth, I think it was the romantic prospect of cycling along this particular route that attracted my two companions to join me more than anything else. Little did they know that the Hexi corridor in springtime is little more than a barren wind tunnel. I could have told them, but then they might not have come along and made four out of every six kilometres much less painful.

The Silk Road also played a big part in my own decision to travel along this route. I spent much of the free time we had in Wuwei reading the *notes* I had Ctrl+C'd and Ctrl+V'd during the winter evenings. The Silk Road's name is as evocative as any historic location. It is more a concept than an intended physical entity, and that concept captures the imagination as much as any of the individual locations dotted along its multiple routes. In fact, the Silk Road is probably the most abstract of all great historical, umm, *things*. The Silk Road, or Silk Route if you prefer, isn't just a single path used by traders to export or import silk. It is so much more than that.

Firstly, it isn't a single path. It isn't even all on terra firma, which perhaps makes Route a more apt name, even if being singular means that it is still imperfect. Broadly speaking, the overland route starts in central China, in Xian[40] and ends in the Mediterranean on Turkey's south coast. However, it is hard to view this as an exact science given that onward trade networks in the Mediterranean distributed goods well beyond Turkey in the same way networks linked Xian to suppliers in cities further east in China.

There are numerous branches and splits in the overland route. Going east to west; the first major branch breaks off just beyond Xian to link with the maritime silk routes in modern-day Guangdong province; next, a complex network of trading routes, also known as the Tea Horse Road, passes through China's south-western provinces, down into India, Bangladesh and beyond to the wider south east Asia region; as did the many maritime routes, which also linked Arabia and Africa to the Silk Road.

The section of the network, which I had always thought of when the Silk Road was mentioned, is the one we joined at Wuwei. It too has its own branches, but at its core, this is the one that travels from Xian, up the Hexi Corridor, splits into northern and southern branches just before Xinjiang and merges again in Kashgar. It was my intention to take the northern route through the ancient cities of Turpan and Kuqa, once the 21st-century road splits at the city of Guazhou in the far west of Gansu. After Kashgar, the road again divides into a system of networks as it passes through central Asia. Before finally running through Persia on its way to the Turkish coast.

This is a gross over simplification of what appears to be the accidental spillage of a bowl of noodles on the right hand page of a world map, an ancient forerunner to Spaghetti Junction if you like. Quite obviously, because trade quite often involves trading, it

---

[40] It was called Chang'an during the Silk Road's glory years.

didn't only move silk. In what politics professors may describe as overspill - in that it wasn't the primary intention of the actors involved but it was a related outcome – the silk road transported religions, ideas, technology, the DNA of Genghis the Shagger and many, many other things. These trade networks brought Buddhism to China and are the origin of the Hui's Muslim faith. In the phenomenal *The Silk Roads*[41], Peter Frankopan teaches us that Kashgar had a Christian Archbishop before Canterbury. To give it a modern political slogan, the Silk Road was an engine for global economic growth, innovation, and cultural exchange. It was a 10th-century Davos PR guy's wettest dream.

It had its dark sides too, just as modern travel and trade has its risks to humankind as evidenced by Ebola, the Silk Road also facilitated the spread of disease. The Black Death is believed to have originated in Issuk-kul[42] in modern day Kyrgyzstan and then spread westwards through these networks.

In the interests of balance, I should point out that the death cart industry was enjoying an unprecedented boon at the time. Unfortunately for every other inhabitant of medieval Eurasia, they didn't have people like Jon sorting out the Black Death. Entire towns and villages were wiped out and the two-thirds of Europeans who survived had little else to do but bring out their dead.

Rodents and mosquitos were the key villains in the spread of plague across the Eurasian land mass. In at least one instance, however, the Mongolians hastened the contagion's spread in the most medieval Mongolian manner. Experiencing a rare defeat thanks to the presence of plague within their ranks, the

---

[41] (Frankopan, The Silk Roads: A New History of the World, 2015)

[42] (Hays, 2005, p. 61)

Mongolian's accidentally stumbled upon chemical warfare[43] by firing the plagued corpses of their number over city walls and infecting the enemy.

Following the Black Death, the collapse of the Mongol empire, the increase in maritime trade and, perhaps most importantly of all, the European discovery of the Americas, the Silk Road broke down into smaller networks and never again has it had the same central role to global trade.

That may change soon as the CCP are trying to revive the Silk Road. Nowadays, the one slogan you can't avoid in China by not reading Mandarin is "One Belt, One Road"; China's vision of a 21st-century reincarnation of the overland and maritime Silk Road. This time though it will reach as far as Rotterdam[44] in the west. Like its predecessor, it will be a series of interlinked networks, which will also operate as a concept as much as a physical entity. Amongst other things, if China and the countries along the way succeed in achieving this, then within my lifetime a modern day British Marco Polo could travel from London to Beijing by train in 48 hours[45]. I can only hope that advancements in pot noodle flavourings have caught up with, if not surpassed, the technological progress made in high-speed rail.

After an early night and with our new found smoothness, we were out on the road by 7am. Even better, by 7.15 we were each eating deep fried spicy lamb patties. Then Mistress Google Maps gave me an almighty spanking as we tried to find an alternative to the dust bowl of a road she suggested we use to exit Wuwei. Through fault of my own, we got lost twice. Eventually, we

---

[43] (Frankopan, The Silk Roads: A New History of the World, 2015)

[44] (CBBC, 2015, p. 4)

[45] http://www.thetimes.co.uk/tto/business/industries/transport/article2696415.ece

thought we'd found our way back onto the glorious G30 on which we'd flown along the day before, but we were stopped by a sullen faced official who simply waved us away each time I tried to talk to her. Only the day before I'd gleefully waved at the police as we transitioned onto the G30. Who knows why we were allowed on that one stretch, but the following day it was confirmed to us in the strictest of terms that bicycles were not allowed on motorways.

By 9am we were finally out of Wuwei and travelling in parallel at frustratingly close proximity to the G30, on a road full of potholes at about half the speed we should have been going. The boys experienced their first real suffering as rain and the Hexi Corridor's famously fierce headwind slowed our progress. Undeterred by time we had lost, we stopped for far too long in the town of Yongchang to eat yet more spicy lamb and noodles.

Yongchang delayed us further with its mural depicting the lost legion of Roman soldiers who were rumoured to have settled nearby in a place that was known as Liqian. Some present day inhabitants of Zhelaizhai, where Liqian once sat, apparently have green eyes and other Caucasian features, sparking a renewed interest in one of history's more romantic theories.

The theory that a Roman stirring of the Gansu gene pool left a legacy of green eyes and other European features originated in the 1940s courtesy of the fantastically named Homer Hasenpflug Dubs; a man who went on to become Chair of Chinese at Oxford University. In 1942, whilst almost everyone else on the planet was busying themselves with Word War Two, Dubs produced an article entitled *"An Ancient Military Contact between Romans and Chinese"*.[46]

---

[46] (Dubs, 1942)

The gist of the story, as explained with great passion by Tom in front of the mural, is this. Just before the biggest clock of all tick-tocked from BC to AD, the Romans, looking to expand their empire further east, took an almighty battering off the Parthians. Following the battle, the victorious Parthians took a great number of Romans prisoner. These captives were converted into mercenaries who fought for their captors. At some point, they were sent to protect the Parthian's own border but were captured once more, this time by the Xiongnu, the nomadic group who dominated the steppes at this time. The Xiongnu also decided to use the Romans as swords for hire. Some time passes, twenty years in fact, before your man Dubs' claim that 100 of same men reappear at the Battle of Zhizhi in what is modern day Kazakhstan. During the battle a Chinese historian, Ban Gu, observed a hundred men fighting in "fish scale formation" something Dubs saw as evidence of Roman warfare practices. Now I hate to be an armchair general but, Roman military technique or not, this hopeless bunch lost again, only this time they were captured by the Chinese.

Of the many stretches of imagination that the theory requires, one of the biggest is that this lost legion of Roman soldiers were then resettled a further 3000km east in Liqian, a name which can mean Rome and sounds an awful lot like legion, another fact used by Dubs as supporting evidence.

The mural in front of us picked up the story from here and painted a picture of the captive soldiers arriving in Liqian; packing in a profession they were clearly unsuited to, they melted down their swords - *which their captors had let them keep* - turned them into shovels and became men of the land. Finally, in a scene depressingly mimicked by obese American businessmen and Filipino teenage girls in Shanghai's worst bars, the ancestors of Berlusconi bunga-bunga'd their way into the hearts and ovaries of

Gansu's fair maidens.

They almost certainly didn't though - there's been DNA tests and everything[47] – but I couldn't stop Tom during his rousing lecture on the subject in front of the mural. I was sorry to break his heart after he had finished.

It is far more likely, what with trade being what it is and humans being what we are, the few Caucasian traits that slipped into the mix, did so in thousands of different *trades* and *exchanges*. Just imagine how many silk sheets and items of silk underwear are on this route after all. Could there be a more lustful trade route?

For example, who's to say Marco Polo didn't leave a little bit of Venice behind a millennium later. Suspiciously, of his time in nearby Zhangye, a young Marco records that he, his uncle and father *"spent a year in this city about their business, which it is not necessary to go into."*[48] Which, quite clearly, is 14th century Italian for 'what goes on tour, stays on tour'.

With the history lesson over[49], we left Yongchang monumentally behind schedule. We began to climb the hills that were topped with a little bit too much snow for comfort. Eventually, we stopped at what we believed was the peak of our ascent towards Zhangye, only to end up sleeping in the vicinity of a graveyard once more. This one was at least clean, and by virtue of its hilltop location had stunning views in every direction.

---

[47] (Zhou Ruixia, 2007)

[48] (Cliff, 2015)

[49] Not quite over, I hadn't reached the full extent of the internet's wormhole on this subject before leaving but as I was writing this up I discovered there was a more recent theory put forward by Dr Christopher Matthew . Dr Matthew, who rather brilliantly is dressed as an ancient soldier on his University's profile page, believes that the lost legion were actually descendants from Alexander the Great's army, who also used similar tactics. (Matthew, 2011)

Better still we had set up camp just outside of a place called Santiaogou, in the Qilian Mountains. Or, to put it phonetically, with a dash of artistic license, we were in Santiago in the Chilean mountains, which is just about my favourite geographical coincidence of all time.

The previous day's homage to the lost legion on the ring roads of Wuwei and celebration of their story in Yongchang had left us with 155km to Zhangye. Though it was established that we had indeed camped at the top of a hill, it quickly became apparent that we were not at the top of the mountain that followed. Things started well, the first few hours of progress saw us 20km further along the increasingly unforgiving road. The Silk Road is not as smooth as the name suggests. If the G30 hadn't been buzzing alongside us then for many, many kilometres it would have felt as if we were retracing the path of traders from centuries past.

Then the Hexi Corridor funnelled a wind so forceful that we couldn't hear one another curse its arrival. The wind turbines around us started spinning and hell broke loose. Three hours of intermittent pushing and cycling earned us only 10km. There was something dramatic about the whole experience that still photographs didn't capture. If the other two had more hair and fewer bandannas the documentation of this part of the trip would have looked like Kajagoogoo were very badly lost. As it was, we just looked like Right Said Fred had kidnapped Limahl.

To add a little extra emphasis as to how bad it was, one of the wind turbines we cycled passed had blown up, presumably from overuse, and had snapped in half. With its blades splayed everywhere, it looked like a defeated warrior who had fallen on his own sword.

The next 30km were thankfully downhill, although we still had to peddle into the fearsome wind to keep moving. We had also spent so long zig-zagging on a surface, which was as bad as the road behind every British chip shop in the late 80s, that it wouldn't be outrageous to imagine we did an extra 10km in pothole diversions alone. We also maintained full contact with the same howling headwind once we returned to the flat. Previously, falling in line had saved time and gained distance, now we formed an orderly queue just to keep moving.

At least at that point, we had a road because by mid-afternoon we didn't. You don't need many things for a road trip but of the absolute necessities, a road is right up there.

It just disappeared. After much tapping of phone screens, a stroll down the motorway into oncoming traffic and a discussion at a nearby petrol station, we discovered that the road had been moved a few kilometres back. Instead of running parallel to the G30 it was now running through nearby villages. Another 5km was wasted.

Though the boys had become proficient cyclists over the last week, this final day was incredibly hard. At 5pm I decided to raise morale by advising all the suffering to now had only got us halfway. Furthermore, we were now only 10km away from the town I had recommended we should stop overnight at during the planning phase, which they had *both* turned down in favour of getting to Zhangye. This reverse psychology worked a treat. Either that or the double Snickers, Ibuprofen and Pepsi cocktail kicked in.

As the wind dropped we attacked, back in team time trial formation we peddled our knees into their fifties. More cycling clichés were confirmed as the big one got to the front on the flat and powered through the remaining wind. Often giving Tom and I so much shelter from the wind that he and I were able to smoke cigars, drink brandy and flirt with flappers in his slipstream.

We reached our interim target of 20km to go by nightfall. Lights were turned on and helmets moved from protecting the back of pannier racks to the heads they were always intended to cover.

We then gently headed off into the full beam glare of oncoming traffic all the way to the finish line.

The circus arrived at the best hotel in town just before 10pm. We proceeded to rip what remained of the boys' cheap panniers off their bikes in front of a growing audience, confusing all but the recently arrived Holly with our actions and communal stench. The day felt like, and in truth was, our greatest achievement of the eight days. If I'd been alone, I would have had to stop well short of Zhangye. Easier days would follow where the lack of camaraderie and sharing of turns on the front would make the experience far less enjoyable and successful than this day. Harder days would come too, where the isolation and relentless headwind made me miss them, but never once did I miss those bloody bandannas.

Unsurprisingly, the last week had drained the three of us. I had also made it to 2000km in 18 days of cycling. So rest day one was a slow affair that started with the dregs of a pitiful hotel breakfast, meandered through life admin but ended with a great meal and handing over the boy's bikes to some Peace Corps volunteers based in Zhangye.

Jon had to finalise his voting by proxy for the general election, Holly had to work, I had to try and remember my own name ahead of a phone interview and Tom had to sleep. Two out of four of these things were a success.

By 17.30 though, we were sat in a most brilliant sunshine, drinking Tsingtao and eating sunflower seeds. For the first time it felt like a holiday. Zhangye had an almost southeast Asian feel to it. At least, it was more relaxing than any other Northern Chinese city has felt to me.

We then met up with Raines and Kelly, two Peace Corps volunteers to whom we donated Tom and Jon's bikes, in order for them to be passed on to their successors who would be arriving in the next couple of months. We had great hotpot and then yoghurt for desert, all whilst admiring the peace Raines and Kelly were delivering to Zhangye.

On my second day of rest and for the boys' final hurrah in China we visited the fantastic Danxia landforms 40km west of Zhangye. These geographic formations are stunning. Stripes of reds, oranges, purples, yellows, reds, greys, browns, whites and blues run through the jagged rock faces.

The different views also come with great names. There's the to-be-expected *Rainbow Hills*; the descriptive *Huge Scallop Shaped Rocks*; and the imagination testing *Monkeys Rush into a Sea of Fire*.

The whole place, names included, was one of those sights of genuine natural wonder that not a single aching bone in our bodies didn't fall in love with. After returning to town, we bid farewell to the boys in the loving way you do when ramming friends into a taxi as the driver hurries everyone along.

On the third Sabbath day, Holly's flight back to Beijing was cancelled so we went off the map to visit a semi-mothballed desert theme park, which had only two remaining attractions – to drive a go-cart in the sand and littering the otherwise beautiful sand dunes.

To compensate for this horror show we then visited China's largest sleeping Buddha, which even more excitingly, for me anyway, may[50] also be the place Kublai Khan was born.

Grandson of Genghis and star of Netflix's Marco Polo, it was Kublai who began the Yuan dynasty by invading and ruling all of China. He extended his grandfather's empire from Vietnam to the edges of central Europe. If the Netflix series is anything to go by, he also did as much as anyone to get that Y chromosome out and

---

[50] Almost certainly isn't

about.

In the evening I checked the weather (rain) and wind direction (20kph headwind) for the following day and decided that Zhangye was worth one more day's rest. With the additional time, I tried to eat myself back up to my natural fighting weight and got down to the miserable business of washing my clothes in a hotel bathroom. These were futile tasks at best. After three rinses my shorts were still emitting the dirt of the three previous provinces and even two trips to KFC and a double portion of dumplings didn't fill me up.

Fully rested, nearly fed, and almost clean, I left Zhangye to the sounds of Alanis Morissette. I thought I'd discovered one of those ultra-rewarding *'oh I didn't know what that was when I was 11'* lyrics. Disappointingly, it turns out that old Alanis doesn't sing "It's like a death row hard-on two minutes too late" in *Ironic*, instead, it's "pardon". I thought it was a brilliant gag about a posthumous erection, which at odds with many other of her examples really would be ironic.

An hour into the day this disappointment dissipated when I met an excitable man on a Giant bike. Shortly after, a Giant branded support vehicle arrived alongside me. It contained a waving, smiling, owner of a Giant shop.

This all led to me joining Zhangye Mountain Bike Club on their May 1 holiday ride for 60km. With the exception of a leg burning 3km jump across to the lead group, the shelter and support they provided were incredibly welcome. Yan, a lady with excellent English and even more impressive calf muscles, and the rest of the group even took me for lunch. All I did in return was pose for the routine photographs, which this time involved me holding up a huge red banner I hadn't read yet, or more accurately, probably won't ever be able to read.

China's economic and social development confuses for the very good reason that it is really confusing, multi-layered and happening in a globalized, internet age. You can't pigeonhole it as being like the 50s, 60s, 70s, 80s, 90s or any other time in another nation's economic development. But what can't be argued with is that China's cycling fashion is at the early 90s stage of development; such colours and shapes on the Zhangye group's clothes were not meant to be put together.

By afternoon I was alone and climbing through fragrant avenues towards the base of the Qilian mountains. It was strenuous but set amongst spectacular scenery. The warm glow of the day dimmed as I came across the losing side in a battle between a dog and a car. I was only 25 days in and I had already seen well over 50 dead dogs, but this was particularly sad as the poor little mite was still breathing. Had I not sent the hammer back after the Pigeon's death on day one, I'd have put him out of its misery in the great British tradition of opposing firearms but being entirely ok with bludgeoning something to death. There can't be a Briton alive who believes Professor Plum fired the gun in Cluedo rather than using the handle to cave in the skull of his victim. As it was, I wasn't armed sufficiently to end this poor dog's pain and (at this stage in the ride) did not possess the constitution to kick a dog to death. So I apologised to the dog, out loud and in Chinese, as if it made any difference, before slowly moving away.

The evening's camping spot had no litter, no graves and thanks to my adoption of Jon's ground mat a lot more warmth. As I cooked up my thousandth pot noodle, I admired the tent as it sat in a golden sunlight that was turning the surrounding earth into a rich gold. I stood back and, as I soaked up the view and atmosphere, I thought to myself that this is what wild camping is meant to be like, as a football podcast blared out in the background.

After 20km of climbing to Alanis, Garbage and other mid-nineties stalwarts before breakfast, I was flagged down by some farmers to help flip over a damaged truck. In this part of planet earth, I am a giant. A great big weird white giant of 173cm[51]. I stepped off the bike and clambered down to the field where the trailer was lying on its side. Under instruction, I flipped the trailer onto its back, which delighted the farmers and their audience. They were much less delighted, though, about how quickly I left upon seeing how utterly devastated the axle was.

In spite of this, my incomplete good deed was rewarded with a long and gentle downhill, which swept me away from the Qilian range. As I hit the first long straight I noticed a man ahead of me riding in an erratic way. He was obviously drunk, worst still, he was clearly using the same 5km marker stones as his rest stops too. We exchanged waves as I passed him on my way to the next marker. In the great Chinese athletic tradition, he was smoking on his rest breaks. I also realised he wasn't drunk but instead, I would guess - and you should feel the British nervousness inside me right now as I speculate on disability without any kind of confirmation – he had a form of cerebral palsy. I think. I mean I don't know. I couldn't, I mean I didn't want to ask, I couldn't ask. I mean I literally couldn't ask him. Would you like a biscuit? Tea? Who wants tea? I'll make some tea. No, no, I'll put the kettle on.

I took my rest at the next stone. In doing so I irritated the part of my mind that finds resting at 901, 906, 911km etc. as infuriating as people who set their alarms for anything other than on the hour, quarter past, quarter to, or half past the hour[52]. Don't get me started on people who set their alarm for earlier than they intend to get up because they like to snooze. For the next 30km or

---

[51] Ok this isn't kilometres, so as a treat, 5 foot 8 **and a half**.

so we repeated a pattern of waving at each other and exchanging encouragement by shouting "Go on!" The only difference in approach was that he would smoke and I would scoff biscuits. Eventually, we parted after I put in a real kick and skipped a few rest stops to get to my target distance by midday.

I hammered it in the way that two full panniers, flat pedals, and cumulative exhaustion will just about allow you to, only stopping for a Pepsi and a five-minute chat with some Gansu old boys who seemed to have taken it upon themselves to run the local bus stop pro-bono. I then pushed hard again before stopping for a chat with two Chinese cyclists who were cycling from Zhangye to Urumqi and held up yet another sign that could have read "this man's ancestors raped my grandmother and our country" for all I know. Then as we took the third of these photos, 50km after I first saw him, my friend from earlier reappeared.

Now, I am fully aware I couldn't compete with any Paralympic cyclist, but this guy was on a shopping bike and was at least five years older than me. Someone from the Chinese Paralympic cycling team needs to pull their stopwatch out of their arse, get down to Gansu, confiscate his cigarettes and see just how fast he can go. He was sustaining 20kph on a shopper with cigarette breaks. How is that even possible?

In a state of amazement, I initially rode on with the owners of the sign. Eventually, we caught the talent, who was smoking again. I then lost touch with them all as I developed a mystery slow puncture, which comprehensively ruined my afternoon. Not least because this misery was compounded by the late arrival of the heat of the day.

As I headed west, China's uniform time for the entire vast landmass, more commonly referred to as Beijing Time, became a right pain in the arse. Not least for delaying the heat of the day until I least wanted it, at the peak of the exhaustion-times-distance-to-go formula. On this particular day it arrived around 2.30pm and for the first, but certainly not the last time, it really hurt me. Pink of face and dry of mouth, I arrived at Jiayuguan, the city at the Western edge of the Great Wall, just as the sun was giving up on producing uncomfortable levels of heat.

Jiayuguan didn't feel like the end of anything, though. The city was alive with commerce. It felt like it was at the sharp edge of China's economic expansion west, rather than the blunt end of a wall. Shops were alive with speakers blaring out offers to a colourful and hectic mix of tourists and locals.

I had opted to stay in a huge tourist-orientated hotel, which came with its own supermarket. I rewarded myself with vast quantities of ice cold Tsingtao to rehydrate my barren mouth before, during and after my shower. The twenty or so minutes after any post-ride shower on this journey were truly special. This one was no exception. The relief at being clean, cool and lying down brought unparalleled joy.

To further replenish and recuperate I went to what must be the only pizza restaurant for 500km. I also drank six different liquids, four of which were genuinely beneficial for rehydration. Once the owner had cleared the teenagers who were asking mundane, if polite, questions, out of the restaurant, I ordered the first of two large pepperoni pizzas. This brought me close to my previous best, when I ate the equivalent of two large pizzas and one extra slice, inclusive of crust – rules is rules, in the great Pizza Hut buffet challenge of December 2001. This time though I didn't spend the next six hours wishing I hadn't partaken in the binge because I couldn't force a single sip of liquid down my throat due to intense nausea. On this occasion, there was room for two pizzas and as much liquid as I could supplement it with. I was merely full by the end of the meal.

I spent the evening lying on top of the hotel bed, smugly tapping my full belly, trying to work out how I could concoct a situation where I could cycle through Italy for two months. Or failing that, the rest of my life.

Whilst some of you filthy capitalist pigs were forking out £19.95 to watch Mayweather v Pacquiao, here in the People's Republic I watched it for free on CCTV 5. This wasn't all good news as it restricted me to my on-the-road diet of pot noodle and Oreos for brunch, but it was nice to watch a sport that common sense and an idea of value now excludes me from watching in the UK.

After watching a taller man beat a shorter man, I headed out to the most touristy part of the Great Wall's western reaches. I'm fully prepared for the sound of thousands of Lonely Planets to be thrown at me by sanctimonious hands, but I really like the way China rebuilds bits of the Great Wall, whilst leaving most of it well alone. I love that you have both the ruins and the recreations, it's a good balance.

The Chinese are also the world's best tourists and fun to be around when they are doing the tourism. They get dressed up like emperors and soldiers, spend a fortune, are consistently excited about something and basically, just love to tourist the living daylights out of everything.

Can you imagine a British husband in his twenties dressing up as a Roundhead, when nobody else was doing so, as he walked around a provincial museum? No of course not, because we're a reserved bunch of dullards. Here at Jiayuguan I spent many happy minutes watching Chinese husbands and dads dress up like emperors for their own and everyone else's entertainment.

This is the place from which people were banished out into the desert, where I would be banishing myself the very next day. I looked over the fortress wall to see the depressing sight of the motorway and its poor cousin, the side road - my road - snaking off into a great big mass of not very much.

Having seen the surface and environment in store for me in the coming days, I decided against visiting a less renovated stretch of wall and instead headed to the Giant shop to buy a pump I could operate with both hands to save me arriving in Kashgar looking like I'd spent a little too long alone in a tent with only thoughts of highly literate TV presenters to entertain me. It was also time to bid farewell to my beloved Howies *Performance Enhancing Water* bottle, which had gone mouldy, the cause of which was almost certainly a result of the Baijiu-Protein Shake Cocktail I endured in Shapotou.

7.1 BLOW ME

The only irritation more prevalent than punctures was the wind. Like punctures, I have tried to only include references to the wind where it changed the character of the day in question. If I hadn't done so, 41 out of my 45 days cycling would have been a diatribe against Gusty McGustface. There was only a single occasion where I had a tailwind for the entire day's cycling.

This is what happens if you ride from east to west across China, almost exclusively into the prevailing wind. As someone who knows the return flight to the UK takes an extra hour, I should have known better, but this permanent headwind is not something any map or atlas had forewarned me of. In fairness, a couple of friends did suggest I was going in completely the wrong direction. Having made my plan, though, it felt too disruptive to change things by the time they intervened, after all, it was only a bit of wind.

In the end, for half of the journey, it really was only a bit of wind. It was just like having a bit of extra resistance on the turbo-trainer. Anything under 10kph could fall into this category. It was a little more tiring, occasionally unwelcome for making me too cold, occasionally welcome for cooling me down.

Somewhere between 10-20kph it became a real strain, where sustained momentum was impossible and the whole day would become a struggle. However, it was possible to make it through these days with the right music and the entire stock of Oreos from a provincial petrol station. I just had to keep moving, set myself mini-targets for the road markers and not give up.

After 20kph and especially above the psychological barrier of 40kph things became very tough. Alternating between pushing and cycling helped, as did pressing on hard during any breaks in the wind. These days were agony, though. The panniers worked as wind breaks, aided by my idiotic inclusion of a 3.2kg laptop and the many litres of water it was necessary for me to carry.

I don't think it would be madness to suggest you could ride across China, without racing, in thirty days, or at least in far greater comfort if you travelled in the opposite direction.

Intermission: An American Mole in China

Welcome to intermission. Why not take this chance to pop to the loo and get yourself an ice cream? For those of you staying, I'd like to briefly address the Gansu Mole. I have spent an age (three or four hours) trying to find out more about this creature without success. The Gansu Mole is a resident of Gansu and neighbouring provinces. It is also at the opposite end of the animal welfare spectrum to extinct. It is a highly successful animal, or pest, depending on how you look at these things.

Where the Gansu Mole becomes truly fascinating, though, is that despite living several thousand kilometres from the sea it is a New World (Scalopini) mole. All of its relatives live in North America. Given that moles aren't renowned long distance swimmers, I spent hours trying to find out how this anomaly has occurred. Infuriatingly no one has yet answered that question. In fact, this "has prompted scientists to occasionally hesitate to continue calling the Scalopini "New World moles" without some caveat to acknowledge this fact."[53] Scientists taking the easy, cautious, way out of the important issues once more.

Did they develop independently with near identical genetics? Are they proof of Zheng He, the great Chinese sailor, reaching America before Columbus and leaving his pet moles there? Did they come the long way round after Europeans made it to America? Did the Romans really make it to America and the Lost Legion then transported the moles to Gansu and the moles are the proof Dubs needed all along? Did they tunnel there?

I'd really like to know. And now, so do you.

Onwards.

---

[53] https://en.wikipedia.org/wiki/Scalopini

8. BANISHMENT

I was now halfway into the journey. Jiayuguan marked the distinction between the half of my trip that was ostensibly a holiday with miserable characteristics and the half that was dangerously close to being an actual adventure.

In preparation for this change of experience, I decimated what would be my last hotel breakfast for three days. Almost immediately outside of Jiayuguan the G312 reverted back to being a G30 service road rather than the village meandering vein of life it was at its best. This baron wasteland is where China's historical naughty boys were sent and it felt as though the G312 was on a mission to recreate some of that historic hostility.

With my eyes facing west, only the road and pylons distinguished the current landscape from its appearance when humans first arrived here. It was barren, the kind of barren where the handful of trees who have survived the harsh conditions look devastated that being here is their lot in life. The scrubland bushes that dot the land look equally perturbed. As if they stay low to the ground so as not to be noticed.

Amongst these depressing surroundings I bounced along the arse-shattering, anti-Christ mixture of gravel and potholes, before the road deteriorated even further by narrowing into one lane thanks to the encroaching sand of the Gobi. This left me with the unpalatable, day-long entertainment of playing chicken with lorries, which is nothing short of unfair if you're on a bicycle.

As ever the lorry drivers of China were first rate and backed down, but the draft they produced in even that extended proximity meant that I too had to swerve onto the sand and gravel regardless of their sound road etiquette. There were some brief moments of relief as the road swerved into the odd village and passed a colourful mosque, but for the most part, the day was as fun as being stuck in a lift with Nigel Farage, with no access to a taser.

I don't believe in fate but I do believe in haphazard preparation. My right forearm will be forever grateful for the new pump I bought only the day before because on my first miserable day of banishment I had five soul sapping and time-consuming punctures.

By punctures number four and five I was doing some world-class swearing. Think Malcolm Tucker, if he was on fire, and being raped by an unforgivably horny giraffe. I screamed into the vast void, but it was a hopeless vitriol, which was merely carried off by the howling wind.

After yet another mono-nutritional afternoon snack of five Oreos, I noticed that despite internet based protestations otherwise, Yumen – roughly my target city for the day – did have a hotel. So, despite the many punctures, I pressed on.

By late afternoon my inner tubes started to behave as I wobbled around the pot holes, with all the grace of a drunken uncle on a bouncy castle. However, it was not to be my day. Over the wind and screams of Scandinavian punk emanating from my headphones I heard a snap and a thud. Two noises even further down on my wish list than pop, hiss or bang. The bike veered violently to one side, meaning only one thing could have happened. Head bowed solemnly, I applied the brakes in the pathetic way a strong headwind requires. As my exhausted arms slowly turned the bike around I noticed a 20-metre gap between my left pannier and the bicycle, which is an unworkable proximity at best. It was starting to feel as if I'd awoken and angered the furious spirits of the banished by cycling over them.

With that, 30km short of Yumen and giving it the full Tucker-Giraffe act in the middle of the road once more, I accepted defeat as the ghosts of banishments past swirled around me. I pitched the tent in a small dell for an indulgent double pot noodle meal within the sanctuary of its grey, plastic walls.

After a decent night's sleep, and with a huge 160km to the next significant signs of life beyond Yumen, I got moving as early as I could. After zip-tying the escapee pannier tighter than a guest on an American rendition flight, I was away. Things started in a dreadful fashion, another puncture was followed by a 6km detour around nowhere, but then the wind flipped and pushed me forwards.

For a while, I was puncture free and flying along the G312. For a brief period, it even reverted to being a road linking farming villages. Soon though the surface worsened again. Within an hour I was on my third puncture, an incident that almost led to a second snapped pannier as a well-intentioned farmer tried to right my bike over too quickly. Fortunately, the pannier unclipped and merely fell off, rather than breaking the plastic clips.

Then the sand hit the fan.

The wind whipped up a treat just as I struggled into the sandy air around Qiaomen Fortress. It was tough going but I made another 10km of progress until I rounded a corner and watched with amazement as the ground became the air. Within minutes the sky was a horrible mix of grey and orange[54], moments later it was dark. I grabbed the waterproof cover for Jon's panniers that he had left me, jumped over a nearby bank to ensure a lorry being driven blind wouldn't run over me, covered myself, and held on for dear life.

The holiday was most definitely over.

if the sight had been one of impending biblical punishment, then

---

[54] Reminiscent of, but not as bad as, that awful Coors sponsored Chelsea away kit from the mid-nineties

the noise of the sand and stones blasting against the plastic cover was worse. It lasted for longer than I'd ever really considered these things could go on for. I had to pull the cover taught to limit the pain of the stones hitting me. This was a proper sandstorm.

I was not quite in the Taklamakan desert, just the entrails that tail off eastwards towards the Gobi. Yet I was having an authentic Taklamakan experience. Albert von Le Coq's (one of the European archaeological raiders of China's many lost arks, who you'll read more about shortly) description of the Taklamakan's *"kara-uran, or black hurricane"*[55], illustrated my predicament and instinctive reactions with alarming symmetry.

"Quite suddenly the sky grows dark...a moment later the storm bursts with appalling violence upon the caravan. Enormous masses of sand, mixed with pebbles, are forcibly lifted up, whirled round, and dashed down on man and beast; the darkness increases and strange clashing noises mingle with the roar and howl of the storm...the whole happening is like hell let loose"

Now, I've not seen hell let loose, but I have spoken to a John Lewis customer who was expecting a clothes rack to be delivered on the day of a Women's Institute clothes sale and had just found out that this was no longer the case. So I think I know what he means.

"Any traveller overwhelmed by such a storm must, in spite of the heat, envelope himself in felts" – no details on whether they should be fuzzy or if a plastic pannier cover will suffice – *"to escape injury from the stones dashing around with such mad force. Men and horses alike must lie down and endure the rage of the hurricane, which often lasts for hours."*[56]

---

[55] (Hopkirk, 1980)

[56] (Hopkirk, 1980)

They really do last for hours. I sat with my back against the bank, with the remaining dim light barely illuminating the yellow of the pannier cover, I could only imagine what the horrendous noise beyond my shell looked like.

After two hours, the ferocity of debris rattling against the cover was reduced to only smatterings, just like the point where microwave popcorn starts to burn. I peeked out from under the sheet into the dark, murky, orange air. The cinnamon blush blanketed all around me. I made a quick assessment and even quicker judgement about my predicament. I was in no way making it to the city of Guazhou and there was at least some shelter where I was now, so I decided to stay put.

For a brief while, I became a highly efficient and rational human being. Important things like torches, compasses and Oreos went into zipped pockets. Water, an extra phone battery, and the waterproof cover I'd just been sheltering beneath went into my rucksack. I ran up to the highest point around me to identify the most sheltered spot I could see, ran back to the bike and wheeled it into the sheltered area I'd identified and set about erecting the tent.

Putting the tent up in a gale was no fun at all, but the alternative was unthinkable. In a scene reminiscent of a Generation Game challenge, I just about succeeded. The tent held some semblance of structural integrity until 2am, when rain, instead of sand, started lashing down and the wind felt like it might take me on a magic tent ride. After twenty minutes it subsided long enough for me to jump out and get the pegs back into the ground.

You have to keep your head in these situations. You also must keep you position. In the modern day this is far less of a danger; only by wandering blind into the road was I likely to put myself in harm's way. So I didn't wander at all. Even when I left to re-peg the tent and urinate I kept one blind hand on the tent, so as to not lose contact with my shelter and also not piss back into it. A century ago, without the security of smartphones, these storms could disorient men to the point of fatal distraction. Von Le Coq also relates the story of 60 Chinese horsemen who were so spooked by the sandstorms that they galloped into the desert and never returned.[57]

Ten minutes later, I was galloping nowhere. Wearing everything I could, with all useful stuff strapped to me or zipped up in something strapped to me, I wrapped my sleeping bag around me and held onto the tent's frame. I was only about 60% sure it wouldn't rip apart and leave me looking for answers that Charles Darwin didn't get round to addressing.

As the tent began to lift I tried a number of positions from the Karma Tentra to keep it grounded; first I went for the *splayed cat* – by pushing my hands and feet into the corners like a feline caught between two fences, or under one lorry; next I tried to centralise my weight in the *I want my mummy crouch*; but finally I settled on the *rickety climbing frame* with my arms firmly locked in the first position of the YMCA to try and reduce the tent's movement at the point it was most exposed to the wind.

It's at times like this you need distraction and perspective. As the violently shaking tent waved my arms from side to side I listened to probably the best episode of *An Irishman Abroad* podcast I've heard yet. This one was with Rory O'Neill, someone I'd not heard of before but will now only forget when the beer takes its toll in later years. It was the perfect mix of positivity and intellectual resilience in the face of entrenched prejudice, which put a windy night in a tent into perspective.

At 5.30am the storm finally gave in and I drifted off to sleep in

[57] (Hopkirk, 1980)

total exhaustion.

After a full 90-minutes sleep, I forced myself to get up and get moving. It took nearly an hour for my exhausted limbs to pack the tent away, but breaks of blue in the sky never looked so good.

I cracked on at a pace and ticked off 15km before I begrudgingly piled yet more Oreos into my mouth. After another 5km I nearly fell off my bike after seeing a monk packing up a plastic sheet in a shallow ditch. How did he sleep through last night without a tent or inspirational podcasts? He was further down the hill and in a fine looking roadside dyke, but talk about zen!

I polished off the rest of the day by lunch, arriving in the pristine and pretty city of Guazhou, only to have my spirits broken by having it confirmed here that the G312 disappears for the next 400km until Hami, leaving only the G30 motorway, which I would not be allowed to cycle on.

I was left with a selection of options, none of which I really fancied. The first was to risk the G30 and gamble on not being removed from it. I decided against this on the basis that the time I would lose if I was caught being a naughty boy it would put the whole trip in jeopardy.

I could take a train for 400km to Hami, something I immediately rejected with prior knowledge of the bureaucracy I would endure, but also because that *really* seemed like cheating.

There was also a Google Maps approved route all the way up to the Mongolian border and back down, but this presented me with very few towns to replenish supplies. If I wasn't going to risk missing my deadline for fear of being removed from a motorway, I certainly wasn't going to risk it to die of dehydration.

Finally, there was the increasingly obvious route to join the southern Silk Road rather than the northern one. This gave me plenty to ponder as the beers I promised myself mid-sandstorm the night before helped mollify the memories of that very same event.

Another day, another disappearing road. 17km beyond Guazhou the G314 disappeared and I joined the G30's little sister the G3010 in an illegal act of such severity that five police cars passed me without so much as a glance and the toll booth guards merely laughed at me as I arrived at the other end. The scenery was stunning, though, the desert became decreasingly scrubland and increasingly golden, which lent itself well to the blue skies above. Every so often I saw mini twisters in the distance and occasionally would be sandblasted by them as they made their way across the road. Both in terms of their appearance and longevity, these little twisters are by far my favourite form of sand and wind-based irritant.

Amongst the day's challenges, which also included a split inner tube and the closely related 10km walk to my hotel, there was one moment of excitement when I met up once again with the monk who slept through the storm without a tent. He was also going to Dunhuang and was, as is to be expected, the happiest man on earth. What bliss enlightenment must be!

He would have slipped down the happiness scale if he'd stayed at the same hotel as me though. I wanted so very little from hotels on my trip, but enough water to shower with was one thing I really needed. The temperature of the water was not important, but the volume was. Standing under the pitiful shower I watched in the mirror opposite as a single trickle ran off my hair, down my face and onto the floor. Too exhausted to complain I resorted to washing myself in the sink, a process that almost cost me an ankle and the hotel a sink.

Not at all clean, I headed out to the huge underground supermarket opposite the hotel. I was forced into a couple of hurried purchases in the supermarket after people started to follow me around out of curiosity. This led to me buying various items without consideration, including a bottle of moisturiser branded Sod. However, I did manage to get a huge naan bread, which caused me to break out into a small celebratory round of applause.

Almost certainly still dirty despite a second dip in the sink, I just about managed to Sodomise myself before falling asleep.

With genuine real life admin to carry out first, I then spent the rest of the day allowing my legs to recuperate, whilst watching the UK election results and hitting refresh on a three-year-old wager on the outcome. A large enough wager that, should it come in, it would be enough to fund a bicycle ride across China for two months. An investment strategy I don't suggest anyone follows.

On the basis of how non-committal my mum was about Ed Miliband, I put a bet on a Conservative majority at odds somewhere around 5/1. There is no better bellwether than my mum for the state of the cumulative British political mind, if she's voting Labour but not happy about it, then the United Kingdom is getting a small Tory majority.

The bet came in. For her part in it, my mum was rewarded with a small olive tree called Ed. This was to mitigate my next accurate political forecast - the UK committing economic suicide and leaving the EU – in case I want something to snack on before a Saturday evening meal back home that doesn't cost twice as much as it did before. I'll end my thoughts on British politics by saying I spent the evening accidentally leaving my rucksack at the supermarket, drinking piss-weak lager that had been chilled by frozen meatballs in a hotel room bin, and falling out of the sink.

If that's not an accurate, if extended, metaphor for UKIP's influence on British politics, I don't know what is.

Despite the do not disturb sign I was awoken the next morning by a hotel maid shouting that she wanted to come in and clean my room. It was, ironically, a real chore to let her in and clean around me but she wouldn't take no for an answer. I just couldn't dissuade her - "please don't clean, it's ok, there's no problem, I don't want it cleaned, please don't clean me, please don't clean my bed" - but to no avail. Interestingly she did not consider the, by now defrosted, meatballs that were still in the bin to be rubbish. So I remained in possession of those for another day.

Dunhuang is just up the road from the ancient Buddhist places of worship at Mogao caves. A fantastic and deserved UNESCO'd place of wonder. After writing off my obliterated rear inner tube – I'm almost entirely sure I had been sold 27.5" tubes in 26" boxes by the way – I pootled the 10km back towards Guazhou to visit the caves, secretly hoping to see my monk friend there.

The monk, perhaps put off by the £22 entrance fee, was not present. I opted to join a Chinese language tour rather than wait an extra hour for the English tour. The visitor centre at Mogao is brilliant and guests first watch a 20-minute film of the cave's history in the full, epic, Chinese cinematic tradition. In China, it seems extras are still cheaper than CGI. This was followed by a 360-degree film, which takes guests on a tour of the site they're about to visit, which was unnecessary but impressive nonetheless. Both films tactfully glossed over – in English at least - the massive thefts that took place here a century earlier.

The full story of the thefts - which quite obviously you're not going to get from me – is part Indiana Jones, part Scott of the Antarctic, and all took place under the auspices of the Great Game.

There was death, duplicity, and moments of barely believable good fortune. I also hope there was a good deal of skulduggery, which was shadowed by mutual admiration too. Peter Hopkirk's *Foreign Devils on the Silk Road*[58] is where you should take your

---

[58] (Hopkirk, 1980)

custom if you want the full picture. Stay here for smut and generalisations.

In the days before Australian girls made gap years what they are today by saying things like "I woke up and saw I had mayonnaise on my tits, but I couldn't remember eating chips last night. Still ate it with my fingers, though, didn't I? Until I realised it wasn't mayo."[59] European chaps like von Le Coq – he of the sandstorm description - had to go on the rob in a Chinese desert to get their kicks.

In the early 1900s, Europeans from Britain, Sweden, Russia, France, and stop me if this sounds familiar, Germany, had an archaeological arms race in the ancient Silk Road cities of Xinjiang and Gansu. On the southern branch, these cities lay some 100km or so north of the present day road that I was following. Buried by the shifting sands of the desert, these cities and their artefacts and mummies, lay preserved and undisturbed for centuries.

Of those who raided the ancient treasures of the Silk Road, Hopkirk posthumously, yet patriotically, awards fellow Britain Aurel Stein the title of "most villainous of the foreign archaeologists" on behalf of the Chinese. Whilst alive Stein had to make do with a knighthood for his exploits. What elevates Stein to the most devilish of the devils is his removal of some 40,000 ancient manuscripts from Mogao after bribing Wang Yuan Lu, the misleadingly-titled, self-appointed, "guardian of the sacred caves"[60]. One of the manuscripts Stein took is the Diamond Sutra, which is believed to be the oldest, dated, printed text in existence. The whole stash, Diamond Sutra included, had been *bought* for £130[61], a rate of just over three manuscripts for every

---

[59] Overheard on a ferry from Santorini to Patras in late August 2008.

[60] (Hopkirk, 1980)

penny.

One man's bribery is another man's tax deductible entertainment allowance, but there comes a point where one man's bribery is theft. That point is some way above £130 when you're talking about the Mogao manuscripts.

One argument goes that, as luck would have it, the Europeans like Stein, actually saved these relics from the ravages of the Cultural Revolution. In part that must be true, though it does a great disservice to the Chinese who may have saved them from that head-smashingly stupid period of their history by either intention, or accident (by stealing the artefacts themselves, rather than outsourcing to Stein & co), but didn't have the chance. They now sit in the British Library where they can at least draw some fire from the Elgin Marbles, half a mile down the road.

The section of Mogao open to visitors nowadays is made up of a selection of small grottoes originally made for monks to meditate in, which had been transformed into beautiful temples full of colour. It is brilliant. I enjoyed being on a Chinese language tour too, not least because our guide had a soothing and easy to understand tone. Though, there was an awful lot of being told Buddha was wearing a red dress, whilst looking at Buddha wearing a red dress. The giant sleeping Buddha that marked the grand finale of our tour looked like he was sleeping with one eye open as sand has sealed off his other one. Mr Sandman must have brought a JCB for this deity.

It is an excessive entrance fee, but well worth it. By the end of our tour a sandstorm was closing in on us, but fortunately, it was a going my way and blew me all the way back to Dunhuang before 5pm.

---

[61] (Hopkirk, 1980)

That evening I returned to the supermarket and purchased a bright pink water flask with glittery, floral decals to allow me to carry extra water through the desert in style. Coincidentally, it was also the cheapest flask available.

My departure from Dunhuang the next morning was meant to be the start of the new normal as I embarked upon plan B. I left a little later than planned but began the day in what I wanted to be my new way of life; spinning gently along in fifth gear on mostly flat roads to reduce the chances of dehydration, taking a big break in the heat of the day and monitoring my water and food consumption carefully.

As the sun was finding its full wattage around lunchtime, I rolled down one of the slight descents and noticed that once again in the heat haze ahead of me, was the monk. About 50 metres before I reached him I began to slow down. As I silently cruised towards him he raised his hand and without turning to face me shouted: "friend, go on, go on, go on!" It was as if he knew of my travails past, present and future.

After a quick chat, which was expedited by the limitations of my vocabulary, I did as I was told and got on with getting on. The 15km before I reached the small town of Akesai in the far south of Gansu's north-western jut, was some of the most glorious scenery of the whole trip. Rippled, golden dunes, hundreds of feet high, sat alongside a winding road in the shadow of huge mountains that I now planned to ride alongside on my way into the desert as part of plan B.

An hour later I rolled through the quiet town centre looking for a place to eat my evening meal. Eventually, I halted at a sparkling clean restaurant run by a young - compared to me and my lack of fertility to date - Hui family. I tried my best not to shovel the delicious food into my mouth in front of the children, whilst fielding the usual questions about myself and my journey.

If the new normal could be like this, then I was happy. If I could get one real meal a day, stay hydrated, and see the monk, then plan B would be great. Full of the goodwill that interactions with young hard-working families can't fail to bring a loafing chancer, I stopped at a petrol station to buy my final top up of water and a head-melting 3.7% can of beer to drink at sunset.

As I approached the till a panicked male attendant called the slightly older female attendant over to serve me. She glanced at him with disdain and said "what? what's the problem, it's £1.20?". I got £1.20 out, causing her to chastise the boy further "look he understands anyway". This prompted my understanding to be tested more fully as a trucker started talking to me at full speed in a far stronger accent. After the girl translated his dialect, it was established that I'd be staying in my tent instead of the town because I wanted to make more distance before dark. The trucker seemed unsure, he didn't think I'd get further than 15km as the road was so steep.

We talked it through a few times, at various speeds and in varying translations of local dialect, Mandarin, Midland's English, Englese and Chinglish. I was sure I had flat roads for many days to come, the trucker was sure of the opposite. Eventually, we agreed to disagree, by me agreeing with him and leaving.

He was right, though. As I headed to join the road that was to be my plan B, two locals flagged me down to explain the road was shut and I must continue on to the G215 instead, which was heading straight into the mountains I'd been smiling at all day long. With that, as the heat was draining away from the day, plan B was dead. Long live plan C.

All I had to do was work out what Plan C was. Without any roaming data flying through the crisp, cooling, air around me, I decided to take spiritual guidance from the monk and just go on. Something that would eventually be as rewarding as it was distressing, but for the immediate future, without any spirituality, my bliss was found in ignorance.

I'm not sure I even made it to the predicted 15km by the time I set up my best camp yet at the foot of the mountains under a sky of a thousand colours. If this was the new new normal then good riddance to the old new normal and its short-lived, half-baked promises.

8.1 CHINESE BUSINESS HOTELS

When I wasn't sleeping in a tent near a graveyard, rubbish tip, or jaw-dropping scenery, I would be frequenting one of China's business hotels. They often award their own stars but by global standards, they're somewhere around two or three. What is not in doubt is the value they provide. I didn't pay more than £35 a night, the average price was under £20, and some were as cheap as £12.

Five-star they may not be, but more often than not you get at least one bed and a clean bathroom with a powerful shower. You don't need more than that, but how best to maximise the Chinese business hotel experience on a bicycle journey I hear you ask.

"How best to maximise the Chinese business hotel experience on a bicycle journey, Simon?"

First, your arrival. I quickly learned during the pollution and coal-heavy days of Hebei, that if you arrive looking like a racist ghost, then you need to start by explaining what you've been up to. Apologise until someone in hotel uniform asks you to stop apologising.

Now, you have a reservation because Ctrip's app is excellent. Only the thing is, 80% of the time they won't find your reservation, but this is irrelevant as there's space in the hotel, because you are in the middle of nowhere. Where it will become irritating is not Ctrip taking loyalty points off you for failing to arrive for a reservation that you did, in fact, arrive for. No, what really grates is them phoning you to ask why you failed to show, requesting your receipt, then putting you on hold after asking for your room number - which you know because you have an alarmingly good memory for all things numerical – then coming back to say there's nothing they can do, you've lost the points you didn't want in the first place. In short, you should never answer a phone call from Ctrip.

You make it to your room, normally assisted by an excitable and brilliant security guard soiling his white gloves with the road filth of one or both of your panniers.

Now through the door, this is where the magic happens. Your immediate priority is to get clean unless you have purchased beer. Then your priority is to take the living room bin and fill it with the frozen meatballs and the strongest cans of beer (3.6%) you found in the nearby shop.

One man's bin is another man's ice bucket. The floor is now your bin. After all, as my right of centre friends always remind me, if you clean up after yourself then other people will be unemployed[62].

Now you can wash, unless of course, you have a shower like the one I had in Dunhuang.

After you've showered, or been forced to bathe in a sink like a massive toddler whose shit himself at playgroup, you need to begin pillaging. The fact you are naked after washing will aid your primitive urges to scavenge. Things you must forage for include: the toilet roll – you're not a bear but you will be shitting in the woods sooner or later; the cotton buds – sand gets everywhere, more often than not places you don't want to, or can't, probe with a finger; sanitary bag – your new mobile bin bag for your futile attempts to save China from litter; the sewing kit – you don't know what clothes/tyre/panniers you'll need to fix, or sadly, what boil you'll need to pop on your saddle punished arse.

Everything else is superfluous or off limits for stealing (see checking out section below).

---

[62] Tidy up after yourself though because you were raised to be better than that.

Always choose the twin room over the double if offered the choice. If staying for two nights, that's a clean bed each night. If staying one night, then you can avoid bending all the way down to the floor to pick stuff up in the morning.

Pillows; search for a spare, because it will be the least used and comfiest. If nothing else, it almost certainly won't contain the weapons grade bean bag balls that make the regular Chinese business hotel pillows so long lasting.

Put the do not disturb sign on, not for any particular reason because from 7am until midnight your desire to not be disturbed is irrelevant. On one day alone I had four visits from hotel staff; including one man who arrived with armed with only a polyfilla gun, looked under a mattress, shrugged, and then left.

Your biggest problem is check out. There is no way round this, I've tried declaring my consumption of two beers, two pot noodles, two bottles of water, two coffees and two Red Bulls, thus offering to pay for all I could have (and had) consumed. It doesn't matter, though, without fail you will suffer at least a ten-minute sweep of your room.

This isn't about your consumption; this is about profit. On the boy's final day, as they tried to check out, a cleaner radioed down to say one of them had 'dirtied a towel'. The cherubs both proclaimed innocence, so in my best Chinese I requested to see the dirty towel. What followed was a magnificently Chinese experience where, within view of us, the duty manager and cleaners kicked all of the 6th floor's towels around the floor to try and find the offending item, which they failed to do.

In short, leave an extra thirty minutes and oppose any charges (also cover your stinky drains with the towels that will never be identified as dirty).

9. THE WILD WEST

I had not intended to go to the province of Qinghai on this journey. In the initial planning stage, during the happy hours I spent tracing my finger along the thin red lines of maps, I had pondered visiting Qinghai Lake, the body of water from which the province takes its name. Sitting due south of Zhangye, it is China's largest lake and by this virtue alone it looked a worthwhile detour. I was further tempted when Apple Maps pointed out I would pass a decommissioned atomic test site.

Yet despite these enticing locations and this being the heady days of the post-Tianjin to Beijing triumph, I still did not fancy being forced to climb over the desolate and unforgiving Qilian Mountains on the Pigeon. Within the first permutations of the possible route, I had written Qinghai off with an immediacy normally only reserved for exiting one of Beijing's public toilets.

This meant I did no prior planning or research on the province; whether that was into the historical colour and geographical wonder that would romanticise bits of it or the more useful logistical research about hotels and places to source food and water.

This turned out to not be much of an oversight, given there was so few of any of these things. Something you might expect of a province deemed worthy of being the testing ground for nuclear weapons. I was going into the barren wilderness of China's Wild West with little more than the knowledge I would be spending much of my time in the mountains. Something I had noticed, because they were handily placed, right in front of my nose.

I awoke to the beautiful sight of them, sitting proud and snow capped under a blue sky. Still naively pleased with what I deemed as my serendipitous change of direction, I finished packing my tent up. As I began pushing back to the road, the wind rose up in every single bit of the wrong direction. It took me an hour to push the first 3km up towards the mountain pass. An amount of time that had allowed Mr Guo to pass me on the way into Akesai and pull up alongside me on his way back up.

With looming deadlines of real life things like job interviews and weddings, and a burning desire to drink Malbec and eat lasagne, my interest in the wholesome integrity of the trip was beginning to dwindle. As I described my situation to friends; I wasn't doing it for charity, I wasn't doing it for any sense of achievement, I was just a twat riding a bike across China. I was already on Plan C after all, and so had decided that from here on in, if I received an offer that would allow me to avoid complete misery, then I was going to take it.

Mr Guo had such an offer. We heaved the Giant, inclusive of its watery excess weight, into the cab of his truck and cleared 10km of headwind hell as he drove me to the quarry he worked at. Though he was in a rush, we almost stopped for a second breakfast after my poor grasp of Mandarin made him think I hadn't yet eaten. If you ever want to panic a Chinese person, tell them you're hungry. If you really want to distress them try telling them you're hungry and cold! If you want them to drive you to a hospital tell them you're hungry, cold and *thirsty*!

We covered *the conversation* before moving on to our favourite types of food as part of his panic over my lack of breakfast and also discussed which countries in Europe had mountains like those we were winding our way through. The desire of the people I met on this trip to compare and contrast China with the rest of the world was unyielding. There was also a real clamour to know more about the world outside China, especially from the mouth of a foreigner. Often it was their own research into purchasing power parity for iPhones and Range Rovers. Every so often, however, as with Mr Guo on that morning, we covered more interesting topics.

We arrived at his quarry, which was still at the base of the mountain pass, too soon for my liking. As he dropped me off, he handed me two bottles of water and wished me good luck. As I looked at the many kilometres of ascending still ahead of me, I wished myself good luck too.

I had to push the rest of the pass. There was no peddling to be done. It felt like the air was thinning and the presence of snow in May gave that feeling some credence. The long johns and scarf were back on by the time I had ascended half way to the top. Shortly afterwards, I received a further water donation from a car full of alarmingly young and affluent people, one of whom was far too beautiful to be touching the same bottle as my filthy hands. I was exhausted by the time I reached the top and actually felt myself falling asleep as I lay down on top of a giant concrete barrier during my final oxygen starved break.

Until Loopie Route produced the map on the magnificent map on the back cover, I had no idea that my total elevation gain was 14145 metres, very nearly the equivalent of ascending evidence twice. I also had no idea that this pass was 3400m, or the equivalent of riding over Snowden, Ben Nevis and Scafell Pike, if you piled them up on top of one another.

The gravity dividend matured in some style in the early afternoon; 25km of pure, joyous descending that was only interrupted by the need to strip down to vest and shorts as I hit scorching hot plateau below.

I made as much progress along the plateau as I could stand, eventually stopping just inside Qinghai province near the western edge of Suqian Lake. I set up camp just in time to discover the whole "the desert is cold at night you know" advice, is not a lie. Why I didn't buy a better sleeping bag in one of Dunhuang's many outdoor shops I'll never know. How I managed to leave my hoody by the desolate roadside as I stripped off that same afternoon I find even harder to fathom.

I also became slightly alarmed at the lack of phone signal and roaming data available. Not just because I'm part of Generation Y and I can't live with not knowing football scores, but because I still didn't actually know exactly where I was, or where exactly I was going, and that *was* a problem.

The night was very cold, especially between 2am and 5am, between which hours I'm not entirely sure I slept. I closed my eyes and tried to sleep but failed like a child on Christmas Eve. Once there was enough warmth to do so, I slept until 9.30am. Once I was up and peddling, a rare tailwind blew me passed glorious windswept scenery that looked as though it could have featured in the film Hero.

This alien scenery marked the end of Schengen China, where borders are (wo)manned by friendly, smiling transport police. Here, as I approached Lenghuzhen, I reached my first police roadblock. The SWAT police stationed here were friendly, especially when you consider the welcome you get at Heathrow, but the security knob had definitely been dialled up a couple of notches. Fortunately, as a lone cyclist, with correct documentation and a hilarious appearance, I was evidently not a threat.

Still conscious I didn't know where I was going, I asked the police if there was a hotel in town. There was indeed a hotel, but I then proceeded to check into the wrong one. There are still hotels in China that foreigners aren't allowed to stay in. A rule that is a throwback to the days of being an old-fashioned authoritarian country, as opposed to a modern authoritarian country. This plays out today in that most modern of ways, whereby it seemed more often than not that it was more about which hotel had the correct software to register a foreigner, than anything to do with security or presentation, which dictated where I was permitted to stay.

I managed to check-in, eat at the restaurant next door and get halfway through a shower before the first knock at the door.

Receptionist: "Can you come out the police are here."

Me: "I'm in the shower."

One minute passed before she tried again. "The police are here please come out."

Me: "Please wait, I'm in the shower."

30 further seconds passed until there was a big bang on the door.

Policeman: "Police!"

Me: "OK, but I'm in the shower."

At this precise moment, I was trying desperately to balance the wild variations in water temperature between scalding hot and freezing cold, in order to rinse the region of my body I wanted to scold or freeze least. To my great annoyance and Graham's great discomfort, only seconds later the door was hit even harder - *bang, bang, bang* - "I'm putting my clothes on" I yelled in surprisingly good Mandarin. Yet it was not enough. *Bang! Bang! Bang!* I then just gave up, reverted to English and calmly said: "OK, you're going to fucking love this."

I opened the door to the policeman, soaking wet and wearing only a pair of Christmas boxer shorts, which invited viewers of said garment to pull me and demonstrate the outcome of doing so with a great big explosive white mark bursting out of my cracker and onto my crotch. He did not look impressed.

This tasteful item of clothing was actually bought for me by my 79-year-old Nan Maureen. It is my most sincere hope that she thought the joke stopped at the 'pull me' element of the garment and was unaware of the explosive ejaculation gag. Since these and the pair with Rudolph's bright red, oversized nose that covers one's trouser snout, were uncomfortably my worst underwear, they were selected to come on the trip due to my eagerness to throw them away at its end.

At first, the Policeman was blunt: I had to get dressed quickly. "No shit son" I replied in deliberately fast and accented English. He couldn't overstate how important it was that I left this hotel immediately. I apologised, showed some faux deference and after we spoke a little in Chinese he relaxed. He even carried one of my panniers down to help expedite things.

Stopping only to pull up the belt-free trousers that had fallen down to my ankles and retrieve my £12 back from the reluctant receptionist, who, thanks to the whole lack of belt thing had also caught sight of the explosive undercrackers, we were out of the hotel in under a minute. The policeman started loading my stuff into his van. I didn't know where I was going but realised it was probably going to be OK given he then instructed me to follow the van on my bike.

I followed the police van a whole 100 metres to a considerably worse hotel that had the correct software to register a foreigner. The policeman had to register me himself as the hotel staff had never done it before, suggesting I was probably Lenghuzhen's first foreign visitor since the advent of the computer, if not ever[63]. I do not expect they'll erect a statue of a foreigner with an exploding crotch to mark the occasion, but it would be nice if they at least considered it. After a prolonged check in I was given the key to a room that for reasons best known to others possessed its own waiting room outside of the bedroom. It looked like a cross between a 1980s doctor's surgery and the world's most orderly, one room, brothel. *Take a ticket and await your number.*

---

[63] Before a pedant can finish raising their hand and inhaling with faux surprise – no, I'm definitely not.

I took a seat in my waiting room, only to be immediately reminded by the sound of a soapy squelch that I still had to finish showering.

Finally soap free, I set about finding where I was and where I would be going. The long view held few surprises and only really one option to reach Kashgar. The final three-quarters would involve trying to skip between the cities, towns, and villages along the G315 road as quickly as possible. As I saved each of them into Google Maps a chain of stars appeared like a child's toy necklace, which led all the way to Kashgar. Alarmingly though the stars didn't have any great frequency in my immediate future. Worse still, as I had expected, I would have to head back over the mountains I had struggled with the day before, to finally enter Xinjiang.

My alarm went at seven but the hotel quilt detained me until nine. With desert to come, I took to my hair with some scissors to thin it out and stop my fringe irritating me. I left the bits that hang over my ears to save them from the sun. Looking somewhere between a snarl-free Liam Gallagher and a hobbit, it was a brave move, but it paid off on days when I forgot to cover my ears in factor 30.

A final liquid break at the last petrol station in town confirmed that the next human settlement would be over 300km away. I filled my new water flask, bringing my total liquid supplies to 15 litres and set off into the unknown.

One of the unknown's great benefits is that it often amazes. Within thirty minutes I had arrived at a stunning scene of wind eroded walls of sandstone. One of the unknown's great failings is that it's often unknown because there's no reason to live there. The stunning scenery was quickly replaced by 40km of monumentally tedious straight road through a bleak monochrome grey landscape, which was complimented by a vicious side-wind that was made all the worse by occasionally alternating with a slightly less angry head-wind.

In mid-afternoon, the third significant sandstorm of the journey arrived in a more beautiful yellow form than its predecessors. After 500 futile metres of trying to push through it. I sat with my back to a huge dune and weighed up my options. Every time I chose a place to camp I was gambling on there not being a better place one, two, or even five kilometres further away. This decision is of paramount importance when it's clear you are about to be bullied by the weather. I struggled on for another 2km or so before I found a dell behind a small dune. It wasn't perfect but I still decided to put all of my chips on it.

I began to dam the wind by building a wall at the entrance to the dell with huge rocks. In the hostile conditions, this took a significant amount of both time and swearing. The wall wasn't perfect but after I had dug a small trench for the tent to sit in, I fancied I had enough protection to not spend the night holding on to the tent and wondering why people far smarter than I have faith in things they can't see.

Once the wall was constructed there was a heart in mouth moment as I unsheathed the tent. As soon as it was out of the bag it was caught by a huge gust that threatened to blow it all the way back to Beijing. Only a misspent youth spent catching coins off my own elbow and bar mats that had been flicked into the air from a table's edge, instead of studying for A-levels, meant I was able to snatch the tent before it disappeared. Sure I could have been a success, but who wants four As and no tent, when you can have four Bs and a tent?

As I unloaded all of the bike's luggage to use as ballast and climbed into the tent, a dark orange sky lit up the violently shaking nylon and it all began to look like a little piece of hell. But at least it was my little piece of hell.

Fed up with the wind I awoke and packed the tent away in record time. I even replaced the rear inner tube, which I couldn't face fixing during the trauma of the previous evening. I then attacked the day for all it was worth to make up for previous day's lost distance. I don't know if there was something in the Oreos, but I was full of aggression.

Did I cash out too soon on the camping location the previous evening? Possibly, but what I lost in larger dunes further down the road, I had made up for in big rocks.

I had my quickest roadside photo of the journey after I noticed the trucker taking my photo was multi-tasking by smoking next to his fume-rich oil tanker. I had just reached Qinghai's oil fields and though I am certain the large state companies must be responsible for them, it looked more like an oil-rush town from the turn of the last century. Nodding donkey oil pumps filled the surrounding mountainsides and fields, with only wooden and tin shacks providing shelter for those few workers who were bussed in each day. It all looked very privateer.

Given the lack of anything nearby, security also appeared to be of a bygone era. In this particular case three Mastiffs of some mongrel form or another. At least I had spotted them well in advance, so I knew what was coming as their muscular legs started to eat up my 200m head start. At first, I didn't look back because I didn't need to, their increasingly loud barking let me know how quickly they were gaining. I managed to drag the bike up to around 35kph before the most irritatingly placed small rise appeared in front of me.

Following cartoon protocol, as we ascended the dogs literally snapped at my heels as I stood and stamped on the pedals. After nearly a kilometre of playing chase, two of the dogs gave up, which isolated the one remaining hunter who too backed down a further two hundred, lung burning, metres up the road. I pushed on as fast as I could manage until the next corner to ensure I was out of sight by the time I stumbled off the bike and gently lowered myself to the floor.

Still riddled with adrenalin, it took well over ten minutes for me to calm down enough to realise I was incredibly thirsty. It had been a lesson in the importance of having a spare match to burn. When cycling long distances, or indeed doing any form of endurance activity, you have the ability to perform a limited number of intense bursts of energy each day before you are totally burnt out - like a match, clever isn't it? Luckily, on this occasion, it was early enough in the day that I had an extra long safety match in reserve, as the three dogs after me were bona fido attack dogs. They were not just angry pets or even strays, but three dogs employed to make my calves look like the leftover Sunday roast that Dad is still picking at with no regard for the ratio of meat to vegetables in Monday night's chicken curry.

At the time, thanks to the adrenaline and elation at avoiding the dogs, I didn't give this incident the thought it deserved. My situation was pretty perilous. I was around halfway between Lenghuzhen and the next town of Huatugou, the nearest medical help would have been 150km in either direction. It would be rude, but probably accurate, to assume this medical care would not have been world class. I hadn't seen another road user for ten minutes. I didn't have a weapon, either real or improvised, that could have dealt with one Mastiff, let alone three. Genuinely, my best implement to take them on would have been my weighty laptop. Had they caught me, the best case scenario would have been an immediate end to the journey. Other possible scenarios include being eaten alive or slowly bleeding to death.

I am not alone in this experience either, the first two people I spoke with about my ride who had also visited rural Qinghai had both experienced this same dog terror too. At risk of being useful, using their experiences and one I had later in Xinjiang, if you're on foot or can't outrun the dogs on a bicycle, throw stones. For whatever reason, this seems to make them back off. Chilli powder could also be a good idea as a stand-in for mace.

After the ride, even around the streets of Beijing, it took me many months to be able to pass dogs again without giving them a wide berth. Almost a year later, two incidents illustrated the imprint this experience had left on a not particularly deep recess of my mind. At the end of a short walk over the Great Wall with Zoe, my housemate from University, we arrived at a farmhouse that also acted as a gateway to this section of wall and therefore a sweet money maker for the elderly couple acting as gatekeepers (£3.50 per person). Before we reached the gate, we arrived at three caged dogs a little larger than those that chased me, but with a vague enough similarity that by the time we met the gatekeeper a few moments later, I was holding a large brick in my hand.

The other incident also happened near the Great Wall. We were spending Easter with friends who rent a house nearby to one of the most spectacular stretches of wall. I had popped out for a late afternoon bike ride over some of the many beautiful hills the Wall decorates just north of Beijing. As I hit the first ascent, two pitifully small dogs ran out of a garage and began to chase me. Despite these being animals so small I could have drop-kicked them back over their owner's house with equal measures of ease and guilt, my mind snapped and I attacked the climb until I was burnt out and on the verge of tears. Crying is an entirely healthy activity. Even if you want to look at it coldly, it's definitely beneficial as a pressure valve. That said, I am just not a person who cries very much. Since the age of 12 I've probably cried less than ten times and when I have done, it's always been around something life-changing in scale. The fact that two runty dogs brought me so close to a roadside meltdown on the weekend after I had got engaged, when I was hanging out with great friends, eating barbecued food, and drinking wine underneath pollution-free skies, tells you all you need to know about how my mind still feels about being chased by dogs.

Back in Qinghai, once my heart rate dropped below 300 I pressed on, clearing my 100km mark for the day by late afternoon. As I did so, my new sparkly pink water flask, briefly known as Rizzo for her short existence, also cracked in dramatic fashion. After an initial few seconds of laughing at my own misfortune, I remembered my water bottles were empty and caught one-third of the leaking contents. As two litres had been lost to the road, I began to ask for water from everyone who stopped for a photo and a chat. The importance of possessing a permanent supply of drinking water to Chinese people is hard to overstate, this nationwide practice meant that almost every car had some going spare and all were generous enough to donate some. My offers of money were always refused.

Late in the day, one driver even gave me four bottles of mineral water; prompting a moral dilemma as to whether it would be right to use some of this unexpected bounty to wash Graham and his close associates. When it came down to it, using mineral water to wash in a desert felt excessive. Like going to Waitrose just to get slightly better cheese. However, being alone meant that washing my bits with water wasn't as important as the quality of mozzarella in a tricolore salad. So I did the understated thing and resolved to stick to baby wipes, which are very much the low fat cow's milk in the breast implant bag, and not the D.O.C. buffalo stuff in the tub, mozzarella of the cleansing world.

I kept pushing on into the early evening, keen to make back some of the lost distance from the previous day. I was compensated with the most spectacular scenery of the trip to date and rewarded with the best camp site I'll ever stay in. Within twenty minutes of getting into my sleeping bag and wrapping my scarf around my head like a hijab for warmth, I lay down for another night of wind-assisted sleep.

So far there had been challenging days, days with moments of fear and frustration but this, my final full day in Qinghai, was by far the worst of the journey. By the end of the day, I'd even go so far as to say that I had lost my patience.

After the dog chase and two nights of inadequate sleep, my nerves were stretched to breaking point. I set off winding around the remaining dunes and down into more of the oil-rich landscape of China's west. Ominously, before the troubles started I saw three vultures. One less than the Jungle Book promised me there would be, but it was enjoyable watching them take off like the sluggish cargo planes of the avian world.

The sight of the vultures had been symbolic. The misery began almost immediately afterwards with 20km of uphill, head-wind hell. The cumulative lack of sleep over the last two nights, a total reliance on Orios and pot noodles, coupled with a general feeling of exhaustion led to the bonk of all bonks at the top of the hill. This wasn't just any bonk, this was an orgy with Genghis and no safety word bonk. My body gave in and my head went.

Whilst reflating yet another mystery slow puncture, as I looked down at the ground the tarmac began to warp in front of me, which is not a welcome experience in the middle of nowhere. I sat myself down by the side of the road and closed my eyes. Fortunately, only a few minutes later two oil workers picked me up and drove me for 45 head-clearing minutes. Despite being hotboxed by strong Chinese cigarettes, my time on the back seat was regenerative. This welcome break made the final 50km to Huatugou possible. I was also spurred on by the fact that this being oil country meant that there'd surely be hotels.

Unfortunately, once my saviours pulled into one of the oil fields, I had to remount and continue on the first road in a very long time that didn't have a cycle lane. Leaving me shoulder to shoulder with lorries that had been loaded up far away from the Emperor and his road traffic regulations. An experience that did nothing for my shredded nerves.

Already emotionally all over the place or, to put it more honestly, absolutely shitting my festive pants, 2km from the centre of Huatugou another dog went for me. With no matches left to burn it was only the dregs of adrenaline and swerving around the road like Kevin Keegan on Superstars that saved me from being bitten. This was the final straw. Panting like a sixteen-year-old asthmatic who'd just lost his virginity to his own grandfather, I resolved to buy an anti-dog weapon the next day.

At just gone six, distressed and destroyed, I arrived at the Western Business Hotel, which seemed a good bet for a foreigner to be able to stay in. I waited in reception for the police and their hurriedly found translator because I couldn't be bothered to unpack only to be moved on. I was advised I could stay, but only for one night, because the town was not yet fully open to foreigners. I wanted to rest for an extra day, but what can you do? The town wasn't ready for me.

I checked in, paid, said goodbye to the police and headed off to have my appetite laughed at as I consumed a four-person stew, an extra bowl of noodles and a side of veg in a Uyghur restaurant.

Washed, fed, and about to get into bed there was an unexpected knock at the door. It was 23.05 and it was the cleaner. I'd been woken up by cleaners at unsociable hours at the other end of the day before but never at 23.05. After three repetitions I understood that she was informing me I wasn't allowed to sleep. A fact that seemed very obvious by her keeping me awake. After a little more discussion, I discovered she meant I couldn't sleep in the hotel. This time I was in a towel rather than festive boxers, but it was awkward all the same. Ten minutes later I headed downstairs, where, unapologetically I was told to go to a different hotel. Unlike my last move the police weren't here to ensure I arrived at the new hotel. No one had any interest in getting me to the right place.

Ten minutes of futility followed as I repeatedly said I didn't know where the new hotel was. Eventually, the cleaner hailed a taxi and at 23.30 I was following it through the streets to my new hotel.

The new hotel was exactly what I was expecting of an oil town. A Beijing registered Hummer indicated the calibre of people my fellow guests would be. It also confirmed just how far out of sight I was from not only the Emperor's road traffic regulations but also the tentacles of his corruption crackdown. As I entered the building, I was made to feel as welcome as a chicken sausage at a barbecue.

The presence of drunk police still in uniform did nothing to assuage my growing prejudices. Though the sheriff is always drinking in the saloon when the outsider arrives in a Western, so I suppose in a way this was a fitting scene for my last evening in Qinghai.

Cinematic or not, it took around an hour to check me in here. Despite the presence of police already in the building and lingering around the reception desk, they sent out for some vaguely sober ones to help with the admin instead. It could have been worse, everyone was friendly and once it was again established I'd leave the town tomorrow all was OK, but it still took an hour of patience that I really didn't have.

I got to bed at 1.30am in a room that smelt of the town's dinners from two nights ago. It had been the kind of farce the hotel rule for foreigners is no doubt in place to avoid: yet all it did was highlight just how ludicrous old China's rules are when applied to new China. Had I been allowed to sleep in the perfectly nice Western Business Hotel, I would not have seen shit-faced policemen, a Beijing registered Hummer, or the town's nouveau riche at their cringe-worthy, neon-illuminated, worst.

This seems as good a time as any to address *China rage*. The French probably have a more evocative term like *seething China wrath*, the Germans probably have a more direct phrase like *China hate*, but for English-speaking foreigners China rage is an all encompassing saying for the moments when China breaks you.

In general, China rage results from the amalgamation of health issues, frustrations with bureaucracy, pollution, restricted freedoms and limited access to cheese. There is a critical mass of China rage any one soul can take before said soul packs its bags and buggers off home. China rage can be stifled or at least briefly forgotten through a number of ways, but once you've had it, it's always within you, lurking, waiting to flare up again like a cold sore on your soul.

As I lay in bed that night, diseased with all of the symptoms of China rage, it was though my blood was boiling. For nearly an hour I lay eyes wide open and sweating anger before eventually exhaustion dragged me off to sleep.

I was still angry at 7am when I awoke and refused to get out of bed until 10am. Instead, I chose to do useful things, which the modern day adventurer is able to do in the Wild West, like buy my Nan's[64] 80th birthday present.

I checked out quickly, only to notice that my latest slow puncture on the front tyre had mysteriously switched to the rear overnight. Once it was fully inflated, I returned to the Western Business Hotel to retrieve my phone charger, bought many litres

---

[64] The other Nan who doesn't buy smutty underwear.

of water, before double dropping baozi, having both meat and veg variations of this delicious dumpling variety. In a moment it was as if the China rage had gone. All was well with the world again; the water had been bought from a friendly family with whom I chatted for several minutes, the same cleaner who had delivered my eviction notice the night before had made a point of keeping my phone charger somewhere safe and the baozi seemed to have medicinal properties. If the dumplings had contained cheese, I'd have married the waitress and applied (unsuccessfully) for citizenship.

I re-joined the G315 and met my first permanent police checkpoint just outside the town. Unlike the temporary one in Lenghuzhen, this one was a bricks and mortar fixture complete with snipers. Again the boys and men manning it were friendly and professional, I was even offered some tea and, obscurely, paracetamol too. I even got a wave off one of the snipers outside.

Should you wave back at snipers? I decided in this circumstance, it was probably the done thing, but bloody hell did it feel counterintuitive.

Having failed to buy an anti-dog weapon in town, I picked up a piece of 2x4 and a small bit of lead piping from the roadside. If a dog was going to die, it was going to meet a very blunt, British end. At the same time, I created my own rule of law. Based on the neo-classical Anglo-Saxon primary school rule of "if they hit you, hit them harder" I adapted this to "if they bit me, I would club them to death". I had decided I must be physically attacked before I battered the dog to death. I was at peace with the idea of giving fair warning that I would harm the animal if it harmed me. I was less at peace with how recently I had a rabies jab – never - but it seemed out of order to kill without a requisite amount of provocation.

The real answer to all of these dog based travails is actually mace, but this is not a product the Chinese authorities are particularly cool with people carrying around. Also, I feel the need to point out that I like dogs, but these were wild animals or dogs that had been trained to harm. I was not preparing myself to club Bouncer, Willard, Lassie, or any of the Blue Peter dogs to death.

By in large, it was an uneventful day on the road. The only notable moment being a big climb passed a huge quarry. And I mean China huge, not just regular huge. I learned a few days later that it was, in fact, a giant asbestos mine. Thankfully the wind was blowing the other way at the time I happened to be riding by.

At the top of the asbestos ascent lay the border with Xinjiang. After successfully avoiding the many dogs guarding mechanic's sheds, restaurants, and petrol stations, I made it to the border, my final frontier. Before I reached the little police tent to register and finally pass into Xinjiang, the local transport police near the border started waving and shouting "watermelon" at me.

After the previous day, this was exactly what I needed. In a flash, I'd been handed a slice of watermelon, shown to a chair and presented with a naan the size of the Charity Shield (or the big plate they give the best girl at Wimbledon if you like your sports with a side of sexism and strawberries). This was exactly what I needed, both spiritually and nutritionally. We had the usual conversation with added questions about the 2x4. "You know there are big dogs, so I have this to hit them on the head" I explained, to which the only response was laughter and the correcting of my pronunciation of dog. I tried to explain how much I love naan and why we eat so much of it in Britain but judging by the confused expressions I'm not sure I succeeded in describing migration and empire. In gratitude, I handed over my

Shrewsbury Town FC badge[65], which could have been used to identify my dog savaged remains, as a token of my appreciation.

The tented border checkpoint, wasn't an electronic affair like the high-tech one at Huatugou. Instead, it was an all paperwork affair. Fortunately, I was allowed to fill my own entry in English. I wonder if they'll ever notice that Steven Gerrard MBE passed through Qinghai to Xinjiang on a bicycle?

Five kilometres beyond the border at Yitunbulakezhen and into the little nub of Xinjiang that sticks eastwards into Qinghai, I found an old quarry. There was evidence of previous habitation (poop) but enough raised windproof spots where somebody couldn't accidentally drive a lorry over a tent.

I set up camp using the 2x4 as an improvised bike stand and got stuck into half of the naan that I had just been gifted, along with the usual noodles. A meal which pretty much counted as hipster fusion food out there in the Wild West.

---

[65] They don't need to know I'm a Liverpool fan who bought that off a Barnet fan under duress whilst drinking in the wrong pub before the annual guilt trip to watch my home town team play away in London. It's the perceived thought that counts.

9.1 EQUIPMENT

As you might expect from a man who cycled across China in a pair of Uniqlo chinos, on a £200 mountain bike with flat plastic pedals; equipment was not my top priority[66]. I took a 3.2kg laptop for pity's sake.

I know that genuine touring cyclists[67] and others often like to list these things in the style of an overly keen, but well-intentioned scout leader, but I will save you from the chore of reading through a comprehensive list of inanimate objects. However, I would like to highlight five pieces of equipment I am incredibly grateful for.

1. My tent. A Decathlon Quechua Ultralight Quickhiker. It never quite saved my life, but it certainly saved me from the complete torture of sandstorms on at least two occasions. Its best feature, by some margin, was the fact it easily fitted in the bag it came in. There was no straining as I tried to fist it back in, no leaving the poles or pegs out and having to strap them to the sides of another bag. It was the first piece of camping equipment I have ever owned, which returned to its container or bag without causing a fight. It also weighed about half as much as my laptop.

2. My jacket. A Howies Helium Lightweight jacket. Unfortunately, I had ordered mine in the lightest colour I think it has ever been available in. Something that the pollution of Hebei and Inner Mongolia couldn't avoid spoiling. I had however bought a £20 (sale price) jacket that blocked the wind, weighed 1/30th of my laptop and quite possibly was the only thing stopping me catching pneumonia at night.

---

[66] Very, very open to sponsorship in the future.

[67] You know, the kind of people not accepting lifts because it's blowing a gale.

3. My gas cooker. An ALOCS gas camping stove. This piece of equipment was a revelation. Surprisingly economical – I left two gas canisters in Kashgar, because I couldn't fly them back – it cooked up at least 35 pot noodles, many coffees and once I realised my pot was non-stick, even scrambled eggs. It was about 1/16th the weight of my laptop.

4. My phone. An iPhone 5 – as if you care – which was on the very brink of death. Smartphones have changed the world. Everyone knows that, but for a journey like this, they really come into their own. But for the times when I was in the middle of nowhere (Qinghai) I always knew where I was, could stay in contact, listen to podcasts, find restaurants, book into hotels, translate words and phrases, take photos, videos and use it as a torch. They don't need any more praise, but they've changed everything. In the case of the kind of journey I was on, they've changed everything for the ~~better~~ easier. They also only weigh a few more grams than my jacket.

5. My panniers. A pair of red Ortlieb Back Roller City. Tough, only broken by my stupidity, and strong enough to carry many litres of water and 3.2kg of laptop.

6. My laptop. Have you ever seen Chinese State TV or tried reading a book? Boring!

10. THE FINAL FRONTIER

There are two good reasons that this book hasn't ventured into Chinese politics. The first and most important reason is that this a book about a journey on a bicycle, not a book about Chinese politics. The second is that I simply couldn't discuss politics with anybody, in any dialect, to a level that would have said anything that hasn't been said a million times before.

There are also two reasons why I didn't want to get into the specific politics of Xinjiang Uyghur Autonomous Region. One, I did not want to conflate a silly story about a silly man doing silly things in silly pants with serious issues. As rich and varied as the emotional swings of life are, it doesn't feel right to have the bombing of civilians and shooting of unarmed protestors sitting next to stories of crass festive underwear and the fictional murder of Jeremy Kyle. Two, there are a number of comprehensive books focused entirely on this subject, which are written by people who are qualified to author such things. So go and read many of them[68] and come to a fluid, informed and open-minded position, on something that is desperately complex and multi-layered.

When it comes to Xinjiang though, politics is depressingly unavoidable. What follows is my best effort to provide as little context as I can get away with, and I'm only going that far because at some point in the next two chapters a large group of heavily armed teenagers come running down a road at me.

Though it was the most marked example, it was not just the tooled up teens causing the change of atmosphere that singled

---

[68] There's many, more, but *The Tree That Bleeds* by Nick Holdstock and *The Emperor Far Away* by David Eimar are two of the less disheartening places to start, since they are humanising and entertaining enough to not cause the audience to entirely give up on humanity as they read.

Xinjiang out as different. The ever present SWAT teams at checkpoints before and after major towns; the barricading of petrol stations and government buildings; the huge police and army presence, complete with riot tanks and automatic weapons; all made for a different atmosphere to the rest of my journey.

***

In late September 2014, as my search for a bicycle began, two protests took place in China. One took place in Hong Kong. The other took place in Xinjiang. The Hong Kong protest dominated global news headlines. First hand reporting of the Xinjiang protest was exclusively the privilege of Chinese state media. The Xinjiang protest took place five days before the Hong Kong protests, yet they were first fully reported on the same day.

In Hong Kong, the world's media descended to watch as yellow umbrellas illuminated mostly young, disaffected faces. Faces that were angry about a wide spectrum of issues, which all coalesced around the proposed formalising of Beijing's control over candidates to run the special administrative region.

This of course, is still more of a choice than my own forefathers ever offered the people of Hong Kong during the colonial era. Would you, for example, rather choose your leader from a group of Beijing-approved candidates or be given a foreign politician who was only available because he had lost his seat in an election where people who were allowed to vote hadn't chosen him?

There were pockets of violence, some police were heavy handed, some protesters overstepped the mark, and there were even rumours of triads in the pay of the government acting as agent provocateurs. Overall, though, given the sheer numbers involved, the cost in terms of human pain and damage to property in Hong Kong was miraculously small. Some British weddings have ended in more devastation.

In Xinjiang, fifty people died and fifty-four were injured. Initial reports of the incident that took place in Luntai county, which had slipped out ahead of the full report suggested only two fatalities. Five days after they occurred, the events in Xinjiang were finally documented in the Chinese media as follows:

"The Xinjiang Uyghur autonomous region's information office released details on a terrorist attack on Sept 21 that killed 10 people, including two police officers and two assistant police, and injured 54.

Forty attackers[69] were shot dead by police or killed in suicide explosions, and two attackers were arrested in Luntai county, the Bayinguoleng Mongolia autonomous prefecture, the regional information office said on the night of Sept 25."[70]

How many explosions? How many died in the explosions? How many were shot by police? Look at the ratios too, when do more attackers die than innocent people in attacks, let alone at a ratio of nearly 4:1?

To cut to the chase, a protest like that which happened in Hong Kong would not have ended the same way if it had happened in Xinjiang. It certainly would not have happened in full view of the world's press as the protests in Hong Kong did[71].

Hong Kong is in the second of China's two systems of governance under the One Country, Two Systems policy. Meaning certain rights are available to citizens, which those living in

---

[69] To also note, originally they had been referred to as rioters, see http://www.nytimes.com/2014/09/26/world/asia/death-toll-in-xinjiang-violence-may-be-higher-than-reported.html?_r=0

[70] http://www.china.org.cn/china/2014-09-26/content_33618457.htm

[71] Though not in mainland China, where BBC World and CNN would have the cable pulled each time the story began, before miraculously returning afterwards.

mainland China do not enjoy. Xinjiang sits firmly within the first system. Yet even for China's first system, the level of control, both in terms of media restrictions and security activities, is exceptionally high.

Regardless of what you decide following the thorough research, which you're going to carry out on the rationale, cause, or complex combination of both cause and rationale for Xinjiang being under tight control, that there has been a significant number of violent incidents is not up for debate.

These incidents are the result of on-going tension between Uyghurs, the authorities, and Han people. This is not to say the violence hasn't impacted the many other minorities in the province or beyond, but it is the principle form of the province's troubles.

These security incidents can be broadly split, with all the caveats broadly splitting requires, into three categories. The first is planned and executed terrorist attacks. The second, like that which occurred in Luntai county is where protests end in violence. The third, which is sometimes a development of the second category, is inter-ethnic violence.

Just a few months before the Luntai protest in May 2014, four Uyghur terrorists blew up Han markets in Urumqi, killing 39 innocent people. Just as there have been many more incidents like the protest in Luntai where protestors are shot by security forces, the bombs in Urumqi were just the latest in a run of attacks by Uyghur terrorists on civilians.

For those of you who can't be bothered with the detail, what follows is an in no way comprehensive summary of the underlying issues. The causation for all variants of this violence has it roots in the transient history of the province. Xinjiang translates as New Frontier; a name it was given by the Qing dynasty in the 18th century in an episode that more than hints at the fact it hasn't always been part of the Middle Kingdom. This is something the CCP refute. Though just as this region hasn't always been part of China, neither has it always been a Uyghur territory. Not least because the term Uyghur has only been active in its current manner since the "1920s (after Stalin started a craze for ethnic labelling)"[72] but also because the original Uyghurs who arrived here some 1200 years ago were originally Mongol Buddhists. The arrival of the Turkic people that added to the genetic mix of the region and brought its Turkic-Islamic culture with which modern-day Uyghurs are associated, began around a century later.

The nub of the modern day issue is the cultural pressures and split in economic fortunes that recent large-scale Han migration has triggered in Xinjiang. In 1955, Uyghurs, constituted 73%[73] of the ethnically diverse population of Xinjiang, the province with a name that promises them autonomy. At the time of the last census in 2010, according to CCP figures they accounted for 43%[74] by which time 41% of the population was Han. It would not take a great leap of imagination to believe that at the time of my journey, after another half decade on the current trajectory, Uyghurs may no longer be the largest ethnic group in the Xinjiang Uyghur Autonomous Region.

The situation is exacerbated by the distribution of wealth between the two largest ethnic groupings. Using Xinjiang's greatest commercial benefit, natural resources, as an example: "just one percent of the workforce of the booming oil and natural gas industries, which account for over half of Xinjiang's GDP, are

---

[72] (Holdstock, 2011, p. 27)

[73] (Bovingdon, 2010)

[74] (National Bureau of Statistics of China, 2011)

Uighurs".[75] Employment opportunities for Uyghurs are further restricted by the world's largest employer, the CCP, requiring its employees to not practise any religion.

Beyond these huge challenges for social integration, international groups like Human Rights Watch[76] and Amnesty[77] also point out that there is significant evidence of disappearances and detention without trial of Uyghurs throughout the province.

Uyghur groups state that this lack of employment opportunities, uneven distribution of wealth, cultural and religious oppression, violent crackdowns and disappearances go beyond just the lack of autonomy the province's title promises and do so to the extent that they infringe upon fundamental rights. The CCP points to economic growth and development, which is pulling millions out of poverty and improving lives throughout the province as proof of the positive effect their policies have in Xinjiang.

This state of affairs has left Uyghurs angry, but disjointed, in response. Though only a tiny minority have turned to violence, it would be misleading to suggest that non-violent opposition to Han migration and CCP governance isn't widespread. In some of the more comprehensive books about this situation, words like "invaders"[78] are often quoted when describing the Uyghur view of CCP governance and Han migration.

This meets head on with the Party's position and challenges their most sacrosanct policy; the unity of China. There is no

---

[75] (Eimer, 2014)

[76] https://www.hrw.org/news/2009/10/21/china-detainees-disappeared-after-xinjiang-protests

[77] https://www.amnesty.org/en/press-releases/2010/07/china-new-testimonies-reinforce-call-xinjiang-riot-investigation/

[78] (Holdstock, 2011, p. 23) and (Eimer, 2014)

compromise on this matter. There is no other way. To question the Party, is to question China and that is unacceptable to the Party. The CCP views itself as the embodiment of China, therefore any criticism - international or domestic - of the Party's behaviour is taken by them as criticism of China. There is no disconnect between criticising a particular policy and criticising the Party and therefore China. They are one and the same. So any kind of separatist act or rhetoric, be that protest or bomb, is met with the heaviest punishment and greater control. To even suggest a different way to achieving peace between different communities to existing CCP policies can lead to a jail term.

At times, as with the restrictions placed on journalists or the presence of armed police, the control in Xinjiang is obvious. Yet it permeates far deeper, sometimes in mind-boggling ways; in the provincial capital's museum Han mummies and non-Han mummies, both of which have been discovered in Xinjiang, are displayed together for "fear of fuelling separatist currents"[79].

For the good of humanity's reputation, it is worth pointing out that even the largest estimates by either official outlets, Uyghur groups, or international sources of the total number of perpetrators from either side, in all three of these broad groupings of violence, represent only a tiny minority of people in the province. The vast majority of people, as they are elsewhere on earth, are peaceful.

In terms of violence, Xinjiang is certainly not Syria; but people are fighting along an ethnoreligious divide and people are dying. For the foreseeable future, Xinjiang will remain restive or troubled, depending on how you take your adjectives, and the CCP's response will always be control.

---

[79]   http://www.independent.co.uk/news/world/asia/a-meeting-of-civilisations-the-mystery-of-chinas-celtic-mummies-413638.html

There is more to Xinjiang than this, it is a stunningly beautiful part of the world, filled with far more warm and friendly people than dick heads. However, it was a different experience compared to the rest of my journey because of the heavy security presence and restricted reporting.

***

One thing everybody can agree on is that Xinjiang is massive. It is China's largest province. In pub quiz fodder, Xinjiang is the eighth largest country subdivision in the world (Sakha Republic in Russia is the largest since you ask). If it was an independent country Xinjiang would be the 18th largest country and that bastion of patronising comparators, the CIA World Fact Book, would have the opportunity to tell you it was approximately the size of Alaska; or six times as large as Wyoming; or 15 times larger than Kentucky; or something equally irrelevant to anything but the Pentagon's end of year quiz. Hypocritically speaking; Xinjiang is just over six times larger than the UK with a population only one-third of the size; or 80 times the size of Wales with a population seven times as large.

In planning the trip, I allocated the same number of days to Xinjiang as I had to the rest of my journey. 2000 of the 5000 kilometres I cycled would be in this one province. They would also be the kilometres with the least access to water, the highest temperatures, all on top of the prevailing head wind; a not exactly ideal combination that raises the question why I didn't make the journey in the opposite direction, from Kashgar to Beijing, thus having a tailwind and avoiding a desert in summer.

This is a question I do not have an answer to. I'm just an idiot who planned a route and stuck to it.

Some hand-freezing descending kicked off my first day in

Xinjiang before the increasing gradient and heavy wind turned the day into yet another festival of pushing and swearing.

Just by breaking up this monotony, lunch was a highlight. I had another fusion dish of Uyghur bread with Han noodles. The best pot noodle noodles too, the wavy ones. In the same inexplicable way crinkle cut chips taste better, so do wavy noodles.

Xinjiang and perhaps the shifting of seasons also marked a change in attitude to temperature. From here on in, the majority of truck drivers were topless. A look that was complimented by the region's fearsome commitment to soup strainer moustaches. This made most cabs look like a corner of Anfield's dressing room in the mid-eighties; where two or three nearly naked, moustachioed men would sit sweating in uncomfortably close quarters. I no longer expected to be asked if I was cold at petrol stations and roadsides. Instead, I imagined my pitiful facial hair would be quizzed.

The wind howled around the warm but barren landscape as the road levelled and I crossed a heat-hazed plateau. On the flat, the basics of Xinjiang's role in China's economy revealed and repetitively reinforced themselves. Empty oil tankers and used cars were heading in, full oil tankers were heading out, sheep were heading in both directions.

Eventually, the gradient raised to a sneaky 2-3%; an acute angle that always seemed to hurt more than its steeper cousins and their open and honest approach to pain.

After hours and hours of heaving the bike uphill, I eventually reached a 14km descent through the mountains. At the bottom was one of the infrequent truck stops that provide water to cool brakes and engines, either of which could be smoking from the exertions placed upon them by the gradient.

These establishments always – and I mean always - possess at least one angry dog. This one was no exception. Smug after successfully passing this particular establishment's dog at speed, another came and attacked from my blindside. I stuck resiliently to the plan to avoid killing a dog unless it was really necessary. I just made it to the next slight downhill out of the reach of its chomping mouth. The gradient provided enough assistance to leave the dog behind. Almost immediately after this sprint, and well aware that this effort had left my last match of the day carbonised and wilted in a crumbly charcoal mess, I resigned myself to the fact that the day's cycling was finished.

I noticed a small stream in the valley below and decided to trade the presence of midges for the opportunity to wash and locate two slow punctures using the stream water. I also swapped the heavily abused rear tyre for the less tortured front tyre. For the first and only time, I cleaned then lubricated the entire group set. It was borderline responsible maintenance.

To counteract these sensible actions, I set up camp below a perilously perched rock of skull crushing proportions. Something I noticed only as I flicked through my photographs later on.

My aim at the start of the day was to leave less than 100km to reach Ruoqiang, but seeing a 34km (thirty fucking four kilometres!!!) of descending sign within the first few pedal strokes indicated that the day was going to be a bit better than that. Headphones in, I flew through the spectacular scenery of rugged and jagged mountains. There really is nothing like going downhill on a bicycle. The winding bends and gradient here were perfect for staying off the brakes. To slow down, I could simply sit up and let the wind hit my chest to scrub off speed. I could stand, I could sit. I could attack, I could relax. I could go at 70kph, I could go at 25kph. I could pull over and take a photo, I could flick the Vs at guard dogs. I could scream "weeeeee" and "wooooo" until I was out of breath.

Out of the mountains, the fun continued as the wind was with me all day long for the first and final time of the entire trip. This was a great way to reunite with the Silk Road on its southern branch. 10km sections flew by in under 20 minutes. By Oreo o'clock I was reassessing the day's target and even decided I could afford a detour. I stopped at Milan, a farming community and home to two of the world's biggest football teams. It was formally a Silk Road trading town and has some ancient Buddhist temples and a fort, which Aurel Stein gave his special excavation treatment.

At the time it seemed as though the farms of Milan were related to the military, but I couldn't make sense of it. It bordered on looking collectivised too. I had places to be and so didn't dwell on it further. The explanation for its military appearance was revealed to me later in *The Emperor Far Away*. Milan was formally Xinjiang Production and Construction Corps' 36 Regiment Farm and began its existence as a forced labour camp[80]. The very next page made me glad I didn't dwell longer and end up staying nearby in the tent once more. "Milan was in the same country where China tested nuclear weapons until 1996."[81] A mountain of asbestos one day, followed by radiation the next; this was not Thomas Cook's best-selling holiday.

Back on the G315 and desperate for a hotel, I pushed on all the way to Ruoqiang. After going to one hotel that didn't admit foreigners, but who at least entertained me by saying it was a "stupid Beijing rule", I eventually made it to the excellent Loulan Hotel. Taking its name from the ancient city just north of present day Ruoqiang, it had all the usual helpfulness. The warm welcome even came with some conversation in English.

---

[80] Forced Labour Camps in China were reportedly eventually closed down in 2014.

[81] (Eimer, 2014)

In reaching Ruoqiang from the border I had cycled a personal best of 225km; the equivalent of cycling from Telford to London, which, incidentally, is probably the best thing you can do if you're from Telford and own a bicycle.

Other journeys of a similar length include: for fans of a good time - Dublin to Galway; for fans of Didcot Parkway - Bristol to Oxford to London; for people on Spring Break - Los Angeles to Tijuana; for EU workers wanting a filthy weekend away - Brussels to Amsterdam; and for residents of North London - It's like cycling around North London a lot, whilst refusing to acknowledge anywhere else exists.

The air in Ruoqiang was thick with the scent of kebabs being cooked over coals. There was little evidence of voluntary ethnic segregation between the different groups, which coloured much of my pre-ride research into the northern Silk Road's towns or the wider province's recent history. Yes, there was definitely a grouping of Han restaurants, but this was in view of the mosque and backed onto Uyghur establishments. These two areas were certainly not ethnically exclusive either.

It is also not unusual for similar establishments to sit next door to one another in China. In one of the most mind-boggling aspects of Chinese capitalism, shops often share a street with many others selling exactly the same product. My favourite of these is in Chengdu where a long line of expensive and shiny shop windows all advertise exactly the same array of safes. The situation in Xinjiang is complex, but if you were to give me four pints and a packet of Sichuan peppercorn flavoured peanuts, I'd have more chance of explaining it than rationalising how ten different shops all selling the same safes ended up thinking it was a good idea to be next door to one another.

Talking of beer, in Ruoqiang it was kept in fridges. Something which is often not the case elsewhere in China. That is to say, that elsewhere the beer is often in a fridge, but the fridge isn't turned on. With spicy kebabs, cold beer and a wonderful hotel room. It was not a hard decision to stay here for three days to recover from the exertions of Qinghai.

I was not the first to find this place a haven either. As I was back on the Silk Road, I had once again crossed paths with Marco Polo. As he pointed out "travellers who intend to cross the desert stay in this city for a week to refresh themselves and their animals."[82] Nearly eight hundred years later Ruoqiang was a place perfectly equipped for the restoration of human and beast alike.

To top it all, at 5am I was awoken by a sand storm rattling against my window. I would have been out in the tent experiencing that had the very same wind not dragged me along at such speed. I pulled the quilt up over my shoulders, which had been chilled by the air conditioning and rolled over wearing the smuggest of sleepy smirks.

Having arrived a day early and not endured any hotel moves it felt like I spent a really long time recuperating in Ruoqiang. Walking round the town in flip-flops and my remaining pair of trousers rolled up above my ankles, whilst smelling of sun cream, tingled my holiday senses. A visit to a museum containing bad taxidermy, the sounds of a language I can't speak and the omnipotence of plastic garden furniture ticked the final boxes – I was on holiday again.

Time itself became exotic, Beijing time was by now completely redundant and people operated two hours behind the official time. Going for breakfast at 9.40 made me one of only a dozen or so people out and about in the town centre.

The Loulan Museum was a reintroduction to the rich history of

---

[82] (Cliff, 2015)

the southern Silk Road. A place of traders and raiders; this is a land of explorers, disappearing towns and stolen artefacts. It sits in Ruoqiang's town square and with its Central Asian architecture, really stands out from the uniform boredom of the buildings surrounding it.

As I entered the stylish building, I asked for one ticket. The girl behind the desk gestured that it was free but came out from behind her desk to walk me over to the lockers immediately behind me. She watched as I put my bag inside and locked the door. She was just doing her job but the history of Xinjiang's archaeology is coloured by theft thanks to Stein and his peers. Theft by strangely dressed Europeans, possessing objectionable facial hair. Europeans like me.

The first European raider to pillage Loulan was not Stein or von Le Coq, but another of the devils. A Swedish devil in fact. As you would expect, he was called Sven, he was bespectacled[83] and he travelled internationally for work.

Sven Hedin was possibly the most interesting of the devils. He was certainly the most devilish by today's standards. Having previously supported Germany in the First World War, his strong nationalist views led him to become a supporter of the Nazis, with the caveat that he didn't particularly like the anti-Semitic elements, what with him being of Jewish descent and all. You'd have thought this would have put him off entirely, but apparently not.

Before he decided to back the losing team in both of history's biggest games and leave an indelible stain on his name by 20th-century Western values, Hedin set about turning his name into dirt in China.

---

[83] (Hopkirk, 1980)

Hedin's first exploration into the Taklamakan led to the deaths of all but two of his team from dehydration[84] and very nearly his own passing. This didn't put him off and he returned to try again almost immediately. It was, however, his third expedition that led him to discover Loulan.

The adventure – and again you should read Peter Hopkirk's book for the full glorious account – makes a mockery of plodding around on a mountain bike and moaning about pot noodles and the wind. The best part of this story is a mixture of coincidence, fortune and forgetfulness. The winter had stopped Hedin and crew short of their destination by freezing the river along which they were travelling. This prompted the ever resourceful Hedin to carry out some land-based exploration.

After nearly three weeks wandering around the desert, the group stumbled across some ancient buildings. After *collecting* some carvings and coins, the team began their return to where the frozen river had halted their journey. At one point Hedin, clearly not fancying any more deaths by dehydration, decided they should stop and dig for water. In doing so, the group noticed they had left a spade behind at the ancient buildings. The man guilty of this memory lapse was sent back for the spade but became disorientated. He returned without the spade, but with tales of beautiful wood carvings. Others were dispatched with him to retrieve them.

Though excited by the finds, Hedin decided against a full excavation of the site. Once more, water supplies were on his mind. Instead, they turned back and headed for Tibet as had been originally intended. Unfortunately for the museum in which I was stood, they faced many difficulties in Tibet and Hedin decided to

---

[84] (Hopkirk, 1980)

return to the serendipitous find.

Hedin's team had accidentally found Luolan, a former garrison town, which the Taklamakan had swallowed up over 1500 years previously. They found the very normal, orderly town, perfectly preserved by sand. It was also full of documents and artefacts for Hedin to take away.

Despite the fascinating back story of Loulan's recent history, by far the most interesting feature of the Loulan Museum was the Tarim mummies. These mummies are the very same group of mummies being displayed elsewhere in united harmony with their preserved Han comrades in Urumqi. The thing that struck me most about the first mummy I saw, with her flowing locks and high cheekbones, was not how likely she was to fuel separatist currents, but how much she looked like my friend Ian when he used to have long hair[85].

My second thought was to question whether they were real or not. That's the thing with three-thousand-year-old mummies, no matter how dry the desert, no matter how talented the embalmer, they all look like something from the pirate ship in the Goonies.

The vague consensus appears to be that the oldest mummies found in Xinjiang are of Indo-European origin. The most famous of all is the Loulan Beauty, who in the great Chinese tradition is in the provincial capital's museum instead of her local house of history. It is likely that the Tarim mummies originally came from Central Asia, probably modern day Iran but possibly further afield. There is even evidence they were even wearing tartan[86]. Though they hadn't come from as far as Scotland, one expert believes the

---

[85] He is still blessed with great cheekbones.

[86] (West, 2008)

cloth is similar enough to link them with Austria[87].

What with Genghis, the lost legion, the Gansu Mole and now the mummies; the journey was beginning to make me wish I'd studied genetics. There's just something fascinating about a group of Austrians, dressed as Celts, ending up in Xinjiang three and a half thousand years ago. What a stag party that must've been.

By the way, for completeness, they have also found "a mummy from the Lop Nur area, the 2,000-year-old Yingpan Man, [who] was unearthed with artefacts associated with an entirely different part of the globe. He was wearing a hemp death mask with gold foil and a red robe decorated with naked angelic figures and antelopes — all hallmarks of a Hellenistic civilisation."[88] Presumably he was on his way to Liqian to further complicate things there, but don't tell Tom.

With the final stretch ahead of me including another three days of desert dwelling, I spent the vast majority of my time in Ruoqiang piling on the fat and protein. By the end of my 48 hours of eating, I had consumed over 24 kebab skewers of lamb. If I was to sell the benefits of long distance cycling on a commission basis, I'd certainly open with "you can eat an average of one kebab every two hours".

The spice mix that is sprinkled over the kebabs in this part of the world is familiar, yet distinctive. Full of chilli, cumin and a mystery combination of other spices, its scent flavoured the hot dry air around the town. Helpfully it also made every cut of meat or offal taste delicious. This was particularly fortunate as my illiteracy provided for some unwelcome variations in my diet by enforcing five skewers of liver and two testicles upon my digestive system.

---

[87] (Barber, 1998)

[88] http://www.nytimes.com/2008/11/19/world/asia/19mummy.html?_r=3

I'm not sure I'd have been able to eat the liver or testes without the spices.

If I'd been a novelty in the smaller towns of Gansu, Ningxia and Inner Mongolia, my presence in Ruoqiang made me a downright alien. Skinny from a week of being a desert rat and mountain goat, my t-shirt hung loosely over my rolled up chinos that were now baggy in a clown like way, complete with feeble facial hair and flip-flops, I was just an eye-patch short of being the world's most misplaced pirate. Among Xinjiang's other pub quiz facts, it is also home to the Continental Pole of Inaccessibility; the piece of land furthest from any coast, which lies north of Urumqi near the Kazakh border.

Amongst the fun and relaxing that came with dressing up as a pirate, there was a first sign of just how on edge the authorities are in China's largest province. As I strolled around on my second evening, what appeared to be a minor situation outside the Han restaurants, was met with armed police, some of whom had their weapons drawn. Outside the establishment five police stood back to back in a star formation, two holding batons so long I'd call them staffs, two with their guns out in front of them, another just watching. The road was closed to traffic at both ends of the street, again by police with weapons held out in front of them by disturbingly rigid and ready hands.

Yet no one seemed bothered, people of all backgrounds chatted and watched the events unfold as if this was a perfectly reasonable response to a minor crime. The older men couldn't be drawn from their Mahjong game and across the road the teenagers continued with their game of pool, only following events when it wasn't their shot. It was all over in a few minutes but a green military riot tank still did a tour of the town afterwards, presumably for the sake of reminding everyone the town still had one.

Fully rested, once more into the desert I went. The grey and grim emptiness beyond Ruoqiang was as dull as the nuclear testing ground that had preceded it. After the blistering speed of my wind assisted entry to Ruoqiang, this felt like my real introduction to the Taklamakan Desert. Ominously Taklamakan means *"go in and you won't come out"*[89], which not only sounds like the invite a church would extend to gay teenagers but also the description of a desert you shouldn't visit.

The Taklamakan also received terrible reviews from the foreign devils. Sven Hedin "called it *'the worst and most dangerous desert in the world'*...Sir Percy Sykes, the geographer, and one-time British Consul-General at Kashgar, called it a *'Land of Death'*...his sister Ella described it as *'a very abomination of desolation'*."[90] Which could just well be my favourite description of anything, ever. So off into the very abomination of desolation I jolly well went.

The Taklamakan's desolate, lunar landscape's one charm was to serve as a great contrast to the handful of oases, which would occasionally enlighten it. Arriving at the small oasis town of Wushixia was like the moment in old Disney movies where the actors pass into a cartoon world. A burst of colour came with the sound of birdsong and sight of butterflies fluttering ahead of me. Mr Bluebird may as well have been on my shoulder.

I stopped for yet another kebab. Mistakenly believing I was going to an old lady's establishment, I ended up sat with Wushixia's answer to the Inbetweeners. The contents of my phone became a source of great interest to these boys. Despite the youngest, who was by some margin also the smartest,

---

[89] (Hopkirk, 1980)

[90] (Hopkirk, 1980)

reiterating the fact I was British, the conversation focused heavily on America. Did I have any dollars? Referring to the photos on my phone; is this America? (it was neighbouring Inner Mongolia), is this America? (it was Thailand) and whilst they briefly left me alone to eat, it sounded like their entire conversation was related to America. The only break in their persistent ignorance was to have a water fight.

Bored of their immaturity I left immediately after the last mouthful and headed out into much prettier golden dunes and heat haze laced roads. I pressed on to 160km before deciding to set up camp. I should, however, have pressed on until sunset. Mosquitoes were everywhere. This led to a horrible situation of me being forced into the tent to avoid them. As the sun was still hot this resulted in me sitting naked in the tent, sweating so profusely that I was sticking to the manmade fibres. Not an ideal situation at the best of times, but even worse when your specific goal is to stay hydrated.

By the time I awoke the following morning, I was incredibly dehydrated and still wet with sweat. This was not conventional preparation for cycling through the desert. I sweated even more as, dressed in trousers to minimise contact with the mosquitoes buzzing around me, I tried to leave the soft sand at speed. Unfortunately, soft sand is one of those surfaces where haste is required rather than speed. I stumbled around and scrambled over dunes, losing yet even more precious bodily fluid before I had even started cycling.

By now I had become spoilt by sand dunes and the sight of yet another small oasis arriving. In hindsight, it was an astonishing landscape to be amongst, but with the heat, the mental focus and cumulative exhaustion that was secretly creeping up on me, I just didn't take it all in. At the time I may as well have been back on the turbo trainer on a day when there wasn't enough internet juice in Beijing to stream a Scandinavian crime drama. I spent more time staring at the tarmac in a dehydrated daze than I did admiring the scenery.

As I approached Qarqan, I was awoken from the monotonous wonder by what seemed to be the winning entries for a school competition to design a propaganda poster. The entries were colourfully decorating the wall to my right-hand side. One depicted a group of Uyghur girls who were wearing colourful dresses berating others for wearing a burka, another seemed to show farmers attacking a terrorist with farm tools.

Dazed and bemused, minutes later I arrived at one of the more salubrious hotels of my trip. The town centre was bustling in the early evening and lovely to wander around aimlessly before I eventually returned to the first place that caught my eye to inhale a meal fit for a family of four.

Aware that another long stretch through nowhere in particular awaited me the following day. I spent the rest of my evening force feeding myself water, which had been flavoured by hops.

I was escorted from Qarqan by dragonflies, who darted around me as I moved through the last stretch of shaded road I would see for a long, long, long time. After a final water and caffeine stop I headed out into what the map promised would be 312km of uninterrupted emptiness. Marco Polo ominously described this stretch of his route as having "nothing worth recording".[91] The first few hours were very pleasant. The gentle headwind actually cooled me down and I made decent progress. The only delay was caused by road maintenance that I wasn't allowed to cycle around despite more than adequate space to do so. I hung about in the shade of the lorries that had also been forced to stop. I provided

---

[91] (Cliff, 2015)

large amounts of entertainment to the otherwise bored drivers just by being alone in the middle of the desert on a bicycle.

This was the only day I saw lorries that had crashed off the road. The fact I had got this far without seeing any others seemed a minor miracle. I guess a mixture of long straights and heat make this stretch of road particularly prone to accidents. The first crash scene was very sombre, with eight or so males crouched around the lorry in stunned silence. On this occasion, the usual chatty nature of Chinese people and the constant noise of the country as a whole amplified the hush surrounding them.

At the second crash site was just one man, presumably the driver, who was wearing an expression that said something stronger than "whoops" as he squatted in front of the overturned vehicle. It was a reminder to stay focused, despite the exhaustion within me and the monotony that lay ahead. It also highlighted why the first rule of wild camping in China is don't camp where someone could drive over your head.

In better news, later that same morning I saw my favourite kind of snake. One that's been mercilessly crushed by many tonnes of lorry.

In the heat of the day the temperature passed 35 and the gentle headwind began to blow only hot air over me. I persevered and made it to the 1000km to go mark, or 4000km completed (sort of, probably) mark but started to become paranoid that my remaining five litres of water wouldn't be enough for the evening and one more day's cycling.

It was the oddest of feelings. All day, not one person had pulled over to talk to me. This had been the only day that this had happened. It was the one and only time I felt alone. The rational thought that five litres of water would be enough to survive for several days was losing the battle with a mind melting through fatigue. Something primitive took over me and an anxiety began to grow. I entered a small village but everyone was still tending the fields. I stared at outdoor taps intended for agriculture but had enough remaining sanity to not to drink from them.

Fortunately, just as I was beginning to get really anxious, I arrived in a town that was not marked on either of my maps. After establishing it wasn't a mirage by touching a pot noodle tub, I purchased enough water to mean I would be leaving the next morning with a full five litres to last me the day, even after drinking another three before bed.

By the time I expertly erected the tent in record time, it was practically dark. I'd made it to just over half way across this stretch of nothing and managed to complete over 100 *miles* of cycling through a desert in late May. A genuine achievement on a journey of few real physical triumphs.

My effort to complete this dash across the desert in two days started well. I was on pace after 90 minutes, until a big, chunky 30kph headwind hit me. With that, my speed dropped dramatically and I took an early lunch to give the wind the opportunity to go away.

It didn't. Two further kilometres down the road I wobbled up to two drivers from Sichuan who were transporting trucks, which were exactly the same size as the vehicles that they were perched on top of, to Kashgar. They invited me to shelter in a location that would turn my mother's stomach but fed up of the wind I joined them in sitting under the overhanging truck to enjoy shade and protection from the wind. We chatted for ten minutes about the weather, the road and naturally whether I'd eaten yet. As the wind raged even harder and dust swirled into our eyes, I was invited to join them for the rest of the journey.

The first time I cheated, it was out of politeness. The second time, it was to avoid misery. The third time, it was because I was in serious trouble. This one was to save you the repetitive story of me pushing – note, not cycling - a bike into the wind for two days, whilst listening to old economics and football podcasts. It wasn't because I couldn't face more wind-related torture or that I'd rather sit in my Rudolph-The-Red-Bell-Ended-Reindeer boxer shorts in an air conditioned room drinking beer all afternoon. Nope, not at all.

Where they put my bike was the most impressive bit. Lifting it by hand onto the top truck, which was already on a truck. A bike on a truck on a truck.

In the cab, I had my longest and fullest discussion in Chinese yet. Selected highlights included: Britain doesn't have deserts and it is much smaller than Xinjiang; Britain does have a lot of sheep.

It took around an hour and a half to cover the 100km to Niya, my intended stopover town. Despite the wind, the weight of the load, and the need for the driver to locate a new cigarette before the previous one ran out, our progress was swift.

This was a first opportunity to take the scenery in at leisure and speed. The marked increase in pace made the view far less monotonous and the windows made the sandstorm swirling and snaking towards us mesmerising rather than demoralising.

As the hypnotic movement of the sand and comfort of the cab's huge seats lulled me to sleep, the driver invited me to use the bunk in the back of his cab. I declined but he insisted I take a look. I didn't need to look. If I learnt one thing from five years at scouts, it's that you don't get into another man's sleeping bag. Ever. Least of all the sleeping bag of a man who has been out on the road for five days. He offered again, but there was no way I was getting into what was little more than a giant wanking sock.

After some minor paperwork infringements were sorted out at the police checkpoint we arrived in Niya. I bid them farewell and handed over my only remaining UK money as a token of my appreciation. Like many people I've met on this trip my driver was especially keen to get his hands on some foreign currency. I didn't tell him what it was worth but I hope he Baidus[92] £20 before he starts lighting his cigarettes with it.

The first hotel I found had the useful signage "Hotel for Overseas Visitors" on the front door. Inside was dark, dingy and dirty. My second-floor room came with two thick lengths of rope in case of a fire or a desire to leave this realm via the wardrobe door labelled *death by misadventure* came over me. Feeling shattered despite the lift, I decided against accidentally ending it all in a manner befitting a backbench MP.

I also wasn't in the mood to socialise that afternoon. I had no interest in being the town's novelty visitor for any longer than absolutely necessary. Instead, I opted to get some beer, naan, and noodles to consume in peace, whilst semi-naked and air-conditioned.

On my shopping spree, I was fortunate to be reminded of Sinkiang Beer, a black beer that must be the most Heavy Metal looking beer in the world. It's black, it's got a big, bold, sharp font with red trim and it's got sin in its name.

Only fifteen minutes after leaving my room, I had already returned, stripped down to the point where my modesty was entirely dependent on a cartoon reindeer and started swigging from a bottle of cold Sinkiang. This was much more my level of misadventure.

Having effectively spent the last few days sanding my throat, I awoke on my first morning in Niya needing to (put your lunch down) dispatch a monstrous load of bloody phlegm. Who knows how much worse it would have been without the aid of my Sichuanese friends and their trucks less than 24 hours before. If

---

[92] One of China's newest verbs, meaning Googles.

there's one place you can't stymie bleeding, it's on the inside.

To medicate, I slept, moisturised and extensively researched which New York bar made the best Dirty Martinis[93] and which restaurant would be the furthest removed from eating a pot noodle[94]. Salivating at the prospect of the following month's money bonfire, I went out for 80p noodles. I returned to fix a puncture, whilst listening to Mogwai so that you'll think I'm cool. Realising Mogwai was probably not enough, I removed the Frodo Gallagher ear covers too.

By mid-afternoon, I felt significantly better and all traces of blood had cleared from my throat. I decided not to waste the whole day and headed out into the town centre. Niya occasionally felt like another world. More so than some of the places even further west in Xinjiang. Ruoqiang had indeed felt like an exotic part of China but sometimes Niya looked like stock footage of a town in peacetime Afghanistan. The town was full of ageing red motorbikes, all Uyghur men were wearing the doppa, the box-shaped Uyghur skull cap, and the women were dressed in vibrant dresses and headscarves.

The colours of China had changed too. There was less intensity but more variety. It seems implausible that anywhere could be more colourful than the neon glow of eastern China, but somehow the attire of southern Xinjiang managed it with the fashion for varied patterns of every conceivable colour combination in the apparel of Uyghur women and the coloured doppas with their intrinsically detailed patterns for men. Things really had started to feel, look, smell and sound like Central Asia with Chinese characteristics and not the inverse of that balance.

---

[93] The Jane Hotel

[94] Eleven Madison Square

10.1 How to Wild Camp in China

Buy tent. Pitch tent. Camp.

Oh, you want to know more. Is it legal? I told plenty of police officers I intended to camp and not one of them cared. That said, if I had camped outside a military barracks in Xinjiang allow me to suggest that nonchalance would not have been officialdom's reaction. Just be sensible about the wider implications of your location.

Assuming you're not an idiot and avoid places that will obviously bring you trouble, then an almighty chunk of beautiful landscape awaits you.

The most important question to ask yourself is this: *can somebody drive over my head if I sleep here?* For once, I'm not patronising you. I'm not talking about parking next to the roadside. In China, especially rural areas, people drive off road with free abandon. Ironically the least safe place to park is next to a speed camera, as people go off-road to drive around them. Obviously, it's a good idea to not park where there are already tracks. The best locations are mounds or ditches significant enough to stop a Toyota 4x4. Should you be forced to stay out in the open, I would recommend leaving one reflective item like a pannier or bicycle covering each side of the tent, with the bike covering the most vulnerable point.

Next down your list of priorities for safety and security is this: *will anything here try and eat me?* This is your time to come over all Ray Mears and inspect the ground for paw prints and piles of shit, the size of each will inform your decision.

Blurring the lines between security and comfort is your visibility. Ideally, you won't be visible at all. The best locations are hidden from view; either in a trench, of which there are surprisingly vast quantities in China; or behind a mound of some sort. If you have no option but to be visible, try and pitch up on a slight slope that will put off the most inquisitive of Chinese lorry drivers from either having to apply their brakes or attempt a hill start.

Safe from predators, inquisitive passers-by and people driving over your head, it's time to think about comfort.

Your number one enemy is the wind. This is the secondary benefit of finding a mound or trench to pitch behind or in. Stopping an hour earlier than you intended because you found such a location is well worth the additional sleep you will gain. Sadly, this will not always be an option, nor necessarily protection enough. If this is the case, all I can advise is to weigh down the corners of your tent externally and internally, put some headphones in, and hold on.

11. THE EYE OF THE STORM

Xinjiang sits north of the Himalayas and alongside the almost equally ginormous mountains of central Asia. Coupled with the mountain ranges within China's borders, the Kunlun, Tian Shan and Altais; these deep layers of peaks frame the Taklamakan Desert in an elliptical form. With the addition of the vast Tibetan plateau and Mongolian desert beyond the mountains, the geographical relief of Western Xinjiang looks just like the eye of a storm.

Which is an elaborate, if hyperbolic, metaphor for the province. In Ruoqiang there'd been a hint of the tension that pervades the region. The level of extra control exerted by officialdom had been obvious since the provincial border but, on the whole, things had felt cheery, relaxed and not like a part of the world that was on the edge.

For my last stint, though, as I rode oblivious through lack of research and restricted reporting, there was another noticeable change in atmosphere. In a disconcertingly rhythmic way my days would yo-yo between tense towns and relaxed towns; but regardless of the atmosphere, I perceived individual towns to have, one thing remained consistent - control.

Metaphorical eye of the storm or not, the second half of my journey through Xinjiang began in the eye of an actual storm. The sound of rain against the hotel room's window did not inspire a prompt exit, but after yet another naan for breakfast, I was soon trudging through grim rain and oily puddles. The only early cheer came from a man on a motorbike who rode alongside me to ask if I knew it was raining. I shouted over the noise of the pouring rain hitting our respective rain coats to advise him that I was indeed aware of the precipitation.

Sodden, I spent an irritating amount of time at a police checkpoint with a not-exactly-elite group of local policemen. As they bumped around trying to look at my passport, automatic weapons slung over their shoulders in a care-free manner, I stood there soaking wet trying to ask what I needed to clarify in order to leave. It is amazing how quickly you can become accustomed to guns in the hands of strangers.

As it turned out, there was no problem, only delight at the word 'Ireland' on my passport. Not because of any historic parallels between here and Northern Ireland, but because they thought it meant I was Irish, which apparently was very exciting. Even here, inside a shed in the least populated bit of the middle of nowhere, everybody loves the Irish.

Here's a low brow dinner party question for you to ask after pudding, what's the biggest road kill you've ever seen? Shortly after I saw my first wild Bactrian camels plodding around the Taklamakan Desert, I saw my first camel road kill. Then I saw my second, then the third and within fifteen minutes I'd seen a fourth. It's hard to fathom how you don't see a camel coming, but I suppose as herd animals who can weigh up to a tonne and run at 40kph, avoidance is a real challenge for a lorry driver on a deadline.

By now I had acclimatised to the stench of decomposing dogs and even the pungent reek of hundreds of rotting sheep, who had not survived the journey to the slaughterhouse, hadn't stopped me eating my body weight in lamb over the last week. The smell of a camel carcass though, is quite something else. The putrid stench brought me to the very brink of re-examining the morning's naan on the side of the road. I can't even begin to describe the odour; it is like nothing to have wafted up my nasal passage before, despite the aforementioned five years of attending scouts.

Once I was clear of the desire to vomit, I stopped for more naan and water. In Xinjiang, when I was out of reach of the kebabs and coals, more often than not I was riding pane e acqua. It was marginally better than noodle e acqua, but as useless for providing adequate nutrition.

With only 20km to go and heavy rain again on the horizon, I put a little air in the back tyre, only to notice the front was totally flat. One of the unique features of having all of my weight over the back was that the front wheel barely touched the floor, often making me oblivious to punctures that were right under my nose. The first spits of rain hit me as I swapped the inner tube for a fresh one. Within two kilometres the tyre was flat again, meaning there must have been something inside the tyre causing the flats. I pulled up again as the torrential rain, as welcome as an invitation to a barn dance, highlighted the key difference between my jacket being shower resistant and water proof.

As the rain bounced off the concrete around me it was impossible to find what was causing the puncture. Before I could choose between trying another inner tube or walking, a police car pulled up alongside me.

You know the formula by now; I wasn't looking to cheat but sometimes, in horrendous situations, I received offers that were too good to turn down. Remember this wasn't for charity or any great sense of personal achievement, I was just a twat on a bike[95]. A twat, who on this occasion, was very bored of being soaking, sopping, sodding wet.

With half the bike hanging out the back of the boot and me desperately trying not to soak the Uyghur policeman I was now

---

[95] At the time of going to press I am still the top result for "twat on a bike China" on Google. Those of a sensitive disposition, should be cautious if searching for this phrase. Those of you keen to see a pedal-powered sex toy being used are in for a treat.

squashed up against with my sodden clothes, we chatted away with some variations on *the conversation*.

The best variation was them saying I looked much better in a photo on my phone than I did there and then. Four years and marathon bike rides will do that for you officer. It was all good natured though and they even took me all the way to my hotel, which was an unexpected bonus.

My destination of Keriya was a mishmash of a town. The poverty in certain places was evident. The tension here, as it often seems only tension can be, was palpable. Whilst on my way to look at the city's mosque a young Han policeman did the now routine 'wow it's a foreigner' double take before smiling, starting to wave, only to suddenly remember where he was and who he was. Without moving his eyes off me, he rapidly moved his hand back to his gun and his finger straight to the trigger. A movement so hasty and precise that it had my flip-flops twitching with a readiness to fail at running away.

I learnt later that there had been an incident during the previous month where six people died in a security operation in a village within the wider Keriya County. Perhaps this was why the town had quite so much weaponry on show. The one bit of violence I did see was heartening, though. A mixed group of boys at that dreadful age just before they're distracted by sexual desire, were having a scuffle in the street. Pleasingly, the fight was not along ethnic lines but was instead over a football. Where football matters most, there's always hope.

At some point in the afternoon, Apple unilaterally updated my phone to what it calls Kashgar time without forewarning me. Causing much confusion as I sat down for some dreadful cold noodles and tripe at what I thought was 15.30 not 13.30.

With two hours to have a second crack at, I did what any intrepid adventurer would do and went to buy a beer. In the shop,

I was taught some Uyghur words, which was really useful given I only previously knew naan and kewab. But, and this is one of the bigger buts you'll happen upon, when my new tutor heard I was British, he performed a perfect Nazi salute and shouted: "Heil Hitler" at me.

Utterly stunned for a moment, I then panicked. In a mutual second language I did my best to say something like "no, that's Germany". Then panicked again and spouted "but not Germany now, Germany is really good now" before taking a breath and clarifying "well, unless you're Greek".

In the early evening, I wandered to the statue of Mao and Kurban Tulum, which apparently is the only statue of Mao with someone else, other than the larger version of the same effigy in Hotan, 170km down the road. The statue celebrates the effort Kurban Tulum, an elderly Uyghur farmer, made in travelling 1500km from Keriya to Urumqi by donkey to present Mao with one melon to thank him for ridding Xinjiang of the Nationalists and other selected baddies.

I followed this propaganda friendly history lesson with my best kebabs yet, alongside my now staple veggie house noodles (with beef obviously) and cardamom tea. I didn't order the cardamom tea, but China, and drinking six or seven litres of plain water a day, was turning me into a real tea ponce. Anything was preferable to plain old water.

Back at the hotel I finally found the tiny fragment that had punctured my front wheel after 30 minutes of searching. I celebrated by fixing the equally tiny hole it had caused and felt fortunate for accepting the ride with the police, as I would have never found something so small in the torrential rain earlier. It would have been an incredibly long walk amongst the camel carcasses without my latest dalliance with motors.

Before bed, I learned from Marco that should a married man

from Keriya leave on a journey of 20 days or more, then his wife can "take another husband immediately"[96]. As with the lost year in Zhangye, Marco doesn't expand on this nugget of information, or how he came to learn it. Suspiciously, he instantaneously protests a bit too much by advising us - as if we'd doubt him - that "she is perfectly within her rights to do this"[97]. No comment is made on the length of Marco's stay in Keriya, but I'd bet the house on him seeing at least 19 sunsets.

With the first rain of the season over, I left to enjoy one of my finest days of the whole trip. It was just about the perfect day for cycling. Sunshine, a gentle breeze, lush green farmland, huge mountains in the distance, wide-eyed toddlers shyly handing back change for refrigerated drinks, the many and varied colours of wild flowers by the roadside, the omnipotent smell of grilled meat, bunny rabbits, though not grilled bunny rabbits. Even the day's single puncture came in the form of a vibrant, bright pink, drawing pin.

As I arrived in Qira it felt as though I'd crossed yet another border. Though the government buildings and petrol stations were still barricaded in a manner they aren't in most other provinces, the police and military presence seemed comparatively non-existent to Keriya. Automatic weapons had really brought the mood down there. Here I didn't see a single gun outside a holster.

Adding to my joy was the location of my hotel. It was above a snooker hall. Here, in the middle of Xinjiang, I had to walk passed images of Stephen Hendry, John Higgins and others to enter the hotel. The world of snooker is tiny; just Britain, China and Tony Drago.

---

[96] (Cliff, 2015)

[97] (Cliff, 2015)

I resurrected my pirate fancy dress and went out into the happy, buzzy centre of town. I was given a garlic bulb for free due to its complete lack of value as a single unit, which allowed me to create garlic naan for dinner. My world was a very happy place as I fell asleep to the combined stench of garlic and cheap cigarettes, which were wafting up from the snooker tables one floor below.

Having decided to take the harder, shorter route to Hotan I waved goodbye to Ken Doherty and friends and headed west through what presumably counts as Qira's suburbs. Quaint farms and small holdings foreshadowed the appearance of orchards, where huge trees provided a shade that wasn't required at such an early hour. After about 15km I was back in the desert. This time I got to see some live camels up close. A mother and calf were on one side of the road and another, particularly stupid looking, camel was on the other. Seeing his gormless expression made it much easier to imagine how they are such prevalent road kill fodder.

After the tedium of another small town police checkpoint, where I'm sure the opportunity to look at a different passport was the main appeal of pulling me over, I passed through more beautiful military farmland under the now much-appreciated shade of the trees lining the road.

From the town of Lop onwards the roads became much busier. I love the modifications made to tuk-tuks in this part of the world. With carpeted and tasselled roofs covering the back, some of the more extravagantly modified vehicles looked like mobile harems. Making the latter part of the day's journey all the more enjoyable as I zig-zagged amongst these opulent machines in the slow lane between Lop and Hotan.

The run into Hotan centre was lined with Chinese flags on every lamppost, just in case anyone dared to forget where they were, which was very easy to do. By now I was now much closer to

Islamabad, Kabul, and Tehran than Beijing. I was even slightly closer to Baghdad.

I arrived to find I was staying at a hotel that had black Range Rovers with personalised license plates (as much as you can with numbers – lots of eights) parked outside. This was good news in terms of pillow quality, but terrible news for the welcome a filthy cyclist would receive. For the first and only time during the trip, the status of my vehicle relegated me to parking it by the bins.

As part of this pretension and in a nod to this being a region with significant concerns about security, there was also a scanner and body search to pass through in the hotel reception. This sounds obtrusive but the security processes of China are often laughable[98]. I walked in, declared I had a knife, got my knife out and continued to hold it out in the open. As I waved the knife around, the guard's detector beeped as it passed over each of my bags. He looked inside none of my them, and only briefly paused to look at my knife with the disinterest of Crocodile Dundee's more relaxed Chinese cousin.

I know there's an element of profiling to even the most pathetic security checks and a weird European on a bicycle is not, at present, the greatest concern in Hotan, but he could have at least taken the knife from me. If only to stop me waving it around and laughing manically as he pretended to search me.

That said, I once found myself in the same Doha hotel where all the many and various Syrian rebel groups, which Qatar was funding at the start of the apocalypse, had gathered. Despite a far more thorough security check and frisk at the entrance than the one I received in Hotan, inside the hotel people were wandering around with their janbiya daggers and, in some cases, even

---

[98] A few months later I was not the slightest bit surprised when somebody managed to take the equipment required to set fire to a plane on board a domestic flight.

swords on display.

In case you hadn't noticed, the world is absolutely bananas.

On the morning of my rest day in Hotan, I went for a cycle around the city. One of the very few times I could be tempted to cycle on my day off. I visited the disappointing museum, which took the security of artefacts to a new level by making visitors lock their belongings up outside.

I then enjoyed the fantastic chaos of Friday prayers around the Juma Mosque and adjacent bazaars. An imposing building surrounded by full, thronging streets. The area was alive in a way only the social moment of the week can deliver. With the road too busy for cars and the noise of a hundred conversations drowning out the wider city, I briefly existed in a time that could have been any point in the last six or seven hundred years. Had I not been looking at my phone for directions to a restaurant.

Eventually I decided against the original eatery I was searching for and instead followed my nose to a small family run restaurant. With the plastic green door curtain filtering the smoky sunlight, the dining room took on a strange lime tinge. At one point, as I waited for my kebabs and sipped pomegranate juice, a row erupted outside. Everyone but the young waitresses and their smallest brother piled outside to spectate as the father shunned a disappointed customer. An act that all played out for me in hazy green silhouettes.

For a digestif I sampled some local pomegranate wine, which was surprisingly tasty. Yet as rewarding as the flavour was, it was nothing on the label's blurb. *"Hotan Pomegranate Wine, like a shining ruby, sparkling with brilliant gloss. Smell the unequal incense, taste the equably mellowness. Made of rare fruit from the southern part of the Taklamakan Desert. High quality raw pomegranate brown with fine grapes and wild roses. Specially designed for successful person, taste the feelings of paradise."* Like any successful person who has drunk a bottle of wine on a weekday lunchtime I drifted off to sleep for a couple of hours.

I awoke with the taste of paradise repeating on me. For my evening meal, I took the short journey across the road to the Han market, whose ethnicity was denoted by a riot tank book-ending each end of it. Each vehicle had two armed soldiers stood on top. I strolled down the middle of the road that the stalls sat astride. Every bit as alive as the bazaars around the mosque, no one paid attention to the gunmen at either end as they shopped.

It felt heavy handed, but Han markets have been attacked elsewhere in Xinjiang. Secure or not, nothing particularly tempted me in the market and I ended up in a Sichuan noodle restaurant round the corner. I entertained the staff and other patrons alike by just asking for the biggest, spiciest, and what probably doesn't translate as meatiest, dish.

After the torment of a record breaking 28 minute check out, I headed north on a road linking attractive villages that will no doubt become the miserable suburbs of an expanded Hotan in the near future. Today though, the villages were full of lush green vegetation and visibly high-yielding small holdings. Colourful bunting flickered in the wind above ornate kebab grills, which stood proud and bronzed in the early summer sun.

In the last of these villages, on the edge of the next stretch of desert, I stopped to pick up a naan for my evening meal and another for breakfast the following morning. As I progressed west it felt like China became more reserved, even shy at times. At the naan oven I met the exception to prove this rule. I was enthusiastically waved over by a man of about my age, who was stood in front of an array of naans as magnificent as his moustache. The naans were piled high behind an upright model of each variant he sold. As he didn't have change, he insisted on giving me an extra naan, despite my protestations that I was happy with two spring onion naans for 50p.

As we chatted I noticed that my honesty test had been failed by Hotan. Throughout the trip, I had left my watch (value £2) on my handlebar. The place it was finally stolen was outside a Public Security Bureau building, only a couple of hundred metres from the riot tanks outside the Han market, and under the gaze of the ~~best~~ most expensive hotel in town's security. Shame on you Hotan.

Out of the oasis and back into the desert once more. I initially made good progress, until your friend and mine Mr Sandstorm arrived. It was a finer grain than its Qinghai or Gansu sisters, which made it less painful to pass through with a quickly fashioned head scarf.

I decided that I had been too much of a sham of late with accepting lifts and got stuck into some outright misery. I put the music on shuffle and told the storm to do its worst. There were as many moments of spine-tingling goodness as there were moments of misguided selections. Des Lynam reading If by Rudyard Kipling followed by Super Trooper by Abba probably summed up that shift best.

Then, as if I was starring in a biopic of my life, You'll Never Walk Alone Came on as the end of the storm was celebrated with a blue circle opening up in the sky. Then it closed in again.

As the wind resurfaced and the surface returned to being part of the wind, I expertly found a hole to hide in for the night and took shelter from the howling winds above. Once I was set up, I shuffled around my tent in order to make a garlic oil dip, the spilling of which would go on to give my mobile home the smell of a mothballed Pizza Express for the remainder of the trip.

I'll also admit to carrying out some old person signal hunting with my mobile, but it worked! Somehow, in a two-man tent, I had black spots and hotspots.

The day started ominously with suicidal lizards who kept jumping in front of my front wheel. It's a miracle I only killed one. They would scurry up to the edge of the road amongst the stray cotton plants, before using their elastic legs to propel themselves into my path like horizontal lemmings. Idiots.

I passed some roadkill watermelons that had been left by an upended truck and were starting to ferment in the desert heat. Seeing something smelly and pink cooking in the sun reminded me that it was time to start working on my tan. Off came the revoltingly dirty shirt and out came the bright white torso. This semi-nudity immediately earned me an iced coffee from one passing driver and a terrifying stare of sexual intent from another.

With my shirt back on, I stopped for a refreshment in a small village and admired the continuing force of Red Bull's marketing domination. In China, their red and gold label is an immediate winner, but bugger me, when will all other brands realise that free merchandise is embraced in China in a way it is in no other country. Want to get your brand awareness up in China? Send people some free, preferably red, merchandise to decorate their shop with.

At 2pm I faced a choice, press on into the brewing sandstorm for another 77km or stop in a place I'd been calling Piss Mountain since I'd first seen its name on a sign in Hotan. Pishan actually translates as something like skin mountain or leather mountain, but with my poor reading ability and childish mind Pi Mountain easily became Pee Mountain and then naturally Piss Mountain.

The first sign that turning into Pishan was probably the wrong choice was the sight of a concrete gun turret on top of a police station. The turret was so new it hadn't even been painted blue and white yet. In fact, the untidy drips gave the impression that it had been built that very morning and the concrete had yet to set.

Then, when I was only 200m from my hotel, a police motorcycle pulled up and stopped side on in front of me, blocking my path. Another pulled alongside me, penning me in against the kerb. The two heavily armed SWAT officers then dismounted, removing all remaining personal space. Piss Mountain clearly wasn't Disneyland.

I hurriedly removed my sunglasses and hat to reveal my 'please don't hurt me, my country has a huge trade deficit with yours' features. Again the SWAT police were firm but professional. They asked me to ride back down the road with them until we were outside the Public Security Bureau station. Here they went through my various bits of documentation and the many hundreds of dull photos on my camera, which seemed to convince them I was not a spy, or worse, a journalist. At least they could be certain I was not a photographer.

All was going well until a child of about eight, started to grab the end of one of the police officer's guns. Remembering that this is a part of China where the police can shoot first and the journalists report five days later, all of the Jason Bourne thoughts ran through my head. You know, the quick hand movements to take a gun off the other officer whilst simultaneously taking him hostage. Basically, all the things you wouldn't do if a shot did get fired because you'd be too busy wondering if your cycling shorts were still tight enough to hold the vast quantities of shat you had just unwittingly released into them.

Fortunately, the officers remained calm and waved the boy's father over to drag him away. I was handed my camera and ID back and sent on to the hotel. At the hotel, I spoke to the police on the phone and then again 30 seconds later when they turned up in person. Initially, this went less successfully as I didn't know the Mandarin name of the place where I was going next. Fortunately, two Uyghurs who were also in the reception translated my next location for me and the police eventually seemed satisfied; once again most of this satisfaction was thanks to my intention to leave at first light on the next day.

There was a final insult to Pishan when the hotel insisted I keep my bike in the room as it apparently wasn't safe to leave it locked up outside. This felt like a boundary had been crossed. The evenings were our own time, a little bit of space from one another. It felt even less appropriate that the only time the bike and I shared a room was under the gaze of a topless woman in a low-quality painting, which hung above the bed.

Once the bike and I had finished smirking at each other about the third wheel on the wall, I checked the internet to see what Pishan's atmosphere was all about. It was revealed that I had accidentally gone on holiday to the centre of terrorist training in Xinjiang[99]. Furthermore, I had done so almost exactly a year to the day after four residents of Pishan committed one of China's worst terrorist atrocities by carrying out the aforementioned bombing of markets in Urumqi.

With the sandstorm - at least I avoided that - raging outside, I popped into the adjacent corner shop, the windows of which were blanked out to hide the alcohol it stocked from the street.

I made my purchases and with Sinkiang beers clinking and sunflower seeds rustling, I strolled back into the room and looked forward to the sun rising.

The doorbell must have already rung once before I awoke because I felt vaguely conscious when I heard it for what must have been the second time. It was 3.15am. Was I about to be kidnapped or worse, made to move hotels? I tip-toed over to the door, against which I had earlier jammed a chair under the handle to improvise a lock as the actual one was broken. I timidly looked

---

[99] http://www.chinadaily.com.cn/china/2014-07/03/content_17639343.htm

through the peep hole but saw no one. I placed my right hand on the door and paused.

In a previous life, I had been on a civil service training course to learn how to be kidnapped effectively. This was ahead of a work trip to post-Sadam, pre-them lot Iraq for a week. Most of the course was common sense, but there were nuggets of advice that have stuck with me. One such piece of good advice was to have a bag of things ready to go in case you need to leave somewhere in a hurry. I had adapted this advice to have a bag of all my important things I would need if the police made me leave in a hurry (trousers top of that pile – no more Christmas boxer short exhibitions for the boys in blue) and a pile of potential weaponry if I was to be kidnapped. Cynics may say the latter pile was actually just the contents of the bin but, delivered accurately and forcefully, three empty bottles of Sinkiang beer could take out three kidnappers.

After thirty seconds there was shouting, it wasn't in Mandarin and there wasn't an overwhelming amount of blue clothing on show, which all but ruled out the police.

Then one of the blurry bodies smashed into my door. He smashed into it shoulder first, which tested my improvised security engineering to the full. The chair rocked back gently and fell pathetically to the floor.

I picked up the chair, stood side on, and prepared to play an orthodox pull shot - you don't switch-hit an intruder - but suddenly there was more shouting and a scuffle in the corridor; through the smears of the dirty keyhole I watched as a second man grabbed the first by his shirt and dragged him away. Moments later, the slam of a door further down the corridor indicated he had been successfully assisted back to his own room.

Despite this commotion, I returned to bed and slept soundly until 6.45 by which time I'd easily had enough of Pishan. I left early enough to miss any police checks, but not so early as to miss fifty or so heavily-armed teenagers running up the road towards me. With numbers on their chests, over their PLA uniforms, it had the appearance of a fun run as the young men chased after the lead runner who was carrying a huge Chinese flag. With their beaming young smiles hurrying after the flag, the front end of this odd scene also looked like a school re-enactment of a red army charge. Their guns were so clean and new that they looked like props. In fact, the combination of their youth and spotless weaponry meant that I wasn't alarmed at first.

This relaxed state of mind shifted quickly once my line of sight travelled beyond their camouflage to the tank and three other military vehicles following after them. As they headed along the main road, passed me, and on into the centre of town, it took a while to process what I had seen.

At the huge police checkpoint just outside of town, the serious police were serious and the silly police were silly. One dipshit tried to push his silly police colleague into me as I entered the building. I stepped around him and made eye contact with the despairing serious police officer who was sat behind the registration desk. I couldn't help thinking that the serious police must hate every minute they spend with the silly police.

Once more I headed straight into a sandstorm. After spurning the offer of a lift only 500m beyond the checkpoint, for two hours I battled through 15km of sandstorm of it before another car pulled up alongside me. A woman in her twenties with a beehive hairdo so tall it looked as though it might actually contain honey, stepped out of the passenger side and into the storm to offer me a lift. With time finally on my side I was happy to take this sandstorm on the chin, especially since the chin and much of the rest of my face was covered with a scarf, so I politely declined. However, Amy Winehouse's Uyghur sister gave me a look that said "look love, I've got my magnificently coiffured hair full of sand from offering you a lift, now you and my husband dismantle your stuff and get in the car". As if secondary to the look I was being given, this demand was then verbalised without reference to her hair style. Once inside the sand-free car, I was consistently fed sunflower seeds and asked friendly questions about my nationality, love life and favourite Chinese food. This was my kind of kidnapping.

At the checkpoint just outside my destination of Kargilik, another small band of PLA youngsters were demonstrating their prowess in taking a man down and pinning him to the floor face first. No point in doing that at their barracks I suppose, just put the mats by the side of the road, in the one place where every car has to stop and make the most of the fresh air.

Despite this threatening introduction, Kargilik felt like another planet from Pishan. Once we were beyond the checkpoint with the scenery passing at car speed, Turkic pop blasting out of the radio, and the husband tormenting his wife in a playful way, it all began to feel like I was starring in one of those indie films you watch on a Saturday night in January, with a bottle of wine, whilst you're not drinking, because it's not really drinking if it's a bottle of wine with an indie film on a Saturday. Sorry. What? Yup. Anyway. It felt exotic, yet warming.

As I rebuilt the bike in the town centre, I glanced up to see a town vibrant with energy and chatter; peace and prosperity always were friends with benefits. There was row after row of bunting, people holding hands and a sort of loved up feel to the place, similar to the evident happiness in the front of the car I had just been sat in. Kargilik could well be the most loved up place I've ever visited in all of China. How this place and Pishan are neighbours I will never know. They felt like parallel universes separated by the cruel lunar desert.

My hotel was, save for non-existent internet, the best I had stayed in since Zhangye. Brand new with helpful staff and even shower gel that didn't smell like the 1970s, whatever they smelt like. I just assume it was soapy and musty like the shower gel of most business hotels in China.

Other than losing my bike lock, the day was a total celebration. For lunch, I visited a restaurant that was absolutely heaving. I had polo, which is pronounced pollo and nothing to do with Marco. It is the quintessential Uyghur dish consisting of big chunks of lamb in saffron rice with sultanas, dates, and berries. I also slipped two extra kebabs on top in order to keep the calorie and protein count up. I also received another Uyghur lesson from the boss, a man with a permanent smile framed by a moustache so strong that I swear I felt my own facial hair burrow back into their follicles like frightened moles. This time I was taught some basic numbers and the names of Uyghur dishes, thankfully without any reference to Hitler.

The town's crowning glory came in the evening as I popped around the corner to buy some eggs and water. As I paid, a policeman came up to me and said: "you must be David". Then the shop owner responded with, "yes David, the man riding the bike". It all sounded very biblical and as if they were a pair of psychics, who were good with situations but not great with names. It transpired it was the policeman who'd done my registration, recording my middle name as my first and the shop owner had seen me ride passed his window. For a very brief moment, though, this surreal situation made it feel as though I was back in that enabling indie film and I was destined to stay in Kargilik to partake in some form of romantic incident, which would ultimately have a feel-bad ending for the sake of art.

If the internet worked, I could have stayed in Kargilik forever. Or one more day at the very least anyway.

Having fallen asleep on Beijing time, I was awake by 6.30am Xinjiang time. It was a tough call to leave Kargilik before Victoria Coren arrived to declare her conditional love for me in the film's heart-breaking final scene, especially since I only had 72km to tick off. But having been caught by enough afternoon sandstorms for one lifetime already, I decided to get moving.

It was arguably the least eventful 72km of the entire journey, but for the routine police checkpoint, all that interrupted my progress was stopping to pick up a doppa that had been lost by another road user. It was dark green with white and red stitching for detailing, which meant its former owner was likely to be from Kashgar.

Continuing to alternate between nice town, nasty town with perfect timing, Xinjiang next served up Yarkant. A grim city, most aptly pronounced in a strong cockney accent. Yarkant was gritty in all senses; shrouded in dust and packed full of miserable architecture. Indoors it was worse. Even the sticker for the local prostitutes was peeling off the wall next to my hotel bed through lack of attention. In addition to peeling prostitute promotions, the air conditioning didn't work, the shower didn't work and my room card didn't work.

The hotel also had one of my least favourite features of China; where men who clearly don't work, through fortune or misfortune, loiter like teenagers in what they deem *the* place to be, which in this instance was the reception of a shite hotel.

On this occasion, that pastime was more irritating than normal as my room didn't have the internet. Following what can only be described as mysterious and magical activity on my phone, I had no credit again. As I tried to use the reception's Wi-Fi to top up my phone, I was pestered by primates with such little respect for personal space that they not only looked over my shoulder and discussed the page I was looking at, but would actually touch the laptop screen with their grubby, moronic, fingers.

All of which hopefully explains why I spent an inordinate amount of time in Mustafa Burger, eating pizza and chips while sipping on nature's sweetest nectar, Mustafa Cola. I dedicated nearly all of my afternoon to failing to guess the passwords to every Wi-Fi network in range. To sum up, how trying Yarkant is for a grumpy Millennial, nobody had set their Wi-Fi password as 12345678 or 88888888. The selfish bastards.

Unable to top my phone up in the preferred manner that involves no human interaction, I visited a China Unicom store. The man behind the desk insisted I couldn't top up my Beijing sim in Xinjiang, which surely can't be true but he wouldn't budge from this position.

To add to my sulky mood, I realised that I, a man who was riding through a desert in sandstorm season had managed to lose his sunglasses. Better to realise that at the time than the next day at least. Serendipitously the search for a new pair also led me to pass a bank with Wi-Fi that was unburdened by a password. The connection lasted just long enough to send Holly a message and ask her to top my phone up online.

There was more farce when I finally returned to the hotel. I was informed that I was unable to return to my room for no particular reason and instead put in another room and not allowed to pick up my belongings until someone came to get me thirty minutes later when my original room would be ready for me to retrieve my items.

Fill in your own gaps or remain none the wiser as to what was going on. It didn't really matter because anything of any interest (the weaponry, the stacks of dollars, the satellite phone) to the kind of person who may have needed me to be kept out of my room for a while, was still in the rucksack I had in my possession. All that was in the room I was banned from returning to was my filthy clothes, toiletries, and Graham cream. I can only hope whoever was in there dipped a curious finger into the white tub and had a taste.

With the exception of an enjoyable conversation with an excitable Pakistani businessman from Lahore, the misery of my time in Yarkant makes it very difficult to address Marco's primary remark on the people of the town with maturity. His stand out observation was that most people in this town had "one very large foot and one small foot"[100].

My grandad always used to say "If you can't say anything sensible, say something that is technically inaccurate but still deeply offensive" but he's dead, so he can get away with that sort of thing and I can't. I imagine he may have said something involving walking in circles and questioned how far from home the inhabitants of Yarkant went to find a life partner. This, of course, is nothing but grossly unfair speculation.

After an unwelcome and unsolicited prank phone call from reception at 5.45am I decided I'd had enough of Yarkant and slowly got my stuff together. Once ready, I joined four men, each of whom was carrying a live chicken, in both the lift and joke that's missing a punchline.

The literal grit had been cleared by overnight rain and I left Yarkant in perfect conditions for cycling. I stopped to stock up on water and enjoyed a heart melting moment as a toddler fascinated with my bike fetched me an offering of sunflower seeds and was brave enough to accept my handshake as thanks.

After the new motorway appeared on my left-hand side, I had the old road entirely to myself for two hours of tailwind. Other than a brief thunderstorm, during which I took shelter under a

---

[100] (Cliff, 2015)

bridge, it was a wonderful day. So wonderful that 100km from the journey's finish line, I finally discovered throwing stones would scare away wild dogs. There was no one around to see this moment of enlightenment. Had there been they would have seen what looked like an angry but elated troll, who was wearing purple tinted, aviator sunglasses, successfully protect his bridge dwelling with a Neolithic military strategy and then do some form of primitive celebratory dance.

Once the storm had passed over, I remounted and continued down the road alone. I cycled passed some desperately poor villages that the new motorway now bypassed. On that afternoon, passing trade was limited to me and only a handful of other cars.

As I began the final hour of the day's journey, I ascended a bridge to cross over the new motorway. From my vantage point, I looked down to see the crushed remnants of a small red car, the colour of which wasn't lucky for someone. Sat on top of a mound of earth, its sole purpose was to warn road users to drive carefully. Sometimes China can be a subtle place of alien nuances flying over a naïve foreigner's head. Famously, the slightest slip of tone can see you describing your girlfriend as someone who looks like a horse, rather than her mother. Less well promoted as motivation for concentration in language schools, however, is just how dangerously close asking for one of the country's most popular beers (Yanjing) is to asking for a penis (yinjing) instead. At other times, though, China does blunt like nowhere else. Short of leaving the rotting corpse at the wheel of the car, the messaging couldn't have been stronger.

Fortunately, I avoided a similar fate to the driver of the red car in my last hour and the penance I served in Yarkant was rewarded with a cute little town in the shape of Yengisar.

I checked-in to a spotless, friendly, smoke-free hotel, run by three very attractive Han women and an arguably even more attractive Uyghur security guard. Compared to Yarkant and me, everybody looked so fresh and healthy. After doling out compliments in my head, I found another burger restaurant where I ate two large adult meals. I was so happy with Yengisar that I even resolved to buy some souvenir knives, which appeared to constitute the town's entire industry, the next day.

Once more the pendulum of nice town, nasty town had swung back towards nice. The individual character each town held is nothing new for the region. Peter Fleming, Ian's older brother and Bob's uncle, wrote in 1936 that the Chinese didn't need to bother trying to divide and conquer the inhabitants of Xinjiang because the inhospitable desert had done it for them[101]. Having experienced the hostile environment between the towns, first-*sand*, it was easy to see why people wouldn't travel between them before the advent of the windscreen. And that this resulting isolation had led the towns to develop distinctive characteristics. Though I'm pretty sure if Yarkant and Yengisar swapped their primary employment opportunities, then the two towns' personalities would also change rapidly.

So to the finale. 67km, that was all I had left. I had a most gentle of mornings. I started by eating the pecan crunch cereal bars from my 'if things get really bad' emergency pouch, which I had held on to through the sandstorms. This really kicked off the last day of school atmosphere. If I'd had them in my possession, I'd have worn some non-cycling clothes and played Guess Who.

First I went to buy one of Yengisar's famous knives. I had no interest in a ceremonial knife or cutlery, I wanted a whopper - a proper multi-purpose, bone-crushing, garlic-slicing, meat-scoring, monster of a cleaver. After screwing my face up at the first ornate

---

[101] (Fleming, 1936)

offerings, the salesman paused and asked me if I was a chef or worked in a kitchen. "Yes, I am a chef!" I lied. With the smell of dishonesty stinking out the place, he brought out a handmade beast of a knife. Overjoyed with this latest offering I blurted out "I'd like two please, my colleague is also a chef" — *obviously, because he is my colleague and I, lest we forget, am a chef. So what else could my colleague do for a living?*

My friend for whom the other knife is a gift, Julian — the star of Chapter Three's 895-pollution-rating bike ride - also isn't a chef, but he is the man more responsible than any other for this trip given that he: A) convinced me to move to China four years before this journey; B) advised Holly on taking the job that led to me returning this time; and C) introduced me to the stupidity of riding idiotic distances between Chinese cities[102].

This knife was the perfect gift because, on one of my very first weekends in China and one of my favourite weekends ever, Julian introduced me to the concept of the Chinese cleaver as he was buying one from a street market in Hunan. He made clear that you only ever need to buy one as they last forever. Within two weeks, his mother-in-law had broken said cleaver, whilst smashing up meat bones.

With such a short distance to cover, the day really was a procession. Just like the needless final stage of a modern day Tour de France. I tried to arrive just after Holly in order for her to nearly fail filming my arrival, something we only just achieved by me staying in third gear and soaking up the scenery and by her finally hitting the right button as I was three seconds away.

---

[102] He suggested we ride from Beijing to Tianjin in the Spring of 2014. The night before he took me to one of Beijing's hidden whiskey bars (this one was in a leisure centre and next door to a massage parlour of confusing moral standing i.e. it seemed legitimate) until 4am. We started the journey four short hours later. It wasn't quite as hard as getting the Pigeon back but it was as troubling as all but four days I had on the Giant.

Kashgar is an evocative name. This is Great Game territory and the gateway to central Asia or China depending on your direction of travel. A town for spies, thieves, and historic figures galore. Stein, Hadin, von Le Coq and friends would almost always pass through here. Approaching slowly from the southeast of the city, though, it had enough uniform, nation-wide, development to remove any sense of the importance or romance Marco Polo attributed to it.

There was no sign of the "splendid orchards and vineyards, and fine farms"[103] that they had in his day. Not that this made things any better for Marco, who had obviously found the journey to this point very tough. In the next but one sentence, he describes the inhabitants as "great misers and live mean lives, with nothing good to eat or drink"[104]. At times it's hard not to speculate that Marco was a bit of a cretin, who the owners of the aforementioned fine farms and splendid vineyards, would rather not feed.

Road works meant a detour away from our hotel, which stood tall, proud and newly built on the edge of the city centre. Eventually, I arrived to the warm welcome five-star hotels in China provide; one that is always dangerously close to being too warm.

Being £500 under budget, I had decided to pre-order champagne to complete that Tour de France procession feeling. It was already in an ice bucket in our room as we arrived. Pop, yey, fizz, pause, fizz, clink, yey!

Once I had removed what I was claiming to be a beard, showered and got into the hotel robe – because that's what you

---

[103] (Cliff, 2015)

[104] (Cliff, 2015)

do, even in summer on the edge of a desert - I phoned my Nan June to wish her a happy birthday and answered the first of many "Simon, answer me this, why did you do it?" themed questions.

Day one of not being on a marathon bike ride began with the destruction of a buffet breakfast. I had four doughnuts in just one of my five courses. With a historical city to see and a bicycle to lose, we set out in an undignified manner as I first failed to transport Holly side-saddle, and then just about managed to transport her legs-akimbo to visit Apaq Xoja's Tomb. It is, without hyperbole, the most beautiful building I've seen in China. There was something about the mismatched colours of the mosaic façade and the uneven slant of the building that gave it a vibrancy and charisma so at odds with its purpose.

Back in the centre of town some of the city's older buildings were still being knocked down. Nothing annoys me more than idiots who bemoan economic development, which offers residents improved safety and greater hygiene ruining the 'real – insert developing location here' and therefore a minor share of the idiots' holiday photo opportunities. They should all be made to live in a Victorian workhouse and have their photo taken with an unnecessarily large camera lens whilst they shit in the street. However, there are ways of doing development well and then there are ways of doing it with the wellbeing of the residents not being the top priority and without sympathy for the cultural heritage the development is replacing. Kashgar's development is not in the first of these categories.

The new old town had already got ticketing gates ready to go at the entrance, which almost exclusively consisted of shops. I am yet to visit a 'cultural tourism' zone, street or village in China, that isn't just shops selling shit from a factory somewhere else in the country. I would also take a punt that the owners of the shops in the new old town would not exactly match the residents of the buildings they have replaced. It wasn't as bad as Disneyland, it certainly wasn't as bad as Sea World, but I couldn't say, hand on empty heart, that it was better than Universal Studios.

We visited the old British Consulate, which disappointingly no longer houses a bar. Now a crumbling Chinese restaurant, which sits in the shadow of a gigantic hotel, this was the launch pad for Stein and friends. Thus we were deprived of the opportunity to have a gin and tonic in the long dark shadow of the many thieves who had proceeded us. As recompense, I had a final kebab in the new old town.

All day Holly and I had been playing a game with the 11-16-year-olds of Kashgar – careful now - whereby the first one to say hello in a friendly manner would win my bike. Perhaps because there was two of us we were less interesting, or maybe it was because Kashgar sees its fair share of tourists, but for the only the second time in the journey no one was interested. We had nearly returned to the hotel by the time the winner revealed himself in the late afternoon. After a brief conversation where I explained why I wasn't keeping the bike, he finally believed it wasn't a wind-up.

Boy: "Hello"

Me: "Hey, small friend, you want my bike?"

Boy: "What?"

Me: "Do you want a bike? This bike? Tomorrow I go to Beijing because I live there."

Boy: "Why don't you take your bike?"

Me: "Because it's too expensive. I sit on a plane tomorrow."

Boy stares.

Me: "I rode it from Beijing. You can have it. No money."

Boy: "You have no money?"

Me: "Yes. No. Yes. You can have the bike. No money"

Boy: "You are giving me your bike?"

Me: "Yes, here."

His face lit up, then he paused to look at Holly and then his mate. After a moment's consideration, he returned to face me.

Boy: "Really?"

I wheeled it towards him until he grabbed the handlebars.

He then said "thank you, thank you, thank you" and then something I didn't understand. I assume it involved swearing. He took the full weight of the bike and I turned away. I said goodbye over my shoulder as he and his friend said lots of other words I've not yet learned. Presumably something like:

Boy 2: "What the fuck was all that about?"

Boy 1: "I don't know. The foreigner spoke like a child. Do you think he's an idiot?"

Boy 2: "Maybe, what are you going to tell your mum?"

Boy 1: "I don't know, probably that I stole it. At least she'll believe that."

With these entirely fictitious remarks, I was without a bike for the first time in two months. The journey was over.

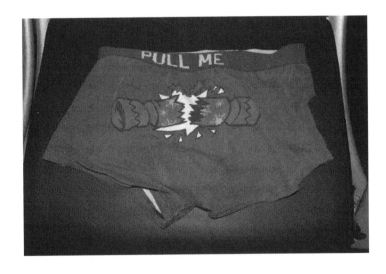

11.1 SUFFIXIES

Less than an hour after handing the bicycle over, I was rolling around the hotel bed in agony. It was as if my body had gone into a state of internalised, apoplectic, grieving for the loss of the bicycle.

The human body is a weird and wonderful thing but sometimes it's too smart for its own good. Since my journey was intended as a once in a life time effort, I had not considered the aftermath of my exertions. It turns out, you may be surprised to learn, that you cannot warm down adequately on kebabs, doughnuts, and two glasses of champagne.

Whatever the scientific ins and outs of it really are. A build-up of over-exertion, lack of sleep, and eating for energy rather than nutrition, had left my immune system broken. First up, it gave in to a particularly vicious case of food poisoning. Whereas normally the only redeeming feature of food poisoning is the haste with which it leaves, my contracting muscles refused to expel the poison, leaving my digestive system in limbo. I was left with one-half of my stomach trying to leave the toilet looking like the façade of a 1960s house, and the other more southerly end acting like the chair of a neighbourhood preservation society and doing all it could to stop that very event.

I remain amazed how quickly the deterioration happened. Whatever chemical changes occurred, or messages my brain sent out to say "it's ok, it's all over now, look he hasn't got a bike anymore", they took effect with an alarming immediacy. Though I'd had rest periods that lasted longer than I'd been in Kashgar, on those occasions my brain was clearly sending whatever signals the rest of my body needed to be prepared for more punishment. This time I went into shutdown.

On top of the awful agony happening in my stomach, a hideous mark, courtesy of the *good* strand of herpes – the one that doesn't come from a laissez-faire attitude to using condoms in coastal towns - announced itself on my face. Barely able to sit upright from stomach pain[105] Holly's surprise purchase of a business class flight (a whole £80 more) back to Beijing was gratefully received as a necessity just for allowing me to lie horizontal, rather than the treat it should have been.

In the immediate aftermath of the journey I was unable to do anything more significant than go for a gentle jog. Even the wholesomeness of a week in Canada and the decadence of a week in New York for Ollie and Jill's wedding failed to cure me. For nearly five months after the journey finished, I had significant issues with my short-term memory. Once again, sorry to everyone I quadruple booked in the autumn of 2015.

So please, if you ever do anything like this, and I'd still recommend it, plan a week of warming down at least. Do not find yourself in the foetal position on a bathroom floor thinking about whether crying is only going to make your stomach muscles hurt more.

You will notice that for a book about a bicycle journey it contains very few references to the bike that completed 4700km of the 5000km. This is incidental in whatever way that something not happening can also be incidental. It is also indicative of what I can only describe as the outstanding performance of the Giant. There was never anything to say about it.

The Pigeon is a thing of romance and history. The Giant was neither of these things. However, for under £200, what it

---

[105] I know, I know, child birth etc. But remember how much lower our pain thresholds are.

achieved without a single fault is astonishing. Nothing wore out to the point of malfunction and nothing mechanical required retuning. It just kept going like the bastard child of a Silk Road camel and a Mongolian horse. Moreover, it wasn't even designed to do this kind of thing. Its weight, its mountain bike tyres, its ride position and its components were all aimed at other disciplines. Yet it achieved what it did in the most modest way it could. It didn't even squeak.

To say more would just cause it undeserved embarrassment. In the end, this really wasn't about the bike.

You will also notice that this story is lacking in any epiphanies or moments where I find myself. Upon my return to Beijing, a new *conversation* developed with friends. How far? How sore is your arse? Are your balls ok? Were you scared? Were you bored? Did you get lonely? Do you really fancy Victoria Coren that much? And inevitably something like "any great life changing moments?"

Answers: 5000km, like 3200 miles or so; it's fine but I can't sit on wooden stools right now; yeah, I used plenty of Graham cream…. Graham as in Graham Gooch because, well, gooch, have you seen *Jackass*? I'm not a huge fan of wild dogs; yes; yes, I mean a bit, but it's mostly for narrative; and finally, no.

As with anyone who has spent 31 years as a human, especially a male one, I possess enough mistakes and regrets to provide further mental torment to any day long slog into a headwind. But then again I'm a Millennial, so I can wash those thoughts away with a podcast. I learned nothing new about myself that changed the things I want from life. It's hard to conceive how people don't already know that by my age. I understand even less how riding a bike could change that situation.

I was also asked if I felt like giving up. The simple answer, if you don't count taking the odd lift as giving up, was no. Even on the edge of Qinghai, with the dogs and the rules for foreigners it didn't cross my mind. Perhaps that's because the occasional short lifts in motorised vehicles had alleviated the pressure when I needed it most. Maybe it's because I'm mentally resilient to the point of being stupid.

The truth is that, even with the sandstorms, frustrations, dogs, and pot noodles; cycling an average of 100km a day is, physically at least, very easy. Any of you who are cyclists will know this. Those of you who are not, I implore you to give it a go. It's really not that hard and incredibly rewarding. I was on a £200 bicycle, if you've wasted money on this book, you can afford £200 on a functioning bicycle. I also had a smartphone, which does the job of a dozen key tools and a dozen new tools that made my journey much easier. If you're buying this as an e-book I can only assume you own a smartphone or you're my parents. In other words, for an outlay of £200 and a bit more on panniers and bits and bobs, you could do this kind of thing for as much time as you have to spare. Why not spend your next holiday being chased by vicious dogs hundreds of kilometres away from the nearest hospital?

I was also lucky. Two weeks before I set off, I had a head-on collision with a motorbike on the outskirts of Beijing after both the motorcyclist and I turned a corner, whilst each trying to read a map on our phones. Fortunately, our balanced weights and the angle of the collision just left a little bruising and a lot of blushes. Yet on the ride, I only had the one crash; the over the bars incident in Gansu, from which I and the bike escaped unscathed. I was also particularly fortunate with illness, as the post ride collapse illustrated in the harshest of lights. I was never truly put in a position to drag myself beyond the parameters of normal endurance sports because of sickness.

A more interesting question is what did I learn about China? The uninteresting and honest answer is not enough; it was always granular, like tiny grains of sand in a weak metaphor. This trip figuratively and literally only scratched the surface. I didn't possess enough Mandarin or speak to enough people to delve deep enough to tell you anything of any genuine intellectual value as I skipped between towns at a modest but still constant rate. So I padded the book out with Genghis Khan's sex life instead.

There were constants; the people were excellent, but then people are excellent everywhere. We have some way to go before we've evolved to a point where all adult genitalia taste like cookie dough ice cream, but we're not doing as bad a job as you might think. China is a likeable country in the extreme but nothing makes a democrat believe in democracy as much as living with one of the alternatives. There was a whole spectrum of contradictions too; far beyond the often discussed yawning wealth chasm and the environmental protection versus economic development debate.

The most irritating aspect of the whole trip was litter. With the exception of large swathes of Ningxia and barren nothings of Qinghai and Xinjiang, everywhere was grubby. In a country where the individual has little to no say on the big things, it baffled me that people had no interest in something they could control, like the litter around their houses and villages. It made no sense.

With perhaps the exception of Hohhot and Jiayuguan, it was certainly possible to sense the slowing of China's economy that was about to come out in the wash immediately after I finished my journey. People were still always on the move, though, only it was now harder to tell how much of that movement was economically beneficial when it was taking place behind the tinted windows of black German cars and not the overloaded mini-vans of years gone by.

Yet these were only hints, only little moments. The odd complaint that business was quiet, but there was no red neon sign of quite how fast the economy was slowing, nor at what speed the consequential changes of a slowing economy would happen. As I finished writing this, almost a year after I began the journey, things were starting to feel a little different already. In the month before I planned to hit upload on this very document, during the CCP's Two Sessions get together, the global internet was turned off and VPNs were being attacked to the extent that they became useless. This isn't unusual but the rhetoric around it and requests for absolute devotion from state media had an unpleasant whiff of a turn for the worse. At the same time exports dropped 25% from the previous year, imports dropped 14% and vast sums of capital were taking flight at an unsustainable rate.

Just like Flying Pigeon is a microcosm of China under the CCP, the CCP itself has lifelike qualities to its own history. The screaming noise of its birth, the teenage years of idolisation, the mid-life crisis that nobody inside the family speaks of but everyone outside does. Is this the CCP's dotage? Allow me to be British and say: *I dunno, probably not*. As an organisation, it doesn't just control, it adapts to survive. Mistakes made by the Party as a whole have not yet been politically fatal. The most exciting prediction I will give you is that before the CCP's centenary in 2049, China will have had a female leader.

A more detailed bet would be that she will still also be head of the CCP and China remains a single-party state. If you want me to go over the top, I would guess that her rise was in part facilitated by the Party in response to changes in society but that ultimately her success was down to her own efforts, both political and intellectual.

Would I put my life savings on it? No. The next five years will be incredibly interesting for China. I've been saying the economy here would implode in 2016 since I first arrived in 2011. This was more guess work around economic cycles and just how false the accounting of provincial governments appeared, rather than sustained, informed economic research. I'm probably wrong, the word implode is probably too strong. However, I think what happens in the next two years will cement what happens for the following twenty-five. As a caveat to all this you should know that when gambling 14/1 are my favourite odds, unless it's the Grand National and the only horse at 14/1 is wearing yellow or purple.

The thing that I hope comes across most from this book is just how great the people of China are. My days were filled with waves, smiles, shouts of "go on" and numerous friendly conversations. I was given gifts, water, food, lifts and offered more of these than I could accept several times over. The only person who dismissed me out of hand was employed by the traffic police and trying to stop me riding down a motorway passed a sign that expressly banned me from doing so, not a totally unreasonable time for her to be frustrated with anyone. Let alone a neon moron, who smelt like the fallout from a catastrophic fire at a pig farm.

Though I had irritations with the regulations, everyone I dealt with was respectful and never threatening. You could argue having an automatic weapon is threatening enough, but in a country where tones really matter and mutual respect tends to keep things calm. I never felt in danger. If China was Star Wars, and remember it isn't because that's Vietnam and America, even the storm troopers who I came into contact with were decent and fair. Even in Pishan, the questioning was proportional, in a public place and only became a bit edgy because a child started to play with a policeman's gun.

What of the Pigeon that started this dream? Well it sits in Beijing, mostly in its cage, causing an overspill of bikes into the living area, which is as beneficial to co-habitational bliss as being caught in bed with £20's worth of sushi again. Would it have made it with a lighter load and more time? Yes, but it would take a minimum of three months and a significantly stronger rear wheel. Maybe one day the Pigeon will rise from the flames, maybe it won't. Maybe its destiny in retirement was always just to be peddled around London by some pub bore who once cycled across China. Only time will tell.

If I could leave you with one thought, it would be this. China is a country with a good coverage of mostly well-tarmacked and fastidiously-measured roads.

THE FINAL STATS

SUSPICIOUSLY ROUND NUMBERS

Total distance: 5000KM
Distance cycled: 4750KM
Distance covered by cheating in a police car, truck, car, and pick-up: 250KM
Average speed: 14KPH

SUSPICIOUSLY ACCURATE NUMBERS

Dead dogs: 67
Dead camels: 4
Dead sheep: 84
Pot noodles consumed: 51
Pot noodles it felt like I consumed: 5151
Kebabs consumed: 45
Naans consumed: 17
Flies consumed: 2
Punctures: 40

LOSING PREFACE

Achtung pedants! Here is your preface. It is a deliberate act of defiance that I've put the preface at the end of the book so as to not piss on the chips of people who are not pedants before they've started reading.

For the most part, I've used the Mandarin name, as it appears when written in toneless pinyin, for people and places. This wasn't a purposeful decision, as the lack of consistency will demonstrate. Anglicised versions of Uyghur and Mongolian place names also appear in the book, but this is only because I called places whatever Google Maps told me they were called. Google's inconsistency is my excuse. I hope this ambivalence serves to highlight just how disinterested I would be in any suggestions that I have any genuine, concrete, opinions on anything. I am, however, aware that for Inner Mongolia, in particular, Google uses the regional name for cities and not always the city's name itself. But what do you want, accuracy?

The names of people appear in these pages either as I heard them or how they appeared on WeChat profiles. This isn't to give people anonymity, because none of them need it. If this provides anonymity, it's because I've misheard or they've decided to use the name *White Pony* or *Jackie Big Todger* for their online persona.

This journey was taken out of a desire to do something interesting, challenging, and fun; with full awareness that some of it would be boring. I hope that you approached the preceding pages with a similar perspective.

It was not done for charity or in search of an epiphany. I just wanted to go on an amazing bike ride. The cycling happened as the book details, there is no miraculous recovery of broken bicycles for the sake of narrative, like some shoddy Sunday night motoring programme on BBC2.

There is no editing in favour of, or against, anyone or anything. In fact, as the poor grammar will prove, there has been very little editing at all. I have spoken about all but one thing I saw or experienced that I deemed of any significance, and many others of no significance whatsoever. The particular moment that I have excluded would have been omitted if I'd seen it in any other country; whether it was a democracy, dictatorship or governed by a magic eight ball.

In regards to the terrible jokes and cultural reference points, I am sorry to all of you who are not 30-35-year-olds from rural Britain.

This is not an academic work. It was a project to fill the many irritating days it takes to sort out visas. That said, I've tried to credit and reference researchers, academics, and authors to the best of my attention span. However, in the age of e-books and audio books, this is a ridiculous task. Where I have been reading an e-book I have not listed the page number because I don't know it. In the case of Peter Frankopan's excellent Silk Road, I was listening to the audio book. However, I'm not going to put audio book timings into a book about a bike ride. Not least because more often than not I was falling asleep to it.

Furthermore, quite obviously this book is not aimed at expanding any contemporary debates around China or as a book for China experts. In my head, this is a book designed for people who've never visited China, been here once, or have the mental maturity to deal with it being written primarily with that audience in mind. I feel this book would go particularly well with a sun lounger and several litres of pina colada.

Oh yeah, before I forget, I don't really hate Telford. I've just always enjoyed the rivalry between Shrewsbury and Telford. It's like watching two ugly brothers at a family wedding, fighting over who gets to dry-hump the least ugly cousin. This is my contribution to that petulance. Long may it continue.

THANKS

The truck drivers of China: If anyone was going to kill me, the truck drivers of China were odds-on favourites. Yet with two rare exceptions, they were exceptional, they gave me room, they waved, they smiled, they gave me water, they offered far more lifts than I accepted. They were just great.

The petrol station attendants of Northern China: Thanks for the relentless cheery faces and unfailing ability to surprise me with a chair.

The other road users of Northern China (excluding those within the second ring road of Beijing): Thanks for the drinks, waves, smiles and roadside chats.

My Fellow Cyclists: Especially the Giant Mountain Bike club of Zhangye, thanks for being great fun.

Mr Wang at Flying Pigeon and Tono in Barcelona: Thanks for all you did to start the dream happening!

Jon, Tom, and Cynthia. Given their preparation (two hours on a Boris bike) and supplies (Sudocreme) it's amazing they're still alive. It was great to have company and no doubt they helped make Ningxia the most fun of all the provinces.

The Mas in Ningxia: For being far too hospitable and taking me for the most fun meal I had on the trip.

Hotel Security Guards: For every time one of the many helpful souls dirtied their white gloves and/or uniform helping me carry my filthy gear into their pristine hotel and almost always insisted I should bring my bicycle too.

Nitai at the Hutong, Raines in Zhangye and Wang Kai at the Merida shop in Yinchuan.

My teachers at That's Mandarin, especially Cai Jingxia, because she's had to put up with me more than the rest.

Podcasts: *An Irishman Abroad* for saving my sanity in a sandstorm; *The Football Ramble* for providing the comforting sound of men in their early thirties talking bollocks about football; *The Bugle*; *Football Weekly*; *The Cycling Podcast*; *Comedian's Comedian*; *RHLSTP*; *Freakonomics*; *China History Podcast*; *The Anfield Wrap* and *The Rider* - especially for playing *If* by The Bluetones.

The Chinese Police. A controversial one because it most definitely isn't always the case, but in all of my direct dealings, they were at the very least polite, professional and, more often than not, friendly too.

www.rfa.org - a very useful source of news in English, especially for Xinjiang where reportage in English is not exactly extensive.

Holly White, for putting up with this, reading through the final draft out loud, topping up my phone from afar and (on the occasions she didn't forget) bringing me spare clothes.

Julian Maccormac for reading a draft of this and continually embarrassing me on cycle rides around Beijing.

Alex Crook for spotting 95% of typos in version 1.0 of the e-book edition.

Wikipedia for its incredible role as a signpost to the literature that enriched the journey. I'm not sure where we are in the Wikipedia fashion cycle at the moment, but I definitely sit on the side of the fence where the rational people are having a barbecue in celebration of Wikipedia's existence. It is not perfect; but for ideas, information, and most of all for its service in flagging the literature around a subject, it truly is a gift.

Finally, thanks to everybody who didn't tell my Nan Maureen what I was up to.

BIBLIOTHEQUE

Barber, E. W. (1998). *The Mummies of Urumchi.* W.W. Norton and Co.

Bovingdon, G. (2010). *The Uyghurs: Strangers in Their Own Land.* Columbia University Press. Retrieved from ISBN 0231519419

CBBC. (2015). *One Belt, One Road.* Retrieved from http://www.cbbc.org/cbbc/media/cbbc_media/One-Belt-One-Road-main-body.pdf

Cliff, N. (2015). *The Travels.* (N. Cliff, Trans.) London: Penguin.

Coyle, T. H. (2013). *The Secret Race.* Croydon: Corgi Books.

Dubs, H. H. (1942). *An Ancient Military Contact between Romans and Chinese* (Vol. 62(3)). Baltimore: John Hopkins University Press. Retrieved from http://www.jstor.org/stable/291665

Eimer, D. (2014). *The Emperor Far Away.* Bloomsbury.

Fleming, P. (1936). *News from Tartary.*

Frankopan, P. (2015). *The Silk Roads.* Bloomsbury.

Frankopan, P. (2015). *The Silk Roads: A New History of the World.*

Hays, J. N. (2005). *Epidemics and Pandemics.* Retrieved from https://books.google.co.uk/books?id=GyE8Qt-kS1kC&pg=PA61&dq=&hl=en&redir_esc=y#v=onepage&q=&f=false

Holdstock, N. (2011). *The Tree That Bleeds.* Luath Press.

Hopkirk, P. (1980). *Foreign Devils of the Silk Road.* John Murray.

Keay, J. (2009). *China: A History.* Harper Press.

Koeppel, D. (2007, January). Flight of the Pigeon. *Bicycling.* Retrieved from https://books.google.co.uk/books?id=isUDAAAAMBAJ&pg=PA60&redir_esc=y#v=onepage&q&f=false

Man, J. (2008). *The Great Wall.* Bantam.

Matthew, D. C. (2011). Greek Hoplite in an Ancient Chinese Siege. *Journal of Asian History, 45*(1/2).

McKay, A. (2003). *History of Tibet.* Routledge Curzon.

National Bureau of Statistics of China. (2011). *Communiqué of the National Bureau of Statistics of People's Republic of China on Major Figures of the 2010 Population Census.*

Ramzy, A. (2013). *A Maker of Bikes Now Makes a Point of Riding Them.* New York Times. Retrieved from http://www.nytimes.com/2013/08/31/world/asia/a-maker-of-bikes-now-makes-a-point-of-riding-them.html?pagewanted=all

Weatherford, J. (2004). *Ghengis Khan and the Making of the Modern World.* New York: Crown Publishing.

West, J. M. (2008). *The Tarim Mummies.* Thames and Hudson.

White, M. (2012). *The Great Big Book of Horrible Things.* W. W. Norton.

WHO. (2013). *Global Status Report on Road Safety 2013: supporting a decade of action.* WHO. Retrieved from ISBN 978 92 4 156456 4

YongGang Yao, Q. K. (2004). Different Matrilineal Contributions to Genetic Structure of Ethnic Groups in the Silk Road Region in China. *Molecular Biology and Evolution, 21*(12), 2265-2280.

Zerjal, T. (2003). The Genetic Legacy of the Mongols. *American Journal of Human Genetics, 72*(3), 717-721. Retrieved from http://www.ncbi.nlm.nih.gov/pmc/articles/PMC1180246/

Zhou Ruixia, A. L. (2007). *Testing the hypothesis of an ancient Roman soldier origin of the Liqian people in northwest China: a Y-chromosome perspective* (Vol. 52). Journal of Human Genetics. Retrieved from http://www.nature.com/jhg/journal/v52/n7/abs/jhg200782a.html

Discotheque

The road is a lonely place and you probably want to block out the noise of your next puncture anyway. Here are the top ten songs/albums of my journey.

10. Yes it's Fucking Political - Skunk Anansie

Why?: That riff, and because you've forgotten Skunk Anansie exist.

Best for: Starting a long slog into the wind or kick starting the next stint.

Special Fact: Contrary to the song's message, not everything is political - Ed Miliband's future being just one example.

9. Adrenaline - Deftones

Why?: 40 minutes of relentlessness.

Best for: The misery of rain, sandstorms, headwind and cold.

Special Fact: White Pony, Deftones' third album, released in 2000 was the perfect soundtrack to walk around Beijing on a sultry spring night in 2015. Not sure why.

8. No Sensitivity - Jimmy Eat World

Why?: Because at times you will either want to remember what it felt like to be eighteen to remind yourself how pleased the eighteen-year-old you would be that you're cycling across China rather than doing anything beneficial for the wellbeing of others or your bank account, or you want to revel in the fact you the following lyrics have no place in your life now that you're an adult.

The world don't spin without you

I'm amazed you're standing still

I'm taking my kisses back (whoa)

I want my kisses back from you

And no your problems, they aren't problems

So be glad they never will

I'm taking my kisses back (whoa)

I want my kisses back from you, from you, you

Best for: For putting a tent up in a sandstorm.

Special Fact: You can't actually take kisses back but you can retrieve a 'borrowed' band hoody as part of some inevitable teenage divorce proceedings.

7. Alanis Morissette and the other songs that sound like Beacon FM from the mid 90s

Why?: Because you'll need to block things out and drifting into dated local radio hits will really help.

Best for: When nothing's happening.

Special Fact: You can also add in your own local radio advertisements. *"Have you got Hohhot hotpot hot-bot? Then why don't you try Andrex Extra Soft?!"*

6. Shakermaker - Oasis

Why?: The intro.

Best for: Riding in deserts; this is the perfect song to cycle through a desert too.

Special Fact: This song does not last as long as most deserts.

5. Welcome To The Jungle - Guns N Roses

Why?: It is impossible not to increase your RPM with this playing.

Best for: Going unnecessarily fast and ensuring you bonk later in the day.

Special Fact: This is the only GNR song I like.

4. A Secret History - The Best Of The Divine Comedy

Why?: Because it's the best distraction going and it's a lot funnier than just a hostess with a massive arse.

Best for: Singing along when happy or sad.

Special Fact: I had breached thirty by the time I became aware Songs of Love was the theme tune to Father Ted.

3. When the Levee Breaks - Led Zeppelin

Why?: Because rhythm is everything

Best for: The relentless slog into a persistent headwind

Special Fact: It's not as good as Kashmir, a song which is actually too good and will lead you to lose focus and drift out of cycle lanes and into lorries.

2. Rave Tapes - Mogwai

Why?: Because you need to relax in a hotel.

Best for: The 45 minutes between stuffing your face and falling asleep

Special Fact: Track 2 - Simon Ferocious, is nothing to do with me. Track 3 - Remurdered, is either the best song you've heard or the best song you're yet to hear.

1. The Boys Are Back In Town - Thin Lizzy

Why?: Dangerously suitable for *Top Gear - The CAPITAL 'T' Tunes For Dads Who Wanna Be Lads III*, but for some reason it always arrived at the right moment on this journey.

Best For: Arriving into a town, as a boy.

Special Fact: My Dad really likes this song.

ABOUT ME

I was born in Shrewsbury in 1984 and grew up in nearby Bayston Hill, a village that would count as a suburb if Shrewsbury was big enough to warrant one. I spent the first 16 years of my life riding bicycles and kicking footballs against walls and over fences. In other words, it was bliss. I then went on to Shrewsbury Sixth Form College, a place so stereotypical of its kind that Wikipedia uses a photo of it to illustrate what a Sixth Form looks like.

I studied Law and Politics at Cardiff University before the legal firms of Britain decided I shouldn't be a lawyer and I went on to study for a Masters in International Affairs at Exeter University.

During these formative years I had eight different employers and wasn't fired by a single one of them; while good for the C.V. this is dreadful for anecdotes. After University I joined the Civil Service and was assigned to BIS. In my last job before moving to Beijing I ran a Government Minister's private office, which is one of the few roles in a ministerial office the *Thick of It* didn't feel the need to satirise.

Redacted Person A: "How many people live in poverty in Pakistan?"

Redacted Person B: "Not really sure, but it isn't a particularly affluent country, DfID do lots there."

Redacted Person A: "Then why, in the name of fuck, have the Pakistani Embassy sent us five kilos of rice for Christmas?"[106]

Then in 2013, Holly moved to Beijing and a few months later I joined her once I'd finished receiving satirical bags of rice for a living. That's how you and I ended up here.

---

[106] You'd be amazed how hard it is to give a charity rice at Christmas.

OH DO ME A FAVOUR

You will notice I have not written the *About Me* section in the third person. You are very welcome. This is because I am self-publishing and therefore you are lucky enough to not be reading the words of an affluent intern pro-bonoing themselves into someone else's job. As thanks for this, I would be incredibly grateful if those of you who have enjoyed the book would review it on the site from which you bought it and share it on social media.

I am inventively called @simondavidclode on Twitter – and yes I'm annoyed I didn't act fast enough to be able to leave my middle name out and must now spend the rest of my online life with a moniker better suited to the bottom half of a scoreboard on a Texan golf course.

You can find more pictures of this journey and feel disgruntled for buying what is essentially just an extended version of a free blog here - www.lastflightofthepigeon.com.

The cover image is by the poly-talented Chris Cantrill, you can see what he's about here - www.christopher-cantrill.com.

The first map was drawn by lead illustrator Oscar, 5 and assistant illustrator Simon, 32. Its production was project managed by Max, 3.

The magnificently detailed map comes courtesy of the outrageously talented Paul Sonley of www.LoopieRoute.com